Microsoft®
Office 2003

SO-BIU-886

Carol M. Cram

Capilano College, North Vancouver, B.C.

THOMSON
———✳———™
COURSE TECHNOLOGY

Australia • Canada • Mexico • Singapore • Spain • United Kingdom • United States

THOMSON

COURSE TECHNOLOGY

Microsoft® Office 2003—Illustrated Projects™

is published by Course Technology.

Executive Editor:
Nicole Jones Pinard

Production Editor:
Pamela Elizian

QA Tester:
Susan Whalen

Product Manager:
M.T. Cozzola

Developmental Editor:
Pam Conrad

Text Designer:
black fish design

In-house Product Manager:
Christina Kling Garrett

Composition House:
GEX Publishing Services

Cover Designer:
black fish design

Associate Product Manager:
Emilie Perreault

Editorial Assistant:
Shana Rosenthal

ISBN-13: 978-0-619-27307-1
ISBN-10: 0-619-27307-0

A Note from the Author

As instructors, what is our goal? I believe that we can and should teach our students to fly—to become independent learners with the confidence to tackle and solve problems. My greatest satisfaction in the classroom comes when my students learn the information, skills, and techniques necessary to function effectively in the workplace and to accomplish tasks related to their own needs and interests.

Several years ago, I was teaching a second-level word processing course to students who had completed the introductory word processing course. These students knew a series of functions and had proven their ability to pass "fill in the blanks" tests. But when I asked the students to produce an attractively formatted business letter, they were at a loss. That's when I realized that teaching a series of functions wasn't enough. Students needed—and deserved—to learn *what* to do with a software application. They needed to "see the forest" and not just the trees.

I developed a philosophy of teaching software applications that has evolved into the Illustrated Projects series. Each text in this series provides students with step-by-step instructions to create documents or perform tasks appropriate to the software package they are learning. As students complete the projects, they learn how a variety of functions combine together to produce a tangible product.

But the Illustrated Projects approach to teaching software doesn't stop with the projects. In my classroom, the significant learning occurs when students are given the opportunity to create their own version of a project document. That's when I feel a kind of magic creeping into my classroom. Students take the structure offered by a project and then, in the Independent Challenges, adapt this structure to explore practical business applications and to express their own interests. Suddenly, my students are willing to take risks, to solve problems, and to experiment with new features as they work toward the creation of a document that belongs to them. Pride of ownership inspires learning!

I hope you enjoy working with the projects in this book as much as I have enjoyed creating them. And I hope that you too can experience the magic that occurs in your classroom when your students begin to fly!

This book owes everything to the talent and dedication of the Course Technology Illustrated team. I particularly wish to thank Pam Conrad, the Developmental Editor of this book, for her encouragement and support and her incredible attention to detail. I am honored to call her not only my colleague but my friend. I also wish to thank my husband and daughter for their endless patience and, as always, my wonderful students at Capilano College.

Preface

Welcome to *Microsoft Office 2003—Illustrated Projects*. This highly visual book offers a wide array of interesting and challenging projects designed to apply the skills learned in any Office 2003 book. The Illustrated Projects Series is for people who want more opportunities to practice important software skills.

Organization and Coverage

This text contains a total of nine units. Six units contain projects for the individual programs: Word (two units), Excel (two units), Access (one unit), and PowerPoint (one unit). Three other units contain projects that take advantage of the powerful integration capabilities of the suite. Each unit contains three projects followed by four Independent Challenges and a Visual Workshop. Students will also gain practice gathering and using information available on the World Wide Web in a variety of the projects and independent challenges.

About this Approach

What makes the Illustrated Projects approach so effective at reinforcing software skills? It's quite simple. Each activity in a project is presented on two facing pages, with the step-by-step instructions on the left page and large screen illustrations on the right. Students can focus on a single activity without having to turn the page. This unique design makes information extremely accessible and easy to absorb. Students can complete the projects on their own, and because of the modular structure of the book, can also cover the units in any order.

The two-page spread for each activity contains some or all of the elements shown below.

Road map—It is always clear which project and activity you are working on.

Introduction—Concise text that introduces the activity and summarizes new procedures. Steps are easier to complete when they fit into a meaningful framework.

Troubles and Tips—Troubleshooting advice to fix common problems that might occur and tips for using Microsoft Office 2003 more effectively. These appear right next to the step where students might need help.

Numbered steps—Clear step-by-step directions explain how to complete the specific activity. These steps get less specific as students progress to the third project in a unit.

Clues to Use boxes—These sidebars provide concise information that either explains a skill or concept covered in the steps or describes an independent task or feature that is in some way related to the steps.

PROJECT 3 Word

BUSINESS CARDS FOR JOSÉ ALVAREZ

Add a WordArt Logo

You need to add a WordArt object to the business card and then modify it.

Trouble
To show the Drawing toolbar, click the Drawing button on the Standard toolbar.

steps:

1. Show the Drawing toolbar if necessary, then click the Insert WordArt button on the Drawing toolbar
   The WordArt Gallery dialog box opens.

2. Select the second option from the left in the third row as shown in Figure A-17, then click OK

3. Type JA, change the font to Comic Sans MS, click the Bold button, click OK, then click the WordArt object to select it
   Black sizing handles appear around the WordArt object to indicate it is selected, and the WordArt toolbar appears.

4. Click the WordArt Shape button on the WordArt toolbar, then click the Slant Up shape as shown in Figure A-18

5. Click the Format WordArt button on the WordArt toolbar, click the Size tab if necessary, change the Height and Width to .5, click the Layout tab, click Square, click the Left option button, then click OK
   By selecting the Square layout, you convert the WordArt object from an inline graphic to a floating graphic that you can position easily on the business card.

6. With the WordArt object still selected, click the Shadow Style button on the Drawing toolbar, then select Shadow Style 9
   The WordArt object is complete.

7. Click next to the J in José, click Format on the menu bar, click Paragraph, change the Before Spacing to 48 point, then click OK

8. Drag the WordArt object to the upper-left corner of the first business card as shown in Figure A-19

9. Click away from the WordArt object, then save the document

Clues to Use

Editing a WordArt object

You can modify a WordArt object in many different ways by selecting different shapes, experimenting with different fill and line color options, and applying various shadow and 3-D styles. To modify an existing WordArt object, click it to show the WordArt toolbar, and then select the tools you require. You can apply one of the preset WordArt styles by clicking the WordArt Gallery button on the WordArt toolbar, and then you can modify the style by selecting new options in the Format WordArt dialog box.

The Projects

The two-page activity format featured in this book provides students with a powerful learning experience. Additionally, this book contains the following features:

▶ **Meaningful Examples**—This book features projects that students will be excited to create, including a personal resume, a marketing brochure, an integrated report, and a sales presentation. By producing relevant documents that will enhance their own lives, students will more readily master skills.

▶ **Start from Scratch**—To truly test if a student understands the software and can use it to reach specific goals, the student should start from the beginning. In this book, students create projects from scratch, just like they would in the real world. In selected cases, supplemental data files are provided.

▶ **Outstanding Assessment and Reinforcement**—Each unit concludes with four Independent Challenges and a Visual Workshop. These Independent Challenges offer less instruction than the projects, allowing students to explore various software features and increase their critical thinking skills. The Visual Workshop follows the Independent Challenges and broadens students' attention to detail. Students see a completed document, worksheet, database, or presentation, and must recreate it on their own.

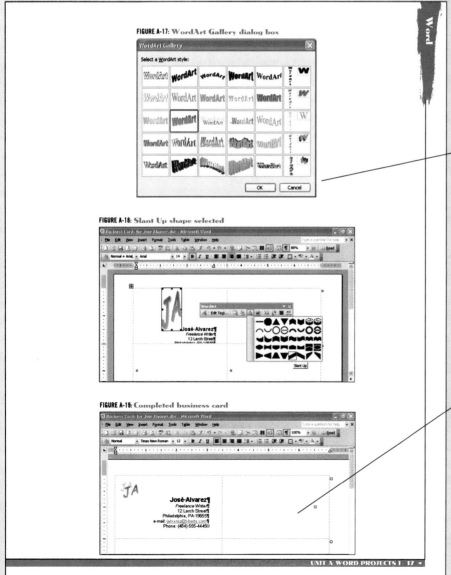

FIGURE A-17: WordArt Gallery dialog box

FIGURE A-18: Slant Up shape selected

FIGURE A-19: Completed business card

Screen shots—Every activity features representations of what the screen should look like as students complete the numbered steps.

Completed document—At the end of every project, there is a picture of how the document will look when printed. Students can easily assess how well they've done.

Instructor Resources

The Instructor Resources CD is Course Technology's way of putting the resources and information needed to teach and learn effectively into your hands. Providing an integrated array of teaching and learning tools that offers a broad range of technology-based instructional options, this CD represents the highest quality and most cutting-edge resources available to instructors today. Many of these resources are available at www.course.com.

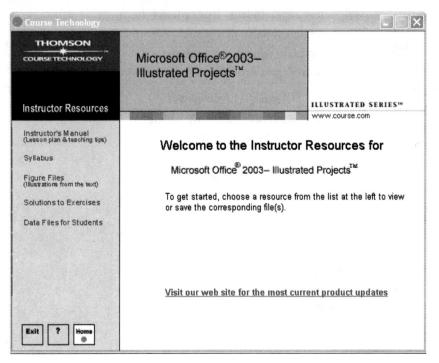

The resources available with this book are:

Instructor's Manual

This includes:

- ► Lecture notes that contain teaching tips from the author
- ► Extra projects
- ► Mapping to skills covered in Office 2003 texts
- ► Alphabetical list of functions covered in the projects

Solution Files

Solution Files contain every file students are asked to create in the projects and end-of-unit material. A Help file on the Instructor Resources CD includes information for using the Solution Files.

Data Files

Data Files contain every file students need to create the projects and end-of-unit material.

Figure Files

The figures in the text are provided on the Instructor Resources CD to help illustrate key topics or steps. Instructors can create traditional overhead transparencies by printing the figure files, or they can create electronic slide shows by using the figures in a presentation program such as PowerPoint.

Also available with this book:

Course Online Faculty Companion

This World Wide Web site offers Course Technology customers a password-protected site where you can find everything you need to prepare for class. Here you can obtain the Instructor's Manual, Solution Files, and any updates and revisions to the text. Contact your Support Service Representative for the site address and password.

Contents

Microsoft
►Word
Projects

Unit A

Word
Projects I

In this Unit You Will Create the Following:

 **Trip Schedule**

 **Newsletter**

 **Business Card**

You can use Microsoft Word to produce many different kinds of documents, ranging from a sheet of business cards to a multi-column newsletter to attractively formatted schedules and lists. Your challenge when using Word is to take the skills you know and apply them to create useful and interesting documents. For example, you can use the versatile Table feature to create forms, questionnaires, schedules, inventory lists, or just about any document that presents information in a grid format with multiple rows and columns. In this unit, you will apply your Microsoft Word skills to create and format a schedule, insert and modify clip art pictures and photographs, create WordArt objects, format documents in columns, and modify a sheet of labels to create business cards.

Schedule for Summit Hiking Club

The Summit Hiking Club in North Vancouver, British Columbia, provides its members with a range of walking and hiking tours in three categories: Strolls, Day Hikes, and Backcountry Adventures. Club members are busy people who want an easy-to-read schedule that shows the monthly tours. As the office manager, you need to create the schedule for August. You will Create Tables, Merge Cells and Add Shading, and Add and Modify a Graphic. The completed schedule appears in Figure A-6 on page 7.

activity:

Create Tables

You need to set up the document in landscape format so that the completed schedule is 9" wide. Then you need to create a small table to contain the legend and a large table consisting of seven columns and 15 rows.

Hint

This unit assumes Show/Hide ¶ is on.

Trouble

If Tahoma is not available, select Arial.

steps:

1. Start Word, close the Getting Started task pane if necessary, click **File** on the menu bar, click **Page Setup**, click the **Margins tab** if necessary, click **Landscape orientation** in the Page Setup dialog box, set a top margin of **.8**, set a bottom margin of **.5**, then verify that the left and right margins are set to **1** as shown in Figure A-1

2. Click **OK**, save the document as **Summit Hiking Club Schedule** to the location where you are storing the files for this book, click the **Zoom list arrow** [100% ▼] on the Standard toolbar, then click **Page Width**

3. Click the **Font list arrow** [Times New Roman ▼] on the Formatting toolbar, select **Tahoma**, type **Summit Hiking Club August Trip Schedule**, then press **[Enter]** twice
   All the text you enter for the schedule will be formatted in the Tahoma font.

4. Click the **Insert Table button** [⊞] on the Standard toolbar, drag to create a table that is **2** columns wide and **3** rows high, then enter text as shown in Figure A-2

5. Click **cell 1**, click the **right mouse button**, click **Table Properties**, click the **Column tab**, select the contents of the Preferred width text box, type **2**, then click **Next Column**

6. Select the contents of the Preferred width text box for column 2, type **.6**, then click **OK**

7. Click **cell 1**, click **Table** on the menu bar, point to **Select**, click **Table**, click the **Align Right button** [≡] on the Formatting toolbar, click the **Outside Border list arrow** [⊞ ▼] on the Formatting toolbar, click the **No Border button** [⊞], then press **[↓]** once
   The table for the legend is right-aligned and the borders are removed.

8. Press **[Enter]** once, click **Table** on the menu bar, point to **Insert**, click **Table**, type **7** for the number of columns, press **[Tab]**, type **15** for the number of rows, then click **OK**

9. Enter the text for row 1 of the new table as shown in Figure A-3, then save the document

FIGURE A-1: **Page Setup dialog box**

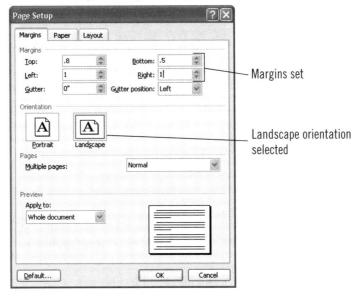

Margins set

Landscape orientation
selected

FIGURE A-2: **Text for the legend**

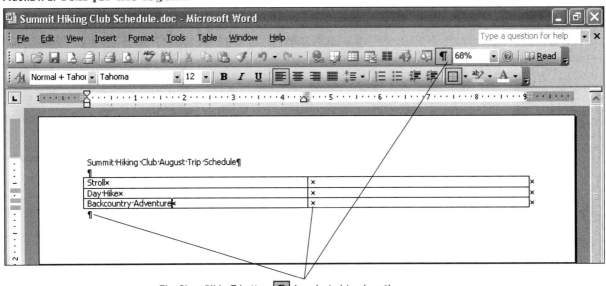

The Show/Hide ¶ button ¶ is selected to show the
paragraph marks and end of cell marks

FIGURE A-3: **Text for row 1**

Summit·Hiking·Club·August·Trip·Schedule¶
¶

Stroll×	×	×
Day·Hike×	×	×
Backcountry·Adventure×	×	×

⊞ ¶

Sunday×	Monday×	Tuesday×	Wednesday×	Thursday×	Friday×	Saturday×	×
×	×	×	×	×	×	×	×
×	×	×	×	×	×	×	×
×	×	×	×	×	×	×	×
×	×	×	×	×	×	×	×
×	×	×	×	×	×	×	×
×	×	×	×	×	×	×	×
×	×	×	×	×	×	×	×

activity:

Merge Cells and Add Shading

In the completed schedule, two or more cells are merged so that the text for the Backcountry Adventure tours—each of which lasts for more than one day—spans the merged cells. In addition, different levels of shading indicate the different trip categories. You need to enter text into the schedule and then display the Tables and Borders toolbar so you can quickly merge selected cells and add shading where required.

steps:

1. Click the cell below Tuesday, type 1, press [Tab], type 2, press [Tab], then continue to enter the date for each day in the first week of August (ending with a 5 for Saturday)

2. Click View on the menu bar, point to Toolbars, click Tables and Borders, select cells 1 to 4 at the beginning of the next row (Sunday to Wednesday) as shown in Figure A-4, then click the Merge Cells button 🖳 on the Tables and Borders toolbar

You use the Tables and Borders toolbar to merge selected cells and add shading where required.

3. Type Skyline Trail to Manning Park, press [Tab] two times, type Deep Cove for Friday, press [Tab], then type Helm Lake for Saturday

You've entered three of the hikes being held during the first week in August.

4. Refer to Figure A-5 to enter the remaining text for the table, including the date for each day and all the hikes

Remember that you'll need to merge selected cells in some of the rows to accommodate the Backcountry Adventure tours. At this point, just enter the text and merge cells. You will add shading in later steps.

5. Click to the left of row 1 (contains the days of the week) to select the entire row, click the Shading Color list arrow 🖳▾ on the Tables and Borders toolbar, click the Black color, click the Font Color list arrow 🅰▾ on the Formatting toolbar, then click the White color

6. Click the cell to the right of the Stroll cell in the legend table, click the Shading Color button 🖳 on the Tables and Borders toolbar to fill the cell with Black, click the cell to the right of the Day Hike cell, click the Shading Color list arrow 🖳▾, click the Gray-30% color, click the cell to the right of the Backcountry Adventure cell, click the Shading Color list arrow 🖳▾, then click the Gray-10% color

7. Format the text in column 1 of the legend table with Bold, change the alignment to Right, then increase the width of column 1 to fit each entry on one line

Hint

To select a cell, click in the upper-left corner; the entire cell is selected when it turns black.

8. Select the cell containing Deep Cove in row 3, press and hold [Ctrl], select only the cells that are filled with Black as shown in Figure A-5, click the Shading Color list arrow 🖳▾, click the Black color, then click the Font Color (White) button 🅰▾ on the Formatting toolbar

9. Refer to Figure A-5 to fill all the cells containing Day Hikes (Helm Lake, Black Mountain, etc.) with Gray-30% and all the cells containing Backcountry Adventure hikes with Gray-10%, then save the document

Remember you can save time by using [Ctrl] to select multiple cells at once.

FIGURE A-4: Tables and Borders toolbar

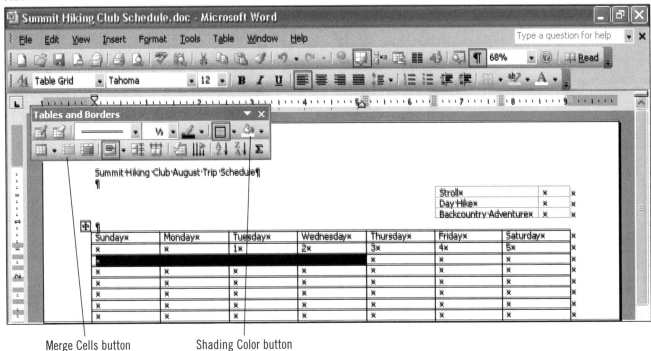

Merge Cells button   Shading Color button

FIGURE A-5: Text for Summit Hiking Club Schedule

						Stroll
						Day Hike
						Backcountry Adventure

Sunday	Monday	Tuesday	Wednesday	Thursday	Friday	Saturday
		1	2	3	4	5
Skyline Trail to Manning Park					Deep Cove	Helm Lake
		Capilano Canyon			Black Tusk	
6	7	8	9	10	11	12
	Panorama Ridge					Black Mountain
Cheakamus Lake		Diamond Head		Mount Seymour	Seymour Creek	Grouse Mountain
13	14	15	16	17	18	19
Maplewood Flats		Garibaldi Mountain				
			West Lion	Ambleside Beach	Crown Mountain	Lynn Canyon
20	21	22	23	24	25	26
Singing Pass to Whistler Mountain						Mount Unnecessary
Goat Mountain	Howe Sound Crest Trail				Shannon Falls	
27	28	29	30	31	Sept. 1	Sept. 2
Rainbow Lake	Mamquam Lake	Golden Ears Provincial Park				

SCHEDULE FOR SUMMIT HIKING CLUB

activity:

Add and Modify a Graphic

The completed schedule is enhanced with a clip art picture that has been modified. In the original clip art, the image of the hiker faces to the left. You need to "flip" the image so that it faces right. Finally, you need to enter the address of the club at the bottom of the page. The completed schedule is shown in Figure A-6.

steps:

1. Click to the left of row 1 of the schedule table to select it, press and hold [Ctrl], select *only* the rows containing hikes (*not* the rows containing the dates), click **Table** on the menu bar, click **Table Properties**, click the **Row tab**, click the **Specify Height text box**, press [Tab], type .4, then click **OK**

2. Click anywhere in the table, click **Table** on the menu bar, point to **Select**, click **Table**, click the **Align Top Left list arrow** on the Tables and Borders toolbar, click the **Align Center button** , then click the **Bold button** **B** on the Formatting toolbar

3. Press [Ctrl][Home] to move the insertion point to the top of the document, select **Summit Hiking Club August Trip Schedule**, format it with **22 point**, **Bold**, **Italic**, and **Right alignment**, then deselect the title

4. Click the Drawing button on the Standard toolbar, click the **Insert Clip Art button** on the Drawing toolbar to open the Clip Art task pane, type **hiker** in the Search for text box, click **Go**, then scroll down to find the clip art picture shown in Figure A-6 (except the hiker will face in the opposite direction)

Trouble

You must be connected to the Internet to download clip art. If you are not connected to the Internet, go to Step 9.

5. Click the **picture** to place it in your document, close the Clip Art task pane, right-click the **picture**, click **Format Picture**, click the **Layout tab**, click **Square**, click the **Left option button**, then click **OK**

6. Right-click the **picture** again, click **Edit Picture**, then click **Yes**
   When you edit a picture, you place it in the Drawing canvas. The picture is then separated into its component objects.

7. Click **Draw** on the Drawing toolbar, click **Group**, click **Draw**, point to **Rotate or Flip**, click **Flip Horizontal**, right-click in a white area of the drawing canvas, click **Format Drawing Canvas**, click the **Size tab**, set the Height at **1.6"**, then click **OK**
   You've regrouped the objects into one object and then flipped it in the opposite direction.

8. Move the pointer over the shaded border of the picture to show the Move Object pointer , click and drag the picture to position it as shown in Figure A-6, then click away from the picture to deselect it

Additional Practice

For additional practice with the skills presented in this project, complete Independent Challenge 1.

9. Press [Ctrl][End] to move to the bottom of the document, press [Enter], type, format, and center the contact information as shown in Figure A-6, save the document, print a copy, then close the document

Summit Hiking Club August Trip Schedule

Legend:
- Stroll
- Day Hike
- Backcountry Adventure

Sunday	Monday	Tuesday	Wednesday	Thursday	Friday	Saturday
	Skyline Trail to Manning Park	1	2	3	4 Deep Cove	5 Helm Lake
6	7	8 Capilano Canyon	9 Panorama Ridge	10	11 Black Tusk	12 Black Mountain
13 Cheakamus Lake	14	15 Diamond Head	16	17 Mount Seymour	18 Seymour Creek	19 Grouse Mountain
20 Maplewood Flats	21	22 Garibaldi Mountain	23 West Lion	24 Ambleside Beach	25 Crown Mountain	26 Mount Unnecessary
27 Goat Mountain	28 Mamquam Lake	29 Singing Pass to Whistler Mountain	30 Howe Sound Crest Trail	31	Sept. 1 Shannon Falls	Sept. 2
27 Rainbow Lake			Golden Ears Provincial Park		Sept. 1	

Your Name, Summit Hiking Club, 1090 Mountain Road, North Vancouver, BC V7H 1A9; Phone: (604) 555-1222

Newsletter for Atlanta Arts Association

The Atlanta Arts Association supports local artists and sponsors several art exhibitions each year. Members of the association want to be kept informed about upcoming exhibitions and other arts-related news. As the publicist for the Association, you are in charge of creating and distributing a newsletter four times a year. To create the newsletter for Spring 2006, you need to Create the Heading, Enter and Format the Text, and Format Columns. The completed newsletter appears in Figure A-13 on page 13.

activity:

Create the Heading

You need to create a heading for the newsletter that includes a picture and two WordArt objects.

steps:

1. Start Word, open the Page Setup dialog box, change all four margins to .5", click OK, then save the document as **Newsletter for Atlanta Arts Association** to the location where you are storing the files for this book

2. Click **Insert** on the menu bar, point to **Picture**, click **From File**, navigate to the location where you are storing files for this book, then double-click **BlueCascade.jpg**
   This photograph of a painting by one of the Association's artists will be featured in the newsletter heading.

3. Right-click the **picture**, click **Format Picture**, click the **Size tab**, change the Height to 2.73, click the **Lock aspect ratio check box** to deselect it, change the Width to 7.6, click the **Layout tab**, click **Behind text**, then click **OK**
   With the layout changed to Behind text, you can now overlay two WordArt objects and some text.

4. Click the **Insert WordArt button** 🅰 on the Drawing toolbar, click **OK**, type **2006**, then click **OK**

5. Click the **WordArt image** to show the WordArt toolbar, click the **Format WordArt button** 🖎 on the WordArt toolbar, click the **Colors and Lines tab**, click the **Fill Color list arrow**, select the **Light Yellow color**, click the **Line Color list arrow**, click **No Line**, then compare the Format WordArt dialog box to Figure A-7

6. Click the **Layout tab** in the Format WordArt dialog box, click **In front of text**, click **OK**, then drag the WordArt object to position it as shown in Figure A-8

7. Create another WordArt object with the text **Spring**, change the Layout to **In front of text**, then drag the object to position it as shown in Figure A-9

8. Press **[Ctrl][Home]** to move the insertion point to the top of the document, double-click approximately .5" below the top of the painting at the left side, type **Atlanta Arts Association**, select the text, change the font to **Arial**, then change the font size to **36**

9. With the text still selected, click the **Font Color list arrow** 🅰▾ on the Formatting toolbar, click the **White color**, apply **Bold** and **Italic**, press **[↓]** once to deselect the text, then save the document
   The completed heading for the newsletter is shown in Figure A-10.

Hint

To show the Drawing toolbar, click the Drawing button on the Standard toolbar

FIGURE A-7: Format WordArt dialog box

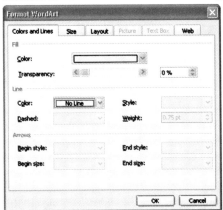

FIGURE A-8: 2006 WordArt object positioned

FIGURE A-9: Spring WordArt object positioned

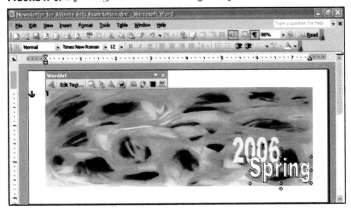

FIGURE A-10: Completed newsletter heading

activity:

Enter and Format the Text

The newsletter consists of three stories. First, you need to create a style that you can apply to each of the three story headings so that the newsletter has a unified look. Then, you need to enter text for the newsletter.

steps:

1. Double-click at the left margin about .5" below the picture, click the **Style list arrow** `Normal ▾` on the Formatting toolbar, click **Clear Formatting**, then, if necessary, press **[Enter]** once or twice more to move the insertion point down so it appears approximately .5" below the picture

2. Click the **Styles and Formatting button** 📑 to open the Styles and Formatting task pane, click **New Style** in the Styles and Formatting task pane, type **Newsletter Story** as the style name, select the **Arial Black font**, then select the **14 point font size**

3. Click **Format** in the New Style dialog box, click **Border**, then click the **Borders tab** if necessary

4. Click the **Width list arrow**, click **6 pt**, click the **Top Border button** in the Preview area, click **OK**, then click **OK**

    The Newsletter Story style includes a solid line above the text.

5. Click the **Newsletter Story** style in the Styles and Formatting task pane, type **Upcoming Exhibitions**, then press **[Enter]**

6. Click the **Show list arrow** in the Styles and Formatting task pane, click **All styles**, select the **Body Text** style from the Styles and Formatting task pane, close the Styles and Formatting task pane, then type the text of the first story in the newsletter as shown in Figure A-11

7. Press **[Enter]** twice, click the **Style list arrow** `Normal ▾` on the Formatting toolbar, click **Newsletter Story** (scroll down if necessary), type **Volunteer of the Season**, press **[Enter]**, click the **Style list arrow** `Normal ▾`, then click **Body Text**

8. Type the text for the Volunteer story and the Featured Work story as shown in Figure A-12

    Remember to format the Featured Work heading with the Newsletter Story style as shown in Figure A-12.

9. Click the **Spelling and Grammar button** 🔤 on the Standard toolbar, make any necessary corrections, then save the document

FIGURE A-11: Text for the "Upcoming Exhibitions" story

Upcoming Exhibitions¶

Spring·2006·will·be·our·best·exhibition·season·ever!·The·Atlanta·Arts·Association·is·proud·to·host·exhibitions· by·three·internationally·acclaimed·artists—all·of·whom·call·Atlanta·home.·First·up·on·April·2·is·Maria·Simpson· with·her·*Landscape·Rhythm*·exhibition.·This·intriguing·series·of·works·is·based·on·video·studies·of·the·unusual· and·historic·landscapes·that·Simpson·often·visits·in·France.·Simpson's·exhibition·runs·to·April·28.·¶
¶
Peter·Moore's·surreal·paintings·take·center·stage·in·the·gallery·from·May·1·to·May·25.·The·paintings·are· inspired·by·the·works·of·the·Italian·Metaphysical·painters·of·the·early·20ᵗʰ·century,·such·as·Giorgio·de·Chirico· and·Carlo·Carra.·Moore's·work·has·attracted·notice·throughout·the·United·States.·In·September,·his·work·will· be·featured·in·two·solo·exhibitions·in·New·York.¶
¶
On·June·2,·photographer·Jay·Singh·presents·*My·Home·Town*,·an·exhibition·of·black·and·white·photographs·of· the·village·in·India·where·Singh·grew·up·before·immigrating·to·America·at·the·age·of·25.·The·haunting· photographs·take·the·viewer·into·the·very·soul·of·the·village.¶
¶

FIGURE A-12: Text for the "Volunteer" and "Featured Work" stories

Volunteer of the Season¶

Janice·Brown·is·our·Volunteer·of·the·Season—the·Spring·Season·in·this·case!·On·more·than·one·occasion,· Janice·has·gone·above·and·beyond·the·call·of·duty·in·her·tireless·efforts·to·communicate·the·activities·of·the· Atlanta·Arts·Association·to·the·public.·We·honor·her·this·season·because·of·her·incredible·contribution·to·our· recent·fund-raising·event.·Thanks·to·Janice,·the·Atlanta·Arts·Association·raised·a·staggering·$50,000—that's· 40%·higher·than·last·year's·total!·Janice·continues·to·inspire·all·of·us·with·her·entrepreneurial·spirit·and·her· enthusiasm·for·art.¶

Featured Work¶

Each·season,·the·Atlanta·Arts·Association·selects·the·painting·that·will·represent·the·association·in·all·its· advertising.·Shown·at·the·right·is·the·image·that·will·be·used·as·the·cover·photo·for·our·spring·ads·in·*Atlanta· Arts*,·*Arts·Alive*,·and·*Art,·etc.*·Entitled·*Cote·de·Granite·Rose*,·this·luscious·canvas·is·the·work·of·Maria·Simpson.· Her·April·exhibition,·*Landscape·Rhythm*,·is·sure·to·be·a·big·hit·with·Atlanta·art·lovers.·At·her·last·exhibition· with·the·association,·Maria·sold·every·single·canvas!·Patrons·raved·about·her·dizzying·array·of·paintings·and· drawings·in·abstract·styles·that·seemed·to·capture·the·essence·of·light·and·color.·¶
¶

activity:

Format Columns

You can achieve some interesting effects by using a variety of column styles to display text in a newsletter as shown in the completed newsletter (see Figure A-13). The "Upcoming Exhibitions" and "Volunteer of the Season" stories appear in two columns of equal width and the "Featured Work" story appears in one column at the bottom of the page. In addition, the "Volunteer of the Season" story is shaded and a picture is inserted into the "Featured Work" story.

steps:

1. Press **[Ctrl][Home]** to move to the top of the newsletter, click to the left of the Upcoming Exhibitions heading, click **Format** on the menu bar, click **Columns**, then click **Two**

2. Click the **Apply to list arrow**, click **This point forward**, then click **OK**
   By selecting This point forward, you set columns only from the current position of your insertion point to the end of the document.

3. Click at the beginning of paragraph 3 in the Upcoming Exhibitions story (begins with the text On June 2…), click **Insert** on the menu bar, click **Break**, click **Column break**, then click **OK**

4. Select the text from **Volunteer of the Season** to the end of the story (enthusiasm for art), click **Format** on the menu bar, click **Borders and Shading**, click the **Shading tab**, click the **Light Yellow color**, then click **OK**

5. Click to the left of the Featured Work heading, click **Format** on the menu bar, click **Columns**, click **One**, click the **Apply to list arrow**, click **This point forward**, then click **OK**
   You have made the last story in the newsletter span one column.

6. Click **Insert** on the menu bar, point to **Picture**, click **From File**, navigate to the location where you are storing the files for this book, then double-click **GraniteRose.jpg**

7. Right-click the **picture** (you will need to scroll to the next page to find the picture), click **Format Picture**, click the **Size tab**, change the height to **1.3**, click the **Layout tab**, click **Square**, click **OK**, then drag the picture to position it as shown in Figure A-13

8. Click at the end of the Featured Work story, press **[Enter]** once, click **Format** on the menu bar, click **Borders and Shading**, click the **Borders tab**, click the **Bottom Border button** in the Preview area, then click **OK**

Additional Practice

For additional practice with the skills presented in this project, complete Independent Challenge 2.

9. Click **View** on the menu bar, click **Header and Footer**, click the **Switch Between Header and Footer button** 🔳 on the Header and Footer toolbar, type and center the contact text as shown in Figure A-13 in **10 point**, save the file, preview the completed newsletter, click the **Shrink to Fit button** 🔳 on the Print Preview toolbar to fit the newsletter to one page if necessary, print a copy, then close the document

Atlanta Arts Association

2006 Spring

Upcoming Exhibitions

Spring 2006 will be our best exhibition season ever! The Atlanta Arts Association is proud to host exhibitions by three internationally acclaimed artists—all of whom call Atlanta home. First up on April 2 is Maria Simpson with her *Landscape Rhythm* exhibition. This intriguing series of works is based on video studies of the unusual and historic landscapes that Simpson often visits in France. Simpson's exhibition runs to April 28.

Peter Moore's surreal paintings take center stage in the gallery from May 1 to May 25. The paintings are inspired by the works of the Italian Metaphysical painters of the early 20th century, such as Giorgio de Chirico and Carlo Carra. Moore's work has attracted notice throughout the United States. In September, his work will be featured in two solo exhibitions in New York.

On June 2, photographer Jay Singh presents *My Home Town*, an exhibition of black and white photographs of the village in India where Singh grew up before immigrating to America at the age of 25. The haunting photographs take the viewer into the very soul of the village.

Volunteer of the Season

Janice Brown is our Volunteer of the Season—the Spring Season in this case! On more than one occasion, Janice has gone above and beyond the call of duty in her tireless efforts to communicate the activities of the Atlanta Arts Association to the public. We honor her this season because of her incredible contribution to our recent fund-raising event. Thanks to Janice, the Atlanta Arts Association raised a staggering $50,000—that's 40% higher than last year's total! Janice continues to inspire all of us with her entrepreneurial spirit and her enthusiasm for art.

Featured Work

Each season, the Atlanta Arts Association selects the painting that will represent the association in all its advertising. Shown at the right is the image that will be used as the cover photo for our spring ads in *Atlanta Arts*, *Arts Alive*, and *Art, etc.* Entitled *Cote de Granite Rose*, this luscious canvas is the work of Maria Simpson. Her April exhibition, *Landscape Rhythm*, is sure to be a big hit with Atlanta art lovers. At her last exhibition with the association, Maria sold every single canvas! Patrons raved about her dizzying array of paintings and drawings in abstract styles that seemed to capture the essence of light and color.

Your Name, Editor, Maple Building, 2000 Olympic Way, Atlanta, GA 30349; Phone: (770) 555-1889

Business Cards for José Alvarez

José Alvarez works from his home in Philadelphia, Pennsylvania, as a freelance writer. José has asked you to create business cards for him. He wants you to combine text and graphics to make his business cards eye-catching. To create José's business cards, you need to **Create Labels and Enter Text**, **Add a WordArt Logo**, and **Format the Label Sheet for Printing**. The completed sheet of business cards is shown in Figure A-20 on page 19.

activity:

Create Labels and Enter Text

You use a business label sheet that you select in the Labels Options dialog box as the basis for José's labels. You enter text in one label and use the Symbol dialog box to insert the é at the end of José's name. Finally, you format the text on the business card so that José's name and position are emphasized.

steps:

1. Start Word, click **Tools** on the menu bar, point to **Letters and Mailings**, click **Envelopes and Labels**, then click the **Labels tab** if necessary
   In the Labels tab of the Envelopes and Labels dialog box, you can select the size and type of label you need to create a sheet of business cards.

2. Click **Options**, then scroll the **Product number list box** until 5371 - Business Card appears

3. Click **5371 - Business Card** to select it, click **OK**, then click **New Document**
   You click New Document because you want to show the label sheet as a table in which you can include both the text and a WordArt object for the business card.

4. Type Jos
   You'll add the é next.

5. Click **Insert** on the menu bar, click **Symbol**, select (normal text) as the Font type if necessary, scroll to the é as shown in Figure A-14, click **é**, click **Insert**, then click **Close**

6. Press [Spacebar] once, type **Alvarez**, then save the document as **Business Cards for Jose Alvarez** to the location where you are storing the files for this book

7. Press [Enter] once, then type the remaining text for the business card as shown in Figure A-15

8. Select the six lines of text, change the font to **Arial**, click the **Align Right button** ▤ on the Formatting toolbar, enhance **José Alvarez** with **Bold** and a font size of **14 point**, change the font size of the remaining text to **10 point**, then enhance **Freelance Writer** with **Italic**

9. Select all six lines of text, click **Format** on the menu bar, click **Paragraph**, change the Right Indentation to .5", click **OK**, deselect the text, then save the document
   The completed text for the business card is shown in Figure A-16.

FIGURE A-14: Symbol dialog box

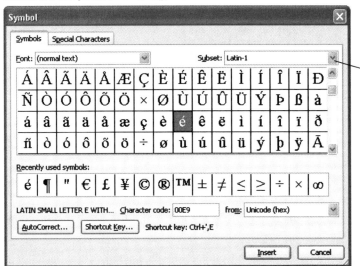

Use the list arrow and navigate to Latin-1 subset

FIGURE A-15: Text for business card

FIGURE A-16: Business card text formatted

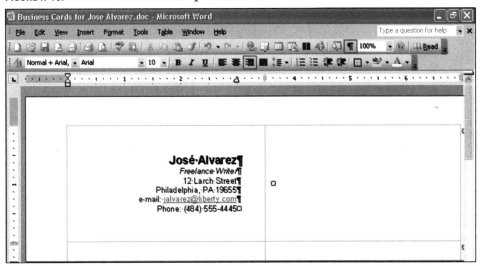

activity:

Add a WordArt Logo

You need to add a WordArt object to the business card and then modify it.

Trouble

To show the Drawing toolbar, click the Drawing button on the Standard toolbar.

steps:

1. Show the Drawing toolbar if necessary, then click the Insert WordArt button ⚞ on the Drawing toolbar

   The WordArt Gallery dialog box opens.

2. Select the second option from the left in the third row as shown in Figure A-17, then click OK

3. Type JA, change the font to Comic Sans MS, click the Bold button, click OK, then click the WordArt object to select it

   Black sizing handles appear around the WordArt object to indicate it is selected, and the WordArt toolbar appears.

4. Click the WordArt Shape button ⚞ on the WordArt toolbar, then click the Slant Up shape as shown in Figure A-18

5. Click the Format WordArt button ⚞ on the WordArt toolbar, click the Size tab if necessary, change the Height and Width to .5, click the Layout tab, click Square, click the Left option button, then click OK

   By selecting the Square layout, you convert the WordArt object from an inline graphic to a floating graphic that you can position easily on the business card.

6. With the WordArt object still selected, click the Shadow Style button ⚞ on the Drawing toolbar, then select Shadow Style 9

   The WordArt object is complete.

7. Click next to the J in José, click Format on the menu bar, click Paragraph, change the Before Spacing to 48 point, then click OK

8. Drag the WordArt object to the upper-left corner of the first business card as shown in Figure A-19

9. Click away from the WordArt object, then save the document

Clues to Use

Editing a WordArt object

You can modify a WordArt object in many different ways by selecting different shapes, experimenting with different fill and line color options, and applying various shadow and 3-D styles. To modify an existing WordArt object, click it to show the WordArt toolbar, and then select the tools you require. You can apply one of the preset WordArt styles by clicking the WordArt Gallery button on the WordArt toolbar, and then you can modify the style by selecting new options in the Format WordArt dialog box.

FIGURE A-17: WordArt Gallery dialog box

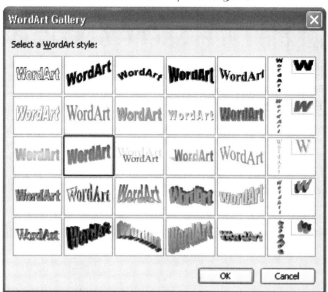

FIGURE A-18: Slant Up shape selected

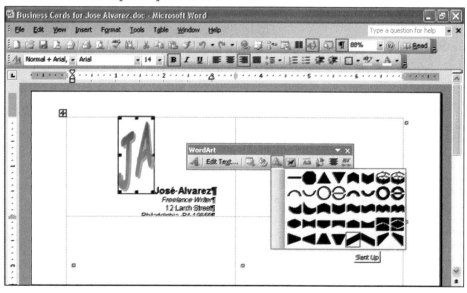

FIGURE A-19: Completed business card

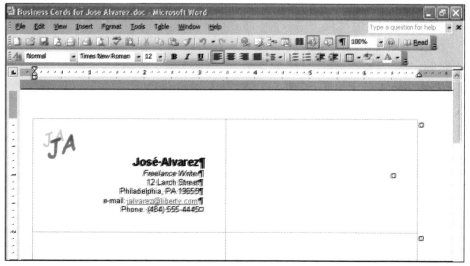

activity:

Format the Label Sheet for Printing

José's business card is complete. Now all you need to do is copy it to the remaining nine cards, and then print the label sheet, which is actually structured as a Word table. The completed label sheet is shown in Figure A-20.

steps:

1. Verify that the cursor is in cell 1, click **Table** on the menu bar, point to **Select**, then click **Cell**

2. Click the **Copy button** on the Standard toolbar, click in the top-right cell, then click the **Paste Cells button** on the Standard toolbar

3. Click **Table** on the menu bar, point to **Select**, then click **Row**

The first row of the business card sheet is selected. Note that you can also click to the left of the first business card to select the entire first row.

4. Click , click in row 2, click , then click three more times

After you paste the last row, a second page of blank cards is added.

5. Click the **Zoom list arrow** 100% on the Standard toolbar, then click **Two Pages**

6. Select all the blank rows on page 2, then click the **Cut button** on the Standard toolbar

A complete sheet of business cards appears on one page.

7. Click at the end of the last line in the last business card, press **[Enter]**, then type your name

8. Save the document, print a copy, then close it

The completed sheet of cards is shown in Figure A-20. If José were really printing his business cards, he would insert several sheets of the pre-punched cards he purchased into his printer before he clicked the Print button.

Trouble

If the rows are not deleted, point the to the left of the first blank row, drag down to select all blank rows, then click the Cut button.

Additional Practice

For additional practice with the skills presented in this project, complete Independent Challenge 3.

Word Pro

José Alvarez
Freelance Writer
12 Larch Street
Philadelphia, PA 19655
e-mail: jalvarez@liberty.com
Phone: (484) 555-4445

José Alvarez
Freelance Writer
12 Larch Street
Philadelphia, PA 19655
e-mail: jalvarez@liberty.com
Phone: (484) 555-4445

José Alvarez
Freelance Writer
12 Larch Street
Philadelphia, PA 19655
e-mail: jalvarez@liberty.com
Phone: (484) 555-4445

José Alvarez
Freelance Writer
12 Larch Street
Philadelphia, PA 19655
e-mail: jalvarez@liberty.com
Phone: (484) 555-4445

José Alvarez
Freelance Writer
12 Larch Street
Philadelphia, PA 19655
e-mail: jalvarez@liberty.com
Phone: (484) 555-4445

José Alvarez
Freelance Writer
12 Larch Street
Philadelphia, PA 19655
e-mail: jalvarez@liberty.com
Phone: (484) 555-4445

José Alvarez
Freelance Writer
12 Larch Street
Philadelphia, PA 19655
e-mail: jalvarez@liberty.com
Phone: (484) 555-4445

José Alvarez
Freelance Writer
12 Larch Street
Philadelphia, PA 19655
e-mail: jalvarez@liberty.com
Phone: (484) 555-4445

José Alvarez
Freelance Writer
12 Larch Street
Philadelphia, PA 19655
e-mail: jalvarez@liberty.com
Phone: (484) 555-4445

José Alvarez
Freelance Writer
12 Larch Street
Philadelphia, PA 19655
e-mail: jalvarez@liberty.com
Phone: (484) 555-4445
Your Name

Independent Challenges

INDEPENDENT CHALLENGE 1

Use the Table feature to create a schedule for a series of activities such as a weekly course schedule or a monthly calendar of events. For example, you could create a schedule that displays all the concerts or plays offered over a six-month period at a local theater, or you could create your personal weekly schedule that includes all your work, school, and leisure activities. To help you determine the information required for your schedule, follow the directions provided below.

1. Determine the purpose of your schedule. Do you want to keep track of your courses each week, or create your personal fitness schedule, or perhaps create a calendar of events for a local community group? Enter the purpose of your schedule in the box below.

    Schedule Purpose _____

2. Determine the column and row labels required for your schedule. If you are creating a weekly schedule, your column labels will be the days of the week; if you are creating a monthly schedule, your column labels will be the months of the year. List the column and row labels required for your schedule in the box below.

    Column Labels _____

    Row Labels _____

3. Calculate the total number of rows and columns required to complete your schedule. For example, if you are creating a weekly schedule, you will need to create a table consisting of eight columns. Column 1 will contain the time increments (e.g., 8:00 to 9:00) and columns 2 to 8 will contain the days of the week.

4. Set up your document so that it prints in landscape orientation. Change the margins, if you wish.

5. Create the table. Note that you can add new rows to the table by clicking in the last cell of the last row, then pressing [Tab]. You can add columns by selecting a column, clicking Table on the menu bar, clicking Insert, and then selecting Columns to the Left or Columns to the Right.

6. Enter the information required for your schedule. Use the Copy and Paste features to minimize repetitive typing time.

7. Show the Tables and Borders toolbar, then shade selected cells with one or more fill colors. Remember that you can use the [Ctrl] key to select and then fill nonadjacent cells with the same shading style.

8. Create an attractive heading for your schedule, using text that describes the content of the schedule (such as "My Fitness Schedule" or "Monthly Events Calendar").

9. Include a clip art picture that you have modified in some way. Remember that you need to convert the clip art picture to a drawing object if you want to rotate it or flip it vertically or horizontally.

10. Enter your name at the bottom of the document, check the spelling and grammar, save the document as **My Schedule** to the location where you are storing the files for this book, then print a copy.

Adapt the newsletter you created in Project 2 to present interesting stories about an organization or company of your choice. For example, you could choose to describe the latest activities of a club you're involved in or you could develop a newsletter for customers of a company. Here are some directions for creating your newsletter:

1. Determine the name of your company or organization and the types of activities you'd like to write about.
2. Develop copy for two or three stories that would be of interest to the people who would read your newsletter. For example, if you've created a newsletter for a gardening club, you could include stories such as "Forever Perennials," "Gardener of the Month," and "Great Garden Tours."
3. Set up your document with .5" margins on all four sides.
4. Create an attractive heading for your newsletter. The heading should include the name of the company or organization and the date of the newsletter publication. You may wish to adapt the heading you created for the Atlanta Arts Association's newsletter. If you wish, include a graphic in the heading. You can choose to include a photograph or a clip art image.
5. Following the heading, enter text for the two or three stories you have written.
6. Create a new style for the story headings. If you wish, include a border line.
7. Format the stories in columns. You can choose to format the entire newsletter in two or three columns, or you can format two of the stories in two columns and one story in one column as you did with the Atlanta Arts Association's newsletter. Experiment with various combinations until you are satisfied with the overall appearance of your newsletter.
8. Include one or two pictures in the body of your newsletter.
9. Include your name as the editor of the newsletter somewhere on the document, then check the spelling and grammar.
10. Preview the newsletter and fit it to one page as necessary, save the newsletter as **My Newsletter** to the location where you are storing the files for this book, then print the completed newsletter.

INDEPENDENT CHALLENGE 3

Use a business card label product, such as 5371 – Business Card, available in the Envelopes and Labels dialog box, to create a sheet of business cards for yourself. Follow the directions to create your business cards:

1. Draw a business-card sized rectangle on a piece of paper, and then spend some time experimenting with different designs for your business card. For example, you could right-align your name and address and include a WordArt logo of your initials in the top-left corner of the business card, or you could center your name and address on only two lines along the bottom of the business card, then insert the logo centered in the middle of the business card. Draw several versions of your business card until you find the one that looks right.

2. In the Labels tab of the Envelopes and Labels dialog box, select one of the Business Card products from the list of available label products in the Label Options dialog box, click OK, and then click New Document.

3. Enter your name and address on the business card. Apply formatting to selected text. For example, you may want your name to appear in a larger font and in bold.

4. Create an attractive WordArt logo based on your initials. Experiment with some of the many options available for formatting a WordArt object. For example, you can modify the fill and line color, add or remove a shadow, or add a 3-D effect.

5. Format the WordArt object so that the layout is Square. By changing the layout to Square, you change the layout from inline graphic to floating graphic. Select an appropriate horizontal alignment option.

6. Reduce the size of the logo and position it attractively on the business card.

7. Modify the Before or After Paragraph spacing of the text, depending on where you've inserted the WordArt logo. You may need to experiment to find the best way to position the text in relation to the WordArt logo.

8. Copy the contents of the first table cell to the second table cell in the label sheet, then copy the entire row down the label sheet until all cells on one sheet contain the text and logo for the business card. Be sure to delete extra rows.

9. Save the document as **My Business Cards** to the location where you are storing the files for this book.

10. Print your sheet of business cards. If possible, print the cards on a sheet of pre-punched business card stock.

INDEPENDENT CHALLENGE 4

Type the text for the confirmation letter shown in Figure A-21, then enhance the letter as directed. Note that the purpose of a confirmation letter is to confirm arrangements related to a specific event or agreement made between two companies or organizations. In the confirmation letter below, Best Communications, a company based in the United Kingdom, confirms a seminar they are hosting for employees of the Midland Counties Bank.

1. Type the text as shown in Figure A-21. Note that you will find the £ symbol in the (normal text) font in the Symbol dialog box.

2. Replace the text "Best Communications, Inc." at the top of the document with a WordArt object. Change the fill color or texture of the WordArt object and modify the 3-D or shadow settings. Your goal is to make the WordArt object different from the preset style you selected.

3. Use your own judgment to enhance the letter attractively, then check spelling and grammar.

4. View the letter in the Print Preview screen, then fit the letter on one page.

5. Save the letter as **Confirmation Letter** to the location where you are storing the files for this book, then print a copy.

Best Communications, Inc.

1603 Woodley Road, Reading, Berkshire, RG22 2RP, England

www.bestcommunications.co.uk

Current Date

Marianne Shaw
Personnel Manager
Midland Counties Bank: Basingstoke Branch
24 London Road
Reading, Berkshire RG30 1TN

Dear Ms. Shaw,

Thank you for your letter of [specify a date one week prior to the current date] confirming a one-day communications seminar at the Basingstoke Branch of the Midland Counties Bank. My colleague, Mr. John McDougall, will be conducting the seminar and supplying all the materials the participants will require.

Here again are the seminar details:

Date:	[specify a date one month after the current date]
Time:	0900 to 1700
Location:	2nd Floor, Administration Building, Reading University, Whiteknights Campus
Cost:	£3000 for 20 participants.

As we discussed, the communications seminar will include the following activities:

1. Warm-up exercises to stimulate a relaxed atmosphere and to determine the general level of communication skills among the participants.
2. Analysis of various communications situations to assess writing strengths and weaknesses.
3. Intensive "hands-on" practice in the communication of clear and effective sales, training, and informational presentations.

I'm very much looking forward to an exciting seminar. Thank you again, Ms. Shaw, for your interest in Best Communications, Inc. If you have any further questions, please call me at 0118 555 2222.

Sincerely,

Your Name
President

Visual Workshop

Create the letterhead shown in Figure A-22 in a new document. Save the document as **Ocean Adventures Letterhead** to the location where you are storing the files for this book. Reduce the size of the WordArt object to .6" high and 4" wide, then change the layout to match the figure. Enhance the WordArt object by experimenting with texture, shadows, and character spacing. Find the clip art picture by searching the Clip Organizer. If you can't find the picture shown, choose a similar picture. Change the layout of the clip art picture to Square and left-aligned, ungroup the picture, click Yes, group the picture, then flip it horizontally. Reduce the height of the drawing canvas containing the marlin so that it appears as shown in Figure A-22.

FIGURE A-22: Letterhead

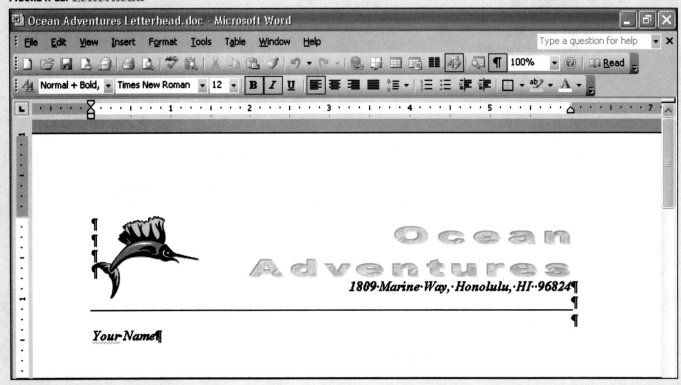

Microsoft Word Projects

Unit B

Word Projects II

In this Unit You Will Create the Following:

 **Five-Page Proposal**

 **Six-Panel Brochure**

 **One-Page Resume**

With Microsoft Word, you can design multiple-page documents such as proposals and reports that include page numbers, headers and footers, charts and diagrams, and an automatically generated table of contents. You can also use Word to create multi-panel brochures containing text formatted in columns, and you can insert a variety of graphics, including clip art pictures, drawn shapes, and WordArt objects. In this unit, you will apply your Microsoft Word skills to modify styles, generate a table of contents, add section breaks, format text in columns, create a diagram, and modify clip art pictures.

Five-Page Proposal for Sage College

The dean of Sage College has asked the Business Department to submit a proposal to request approval for a new program designed to train executive assistants and office administrators. You will **Set up the Document, Create Page 1, Create Page 2, Create Page 3**, and **Create the Table of Contents and Title Page**. Figures B-3 through B-7 on pages 29 through 35 show the five pages that you'll create for the proposal.

activity:

Set Up the Document

You need to set up a header and a footer and then you need to modify heading styles.

steps:

1. Start Word, click **View** on the menu bar, click **Header and Footer**, type **Executive Assistant Program Proposal**, press **[Tab]** twice, click the **Insert Date button** on the Header and Footer toolbar, then press **[Enter]**

2. Click the **Switch Between Header and Footer button** on the Header and Footer toolbar, type your name, then press **[Tab]** twice

3. Click the **Insert Page Number button** on the Header and Footer toolbar, click **Close**, then save the document as **Sage College Proposal** to the location where you are storing the files for this book
The document now includes a header and a footer containing text that will appear on the top and bottom of every page.

4. Click the **Styles and Formatting button** on the Formatting toolbar to open the Styles and Formatting task pane, right-click **Heading 1** in the Pick formatting to apply list, click **Modify**, then change the font size to **18 point**

5. Click **Format**, click **Border**, select the Double border style, click **None** in the Setting area, then click the **Bottom Border button** in the Preview area as shown in Figure B-1

6. Click **OK**, then click **OK** to exit the Modify Style dialog box

7. Click **Heading 1** in the Styles and Formatting task pane, type **Introduction**, then press **[Enter]**

8. Right-click **Heading 2** in the Styles and Formatting task pane, click **Modify**, click the **Increase Indent button** once, then click **OK**

9. Save the document
Your screen should look like Figure B-2.

FIGURE B-1: Borders and Shading dialog box

None ——

Double border style ——

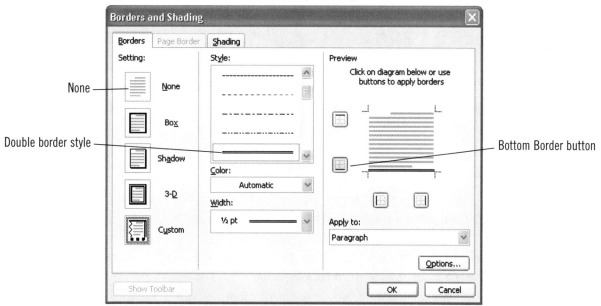

—— Bottom Border button

FIGURE B-2: Heading styles

Heading 1 style applied ——

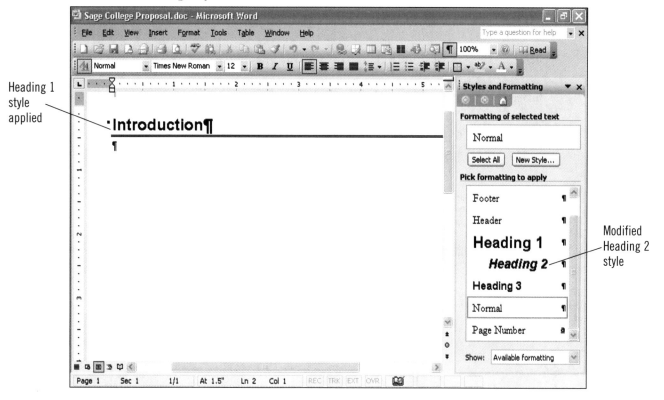

Modified Heading 2 style

activity:

Create Page 1

First, you need to create a new style to format the proposal text. The new style, which you name Proposal Text, changes the text indent to .5, the line spacing to 1.5, and the before paragraph spacing to 12 point. Then, you need to enter the text required for page 1 and create a footnote. The completed page 1 is shown in Figure B-3.

Hint

A ScreenTip appears when you move the pointer over a button.

steps:

1. Click New Style in the Styles and Formatting task pane, type Proposal Text as the style Name, then verify that ¶ Normal appears in the Style based on text box

2. Click the 1.5 Space button, click the Increase Paragraph Spacing button twice, click the Increase Indent button, then click OK

   All text formatted with the new Proposal Text style will have 1.5 spacing between lines and 12-point spacing between paragraphs, and be indented .5".

3. Click Proposal Text in the Styles and Formatting task pane, then type the introductory paragraph as shown in Figure B-3

4. Press [Enter], click Heading 1 in the Styles and Formatting task pane, type Scope of the Program, press [Enter], click Proposal Text in the Styles and Formatting task pane, then type the next paragraph as shown in Figure B-3

5. Press [Enter], select the Heading 2 style, type Description of Need, then press [Enter]

6. Select the Proposal Text style, then type the next two paragraphs as shown in Figure B-3

7. Click Insert on the menu bar, point to Reference, click Footnote, then click Insert to accept the default settings

8. Press [Tab], press [Ctrl][T] to create a hanging indent, then type the text for the footnote as shown in Figure B-3

9. Save the document

Executive Assistant Program Proposal   Current Date

Introduction

This proposal presents a request to develop the Executive Assistant program to train students for employment as Administrative and Executive Assistants, Office Managers, and Office Administrators. Included in the proposal is a discussion of three factors related to the development of the program: Scope of the Program, Proposed Courses, and Funding Requirements. If approved, the Coordinator of the Business Department will develop course outlines and begin to recruit students for entry into the program in September 2007.

Scope of the Program

The proposed program will provide students with extensive training in computer applications and business-related skills. The goal of the program is to train students for employment. The program will run for nine months—from September to May and include a two-week work practicum. Students who graduate from the program will be prepared to enter the workforce.

Description of Need

At present, none of the local community colleges offers an Executive Assistant program. Westview College, the closest competitor to Sage College, offers an Administrative Assistant program that primarily attracts students who have just graduated from high school. The proposed Executive Assistant program will target candidates who have either several years of college or considerable work experience. These candidates require practical skills that will help them gain employment in an office environment.

The marketing survey conducted by Joanne McLean, Coordinator of the Business Department, is attached to this proposal.[1]

---

[1]   Personnel agencies, human resources professionals, and businesspeople responded to the survey. The results show a need for candidates with the skills offered by the Executive Assistant program.

Your Name   1

activity:

Create Page 2

You need to insert a hard page break so that the text and headings you enter next appear on page 2. When you have finished entering the text and headings, you insert the table for the list of courses and enclose it in a rounded rectangle. The completed page 2 is shown in Figure B-4.

steps:

1. Click at the end of the last paragraph on page 1 after the footnote marker, click Insert on the menu bar, click Break, click OK to accept Page Break, select the Heading 1 style, type Proposed Courses, then press [Enter]

2. Select the Proposal Text style, enter and format the text required for the rest of page 2, with the exception of the table in the Course Descriptions section as shown in Figure B-4, then press [Enter] twice

Remember to format the two subheadings with the Heading 2 style and paragraphs of text with the Proposal Text style.

Be sure to hold down the left mouse button as you drag.

3. Click the Insert Table button ▦ on the Standard toolbar, drag the pointer to create a table consisting of nine rows and two columns, then enter and format the text for the table as shown in Figure B-4

The text will wrap to page 3. You'll fix this problem in the next step.

4. Scroll up to the top of the table, move the pointer over the upper-left corner of the table to display the table move handle ⊞, then click ⊞ to select the entire table

5. Select the Normal style in the Styles and Formatting task pane, drag the left edge of the table to the right to reduce the width of column 1 to approximately 1.5", click the Outside Border list arrow ▦▾ on the Formatting toolbar, then click the No Border button

6. Click the ¶ mark above the table to deselect the table, close the Styles and Formatting task pane, click the Drawing button ✎ on the Standard toolbar to show the Drawing toolbar, click the Zoom list arrow 100% ▾ on the Standard toolbar, then click 75%

In 75% view, you can easily see the entire table.

7. Click the AutoShapes button AutoShapes▾ on the Drawing toolbar, point to Basic Shapes, click the Rounded Rectangle button (second row of the first column), then click below the Create Your Drawing Here drawing canvas

When you click below the drawing canvas, a small rounded rectangle appears.

8. Click the Fill Color list arrow ◇▾ on the Drawing toolbar, click No Fill, use your mouse to adjust the size and position of the rounded rectangle so that it encloses the table like a border as shown in Figure B-4, then save the document

Executive Assistant Program Proposal   Current Date

Proposed Courses

Martha Travis, an instructor in the Business Department, developed eight new courses for the proposed Executive Assistant program. She was assisted by Dr. Roy Devaux, a Management Consultant and former faculty member at Sage College.

Course Overview

Students in the proposed Executive Assistant program will take eight courses over two terms: September to December and January to May. The courses are evenly divided between theory-based and application-based courses. During the program, students become proficient in several software applications. In addition, students improve their written and oral communication skills, develop project management skills, and learn how to plan and run special events.

Course Descriptions

The following table lists the eight courses offered to students in the proposed Executive Assistant program.

Course	Description
Basic Business Skills	Learn the fundamentals of business
Document Design	Develop expert-level skills in Microsoft Word
Project Management	Learn the fundamentals of project management
Budgeting & Analysis	Develop spreadsheet skills using Microsoft Excel
Web Page Design	Use HTML to design Web pages
Event Planning	Organize special events
Data Management	Develop database skills using Microsoft Access
Communications	Develop written and oral communication skills

Your Name   2

PROPOSAL FOR SAGE COLLEGE

activity:

Create Page 3

You need to include a radial diagram that illustrates the various sources of revenue required to run the Executive Assistant program. In addition, you need to include information about estimated expenses and a conclusion. The completed page 3 is shown in Figure B-5.

steps:

1. Click below the table on page 2, press **[Ctrl][Enter]** to insert a hard page break, then click the **Styles and Formatting button** 🔠 on the Formatting toolbar to open the Styles and Formatting task pane

2. Select **Heading 1**, enter the headings and text required for the Estimated Costs and Estimated Revenue as shown in Figure B-5, press **[Enter]**, then close the Styles and Formatting task pane

3. Click the **Insert Diagram or Organization Chart button** 🔘 on the Drawing toolbar

4. Click the **radial diagram** (far right selection in the top row), then click **OK**
   A diagram with four circles is inserted, and the Diagram toolbar is displayed.

5. Click the **middle circle**, type **Funding Sources**, click the **Insert Shape button** on the Diagram toolbar twice to insert two new circles, then enter text in the five perimeter circles as shown in Figure B-5

6. Click the **AutoFormat button** 🔷 on the Diagram toolbar, click the **Thick Outline** diagram style, then click **OK**

7. Right-click a white area of the diagram, click **Format Diagram**, click the **Layout tab**, click **Square**, click the **Center option button**, click the **Size tab**, set the height at **4"**, then click **OK**

8. Select **College Grant** in the top circle, click the **Bold button** 🅱 on the Formatting toolbar, select the **10-point** font size, double-click the **Format Painter button** 🖌 on the Standard toolbar, use the Format Painter to apply formatting to the text in the rest of the circles, then click 🖌 to deselect the Format Painter

9. Double-click at the left margin below the diagram, type **Conclusion** and apply the **Heading 1** style, enter the concluding paragraph in the Proposal Text style as shown in Figure B-5, then save the document

Executive Assistant Program Proposal   Current Date

Funding Requirements

Estimated Costs

The total estimated cost for the proposed program is $138,000 broken down as follows: $80,000 for faculty (based on a $10,000 cost per course), $35,000 for administrative support, $10,000 for advertising, and $13,000 for new software.

Estimated Revenue

The radial diagram shown below displays the various funding sources available:

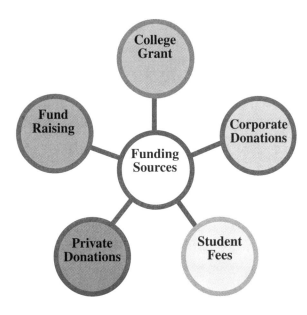

Conclusion

The Executive Assistant program will enroll 36 students at a cost of $3,000 per student for total student fees of $108,000. The remaining funding should break down as follows: College Grant: $15,000, Corporate and Private Donations: $10,000, and Fund Raising: $5,000.

Your Name   3

activity:

Create the Table of Contents and Title Page

You need to insert a section break above the first page of the proposal text, generate a table of contents, and create a title page.

steps:

1. Press **[Ctrl][Home]** to move to the top of the document, click **Insert** on the menu bar, click **Break**, click the **Next page option button**, click **OK**, press **[Ctrl][Home]** again, click the **Style list arrow** [Normal ▾] on the Formatting toolbar, then click **Clear Formatting**

2. Type **Table of Contents**, press **[Enter]** four times, then enhance Table of Contents with **Bold**, a font size of **16 point**, and **Center alignment**

3. Click at the second blank line below Table of Contents, click **Insert** on the menu bar, point to **Reference**, click **Index and Tables**, click the **Table of Contents tab**, click the **Formats list arrow**, click **Formal**, then click **OK**

   The table of contents is automatically generated based on the styles you applied to the various headings.

4. Press **[Ctrl][Home]**, insert another **Next page section break**, move to the top of the document again, click **View** on the menu bar, click **Header and Footer**, click the **Page Setup button** 🔲 on the Header and Footer toolbar, click the **Layout tab**, click the **Different first page check box** to select it, then click **OK**

   This step returns the header and footer on the first page to blank.

5. Click the **Show Next button** 🔲 twice on the Header and Footer toolbar to move to the header for section 3 (which contains the three pages of the proposal text), click the **Link to Previous button** 🔲 on the Header and Footer toolbar to deselect it, click the **Switch Between Header and Footer button** 🔲, click 🔲 to deselect it, click the **Format Page Number button** 🔲, click the **Start at option button**, verify that 1 appears in the Start at text box, then click **OK**

   By deselecting the Link to Previous button in Section 3, you ensure that any changes you make to the header and footer in Section 2 will not affect the header and footer in Section 3.

6. Click the **Show Previous button** 🔲 to move to the footer for section 2 (the table of contents), click 🔲 to deselect it, click 🔲, click the **Number format list arrow**, click the **i, ii, iii number format**, click the **Start at option button**, verify that i appears in the Start at text box, then click **OK**

7. Switch to the header, click to the left of the header text to select it, press **[Delete]**, then click the **Close button** on the Header and Footer toolbar

   The table of contents page appears in its own section. You can delete the header text without deleting it from the rest of the proposal text because you deselected Link to Previous in section 3.

8. Scroll to the table of contents page, right-click the **table of contents**, click **Update Field**, click the **Update entire table option button**, click **OK**, click below the table of contents to deselect it, then compare the table of contents to Figure B-6

9. Scroll through the document to verify that "i" appears in the footer on the Table of Contents page and "1" appears in the footer on the first page of the proposal text, press **[Ctrl][Home]**, enter and enhance the text for the title page as shown in Figure B-7, check the spelling and grammar, save the document, print a copy, then close the document

Additional Practice

For additional practice with the skills presented in this project, complete Independent Challenge 1.

FIGURE B-6: Completed table of contents

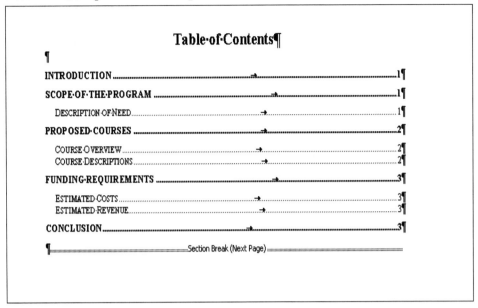

....Section Break (Next Page)...................................

FIGURE B-7: Completed title page

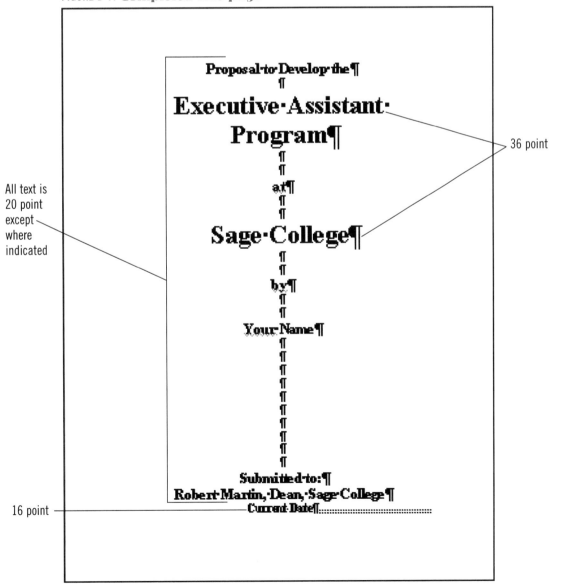

36 point

All text is 20 point except where indicated

Proposal to Develop the¶
¶
Executive Assistant Program¶
¶
¶
at¶
¶
¶
Sage College¶
¶
¶
by¶
¶
¶
Your Name¶
¶
¶
¶
¶
¶
¶
¶
¶
¶
¶
Submitted to:¶
Robert Martin, Dean, Sage College¶
Current Date¶

16 point

Six-Panel Brochure

You need to create a six-panel brochure on tours of the United Kingdom. Page 1 of the document consists of the inside three panels of the brochure (panels 1, 2, and 3), and page 2 consists of the folded-over panel, the back panel, and the front panel (panels 4, 5, and 6). To create the brochure for UK Castle Tours, you need to Set Up the Brochure, Create Page 1, and then Create Page 2. The completed brochure is shown in Figure B-11 and Figure B-12 on pages 39 and 41.

activity:

Set Up the Brochure

You need to set up the brochure in Landscape orientation, create a header and footer that appear only on the first page of the brochure, and then insert and modify a clip art picture in the footer.

steps:

Hint

To modify a style, right-click the style name in the list of styles, then click Modify.

Hint

You press and hold the [Shift] key while you draw the line to keep the line straight.

1. Start Word, open the Page Setup dialog box, select Landscape orientation on the Margins tab, set all four margins at 0.5", click OK, then save the document as UK Castle Tours Brochure to the location where you are storing the files for this book

2. Click the Styles and Formatting button 🅐 on the Formatting toolbar, modify the Normal style so that the font is Arial, then close the Styles and Formatting task pane

3. Switch to Page Width view, show the Header and Footer toolbar, click the Page Setup button 🔲, click the Layout tab, click the Different first page check box to select it, then click OK

4. Click the Drawing button 🔳 on the Standard toolbar to show the Drawing toolbar, click the Line button ◢ on the Drawing toolbar, hold down [Shift], scroll down and click at the left margin below the drawing canvas, then draw a straight line to the right margin as shown in Figure B-8

5. Drag the line up to the First Page Header area as shown in Figure B-9

6. With the line still selected, click the Line Color list arrow 🖉⏷ on the Drawing toolbar, click the Blue color, click the Line Color list arrow 🖉⏷ again, click Patterned Lines, select the Light upward diagonal pattern (second row of the third column), click OK, click the Line Style button ▤ on the Drawing toolbar, then select the 6 pt solid style

7. Click the Switch Between Header and Footer button 🔲 to move to the footer, click the Insert Clip Art button 🔳 on the Drawing toolbar, type United Kingdom map in the Search for text box, click Go, then find and insert the picture of the map shown in Figure B-10
   You will need to scroll down to find the required picture, which shows the United Kingdom map filled with pink shading. When you insert the picture, it will appear much larger than the picture shown in Figure B-10.

8. Right-click the picture, click Format Picture, click the Size tab, enter 1" as the height, click the Layout tab, click In front of text, click OK, then drag the clip art picture to position it as shown in Figure B-10

9. Click Close on the Header and Footer toolbar, close the Clip Art task pane, then save the document

FIGURE B-8: Drawing a line

Start drawing the line here

Line button on the Drawing toolbar

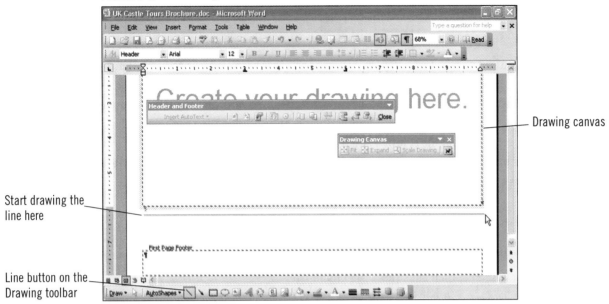

Drawing canvas

FIGURE B-9: Line positioned in First Page Header area

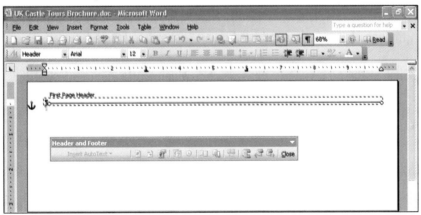

FIGURE B-10: First page footer

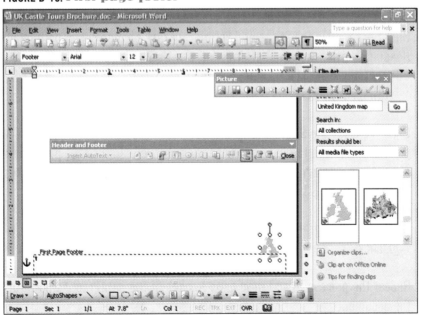

SIX-PANEL BROCHURE FOR UK CASTLE TOURS

activity:

Create Page 1

You can choose to display the inside panels in a brochure in a three-column format, or you can create a more interesting effect by formatting the text in two columns of uneven width. Page 1 of the UK Castle Tours brochure appears in Figure B-11. As you can see, the text appears in two columns of uneven width. Column 1 is about 3" wide, and column 2 is a little more than double that width. You need to format the columns, then enter the text for columns 1 and 2. After you create the text for column 1, you need to insert and modify a clip art picture, and after you create the text for column 2, you need to insert drop caps to spell "Castle."

steps:

1. With the insertion point positioned at the top of the document, click **Format** on the menu bar, click **Columns**, then click the **Left** column type

   The Left column type appears in the Presets section at the top of the Columns dialog box. The Left column type formats the document in two uneven columns, with the narrower column to the left.

Trouble

The text will flow to column 2 as you type. You will adjust how the text wraps in Step 4.

2. Click **OK**, switch to 100% view, click the **Style list arrow** Normal on the Formatting toolbar, click **Heading 1**, type **Tour Description**, press **[Enter]**, then type the first four paragraphs of text (through "bacon, eggs, and fried bread.") shown in Figure B-11

3. Click at the **beginning of paragraph 3** (which starts "Sharon McCarthy..."), click the **Insert Clip Art button** on the Drawing toolbar, search for **castle**, insert the **clip art picture** shown in Figure B-11, right-click the picture, click **Format Picture**, click the **Layout tab**, click **Tight**, click the **Right option button**, click the **Size tab**, set the height at **1.2"**, then click **OK**

4. Click at the **beginning of paragraph 4** ("After a day..."), click **Insert** on the menu bar, click **Break**, click **Column break**, click **OK**, then press **[Enter]**

5. Click at the **end of the fourth paragraph** ("...fried bread."), press **[Enter]** twice, click the **Styles and Formatting button** on the Formatting toolbar, click **Heading 1**, then type **Moments to Remember**

Trouble

The list arrow appears when you move the pointer over a style in the Pick formatting to apply list.

6. Click **Select All** in the Styles and Formatting task pane to select both headings formatted with the Heading 1 style, click the list arrow next to **Heading 1**, click **Modify**, then change the font size to **20 point**, the font color to **Blue**, and the font style to **Comic Sans MS** (or a similar font)

   You can modify a Heading style at any time in the document creation process.

7. Click **OK**, close the Styles and Formatting task pane, click to the right of **Moments to Remember**, press **[Enter]**, type the paragraph that begins "Here are just...", press **[Enter]** twice, then type the remaining six paragraphs of text, typing the letters that appear as drop caps normally, and pressing **[Enter]** three times between each paragraph

8. Click in the paragraph that begins "Chart a course...", click **Format** on the menu bar, click **Drop Cap**, click **Dropped**, then click **OK**

9. Repeat the process to add drop caps to each of the paragraphs shown in Figure B-11, then save the document

Tour Description

UK Castle Tours, Inc., is proud to offer two-week tours of the great castles and stately homes of England, Scotland, and Wales. These tours will appeal to you if you are longing to experience the United Kingdom and its wealth of history, but you *don't* want to worry about arranging transportation and accommodations, and you *don't* want to spend your vacation on a crowded tour bus.

Each UK Castle Tour is limited to 20 people. To keep costs down and make your travel experience as authentic as possible, you travel on local buses and trains and stay in comfortable one- and two-star bed and breakfasts.

Sharon McCarthy, our experienced guide and art expert, takes care of all the travel details as she escorts you through the great houses and castles of the United Kingdom. Our tour takes you from Windsor Castle, home of the Queen, north through the heartland of England to mystical Edinburgh Castle in Scotland and from there to the castle strongholds of Northern Wales.

After a day touring the stately homes and castles of Britain, you can relax with a pint of best bitter in a charming pub and then take a stroll down winding country lanes. Sleep comfortably in cozy bed and breakfasts and awake each morning to the legendary full English breakfast complete with bacon, eggs, and fried bread.

Moments to Remember

Here are just some of the moments you will share with other history lovers on our UK Castle Tour:

Chart a course through British history as you wander the crumbling hallways of castles that were new a thousand years ago.

Appreciate firsthand the warm hospitality of your British hosts at family-run bed and breakfasts where the beds are comfortable and the company is cheerful.

Settle down with a good book by a roaring fire in an Elizabethan inn, then sleep in a four-poster bed straight out of a Jane Austen novel.

Take time out to sample the lagers and ales of a typical British pub, enjoy an English cream tea, and feast on the best salmon in the world—caught fresh from a Scottish mountain stream.

Linger atop the battlements of Carnarvon Castle and imagine ancient sieges as the sun dips below the Welsh hills.

Enjoy touring sumptuous gardens and marveling at the wealth of art treasures in stately homes and palaces.

activity:

Create Page 2

Page 2 of the UK Castle Tours brochure is shown in Figure B-12. You need to insert a column break after page 1 and select the three-column format. The page includes a table, text enclosed with a border, a WordArt object, and a photograph of the Tower of London.

steps:

1. Click at the **end of the final paragraph** on page 1, click **Insert** on the menu bar, click **Break**, click the **Column break option button**, click **OK**, click **Format** on the menu bar, click **Columns**, click **Three**, click the **Apply to list arrow**, click **This point forward**, then click **OK**

2. Select the **Heading 1** style, type **Tour Itinerary**, press **[Enter]**, then type the first two paragraphs of text as shown in Figure B-12

Hint

To create the table, click Table on the menu bar, click Insert, enter the number of columns and rows required for the table, then click OK.

3. Press **[Enter]** twice after the second paragraph, create a table consisting of **3 columns** and **17 rows**, select the table, change the font size of the table text to **9 point** and the line spacing to **1.5**, enter and format the table text as shown in Figure B-12, then use the pointer to modify the column sizes

4. Click below the table, insert a **column break**, type and center the text as shown in the box at the top of column 2 of Figure B-12, press **[Enter]** twice, select all the text from **Tour Cost** through **...meals are not included.**, click **Format** on the menu bar, click **Borders and Shading**, click **Box**, select the **Single line style** and a line width of **½ pt** if necessary, click **Options**, set the From text Top and Bottom settings to **4 pt**, then click **OK** twice

5. Click at the **last paragraph mark** in column 2, press **[Enter]** three times, then enter the remaining text for column 2 as shown in Figure B-12, formatting **UK Castle Tours, Inc.** with **Bold**, the **Comic Sans MS** font, and the **16 point** font size

6. Insert a column break, click the **Insert WordArt button** 🄰 on the Drawing toolbar, select the style in column 1, row 5 (the last row), type **UK Castle Tours** on three lines, select the **Arial Black font**, then click **OK**

7. Right-click the **WordArt object**, click **Format WordArt**, click the **Size tab**, set the height at **3"** and the width at **2.5"**, click the **Colors and Lines tab**, click the **Fill Color list arrow**, click **Fill Effects**, click the **Preset colors list arrow**, click **Brass**, click **OK**, then click **OK**

8. Click to the right of the WordArt object to deselect it, press **[Enter]** four times, click **Insert** on the menu bar, point to **Picture**, click **From File**, navigate to the location where you are storing the files for this book, double-click **Tower.jpg**, then set the height of the picture at **3"**

Hint

Verify that the Exclude label from the Caption check box is not selected.

9. Right-click the picture, click **Caption**, click **New Label**, type **Tower of London**, click **OK**, click **OK**, then press **[Backspace]** three times to remove the "1" and the extra spaces

Additional Practice

For additional practice with the skills presented in this project, complete Independent Challenge 2.

10. Compare page 2 to Figure B-12, make any spacing adjustments required, check the spelling and grammar, then save and print a copy

   If possible, print the brochure on two sides of the same sheet of paper. If you cannot do so, place the two printed pages back to back, staple them, then fold them so that "UK Castle Tours" appears on the front panel and the contact information appears on the back panel.

UK Castle Tours

Tower of London

Tour cost: $4,400 per person

Cost includes travel insurance, accommodations, transportation, museum entrance fees, and six full-course dinners. Airfare to London and all additional meals are not included.

Call (416) 555-1223 to book your UK Castle Tour

UK Castle Tours, Inc.
230 Dundas Street West
Toronto, ON M5W 1E6
www.UKCTours.ca

Tour Itinerary

You can choose from four tour dates: May 16 to May 31, June 15 to June 30, July 16 to July 31, or September 15 to September 30.

The tour starts and ends in London. The following itinerary lists only those activities in which your guide accompanies you. You will also have plenty of time to explore on your own.

Day	Overnight	Sites
Day 1	London	Tower of London
Day 2	London	Westminster Abbey
Day 3	Arundel	Arundel Castle
Day 4	Maidstone	Leeds Castle
Day 5	Windsor	Windsor Castle
Day 6	Oxford	Blenheim Palace
Day 7	Stratford	Warwick Castle
Day 8	Durham	Durham Castle
Day 9	Edinburgh	Edinburgh Castle
Day 10	Aberdeen	Craigievar Castle
Day 11	Stirling	Stirling Castle
Day 12	Carnarvon	Carnarvon Castle
Day 13	Conwy	Conwy Castle
Day 14	Harlech	Harlech Castle
Day 15	Cardiff	Cardiff Castle
Day 16	London	Farewell Banquet

PROJECT 3

One-Page Resume for Andrea Leriche

Andrea Leriche recently earned an Office Management certificate from North Shore College in Sydney, Australia. Now, she needs to create an attractive one-page resume to include with her job applications. For this project, you will **Create and Enhance the Resume**. The completed resume is shown in Figure B-13.

activity:

Create and Enhance the Resume

You need to set up the resume heading, modify styles, and then create a table to contain the resume text. Finally, you need to enter and format the text.

Hint

Andrea's name is enhanced as 20-point Arial Rounded MT Bold.

steps:

1. Start Word, type and center the name and address as shown in Figure B-13, press [Enter] twice, click the **Align Left button** ▤ on the Formatting toolbar, type **Objective**, press [Enter], type **To apply my organizational and computer skills as an Office Manager in a service-based company or organization**, press [Enter] twice, then save the resume as **Andrea Leriche Resume** to the location where you are storing the files for this book

2. Modify the **Heading 1** style so that it formats text with **14 point**, **Bold**, and **Italic**, and includes a bottom border line with a width of 1½ **point**, verify that the Before Spacing is set to **12 pt** and the After Spacing is set to **3 pt**, then apply the **Heading 1** style to **Objective**

3. Click at the **second blank paragraph**, then create a table consisting of **two columns** and **nine rows**

4. Click **Table** on the menu bar, click **Table Properties**, click the **Column tab**, enter **1.5** as the preferred width of column 1, click the **Next Column button**, enter **4.5** as the preferred width of column 2, then click **OK**

5. Select the **entire table**, click the **Outside Border list arrow** ▦▾ on the Formatting toolbar, then click the **No Border button**

6. Select the **cells in the first row** of the table, click **Table** on the menu bar, then click **Merge Cells**
   The two cells in the first row are combined into one cell.

7. Using Figure B-13 as your guide, type **Education**, apply the **Heading 1** style, press [Tab], type **2005-2006**, press [Tab], type **North Shore College, Sydney, NSW**, press [Enter], then type and format the text that appears under North Shore College
   You will need to format North Shore College with Bold, format Office Management Certificate with Italic, and apply bullets to the list of skills.

8. Complete the resume as shown in Figure B-13
   Remember to merge the rows containing headings (e.g., "Work Experience"), to apply the Heading 1 style to the headings, and to apply bold, italic, and bullets where required.

Additional Practice

For additional practice with the skills presented in this project, complete Independent Challenge 3.

9. Check the spelling and grammar, print a copy of the resume, then save and close it

Andrea Leriche

1600 Shoreline Drive
NSW 2042, Sydney, Australia
Phone/Fax: 0400 555 544
E-mail: AndreaLeriche@webplace.com.au

Objective

To apply my organizational and computer skills as an Office Manager in a service-based company or organization

Education

2005-2006	**North Shore College**, Sydney, NSW
	Office Management Certificate

- Computer skills: Microsoft Office 2003: Word, Excel, Access, PowerPoint, FrontPage, Project, and Publisher
- Business Communications and Organizational Behaviour
- Accounting and Bookkeeping
- Project Management
- Supervisory Skills

2004	**Allenham High School**
	School Leaving Certificate

Work Experience

2004-Date	**Branson's Bookkeeping**, 3100 Walloonga Street, Sydney
	Office Assistant (part time)
	Responsibilities include:

- Maintain company records
- Format documents in Word 2003
- Organize company database with Access 2003

2000-2003	**Camp Koala**, Hart Valley, Queensland
	Camp Counselor (summers)
	Responsibilities included:

- Supervised groups of 10 campers aged 9 to 11
- Organized crafts and sports activities
- Assisted with general office duties

Volunteer Experience

2005-2006	**North College Applied Business Technology Department**
	Student Activities Coordinator
2002-2004	**Food Bank**, South Sydney

Independent Challenges

INDEPENDENT CHALLENGE 1

Write a multiple-page proposal that requests a significant change in a course, program, or company procedure. For example, you could request more hours of computer training as part of a college course or propose the setting up of a day care facility at your company. Alternatively, you could write a proposal to purchase new computer equipment or to establish a more equitable procedure for allocating holiday time. If you are a student, you may want to request that more classroom time be allocated to a specific topic such as the Internet or computerized accounting. If you are in the workplace, you could propose a new marketing strategy for a particular product or you could request new computer software (such as the latest Office upgrade). The possibilities are endless! Fill in the boxes provided below with information about your proposal and then follow the steps to create and format the proposal, a title page, and a table of contents page. The completed proposal should consist of approximately three pages of text (excluding the title page and table of contents).

1. Determine the subject of your proposal. To help you focus on a subject, ask yourself what changes you would like to see happen in your own workplace or at college. Write the principal request that your proposal will make in the box below:

Proposal request:

2. Determine the three or four principal sections of your proposal in addition to the introduction and conclusion. These sections will form the basis of your outline. For example, suppose you decide to write a proposal that requests changes to a college course on computer applications that you have just taken. You could organize your proposal into the following three sections:
   I.   Recommended Software
   II. Laboratory Hours
   III. Learning Materials
   Under each of these headings you would describe the current situation in the course and then offer your recommendations for improvement. Write the three principal sections of your proposal in the box below:

I.

II.

III.

3. After each of the principal topics you listed above, add subheadings and even sub-subheadings that will further organize your proposal. Limit the number of additional headings to one or two for each section.
4. Start a new document in Word, create a header that includes the name of the proposal at the left margin and the current date aligned at the right margin. Include a single border line under the header text.
5. Create a footer that includes your name at the left margin and the page number at the right margin.

6. Save the proposal as **My Proposal** to the location where you are storing the files for this book.

7. Modify the Heading 1 and Heading 2 styles. You choose the settings you prefer.

8. Create a new style for the proposal text that is based on the Normal style and will format text with 1.5 spacing, a left indent of .5" and 12-point after-paragraph spacing.

9. Type **Introduction**, apply the Heading 1 style, press [Enter], apply the new Proposal Text style you created, then type the text for your introduction.

10. Enter headings and write the text required for your proposal. As you write, try to visualize your reader. What information does your reader need to make an informed decision concerning your request? How will your request directly affect your reader? What benefits will your reader gain by granting your request? What benefits will other people gain? All of these questions will help you to focus on communicating the information your reader needs in order to respond positively to the principal request your proposal makes.

11. Insert up to two footnotes in appropriate places in your proposal. Remember that a footnote is used to reference any books, periodicals, or Web sites you mention in your proposal or to add additional information.

12. Include a chart or a diagram in an appropriate section of your proposal. For example, you could include a Target diagram that shows the steps toward a specific goal related to your proposal, or you could include a chart that shows statistical information.

13. Insert a Next Page section break above page 1 of your proposal, clear formatting, enter and format **Table of Contents**, then generate a table of contents.

14. Show the Header and Footer toolbar, move to the footer for the first page of the proposal (starts with "Introduction"), deselect the Same as Previous button, then start the page numbering at 1.

15. Show the footer for the Table of Contents page, then change the page numbering style on the Table of Contents page to lower-case Roman numerals that start at "i".

16. Add a Next Page section break above the Table of Contents page, then create an attractive title page for your proposal.

17. View the Header and Footer toolbar, click the Page Setup button, then select Different first page so that no text appears in the header and footer on the title page of your proposal.

18. View the proposal in Two Pages view, make any spacing adjustments required, check spelling and grammar, then save the document and print a copy.

INDEPENDENT CHALLENGE 2

Create a two-page, six-panel brochure that advertises the products or services sold by a fictitious company of your choice. For example, you could create a brochure to advertise the programs offered by a public television station or to present the products sold by Quick Buzz, a company that sells high-energy snack foods. If you are involved in sports, your brochure could describe the sports training programs offered by a company called Fitness Forever, or if you are interested in art, your brochure could list the products sold by an art supply store called Painting Plus. For ideas, check out the pictures in the Clip Art task pane. A particular clip art picture may provide you with just the subject you require.

1. Determine the name of your company and the products or services that it sells. Think of your own interests and then create a company that reflects these interests.

2. Select two or three products or services that your brochure will highlight. For example, a brochure for a landscaping company called Greenscapes could present information about bedding plant sales, landscaping design, and garden maintenance services.

3. Allocate one of the three inside panels (1, 2, and 3) for each of the products or services you have selected. For example, if you wish to create a brochure for the Painting Plus art supply store, you could devote one panel to each of the three main types of products sold: Painting Supplies, Papers and Canvases, and Drawing Supplies. Alternatively, you could include two sections in panels 1, 2, and 3 of a brochure that advertises the sports training programs offered by Fitness Forever. Panel 1 could describe the sports facilities, and the weekly program schedule could be spread over panels 2 and 3.

4. Determine the information required for page 2 of the brochure. This page includes panel 4 (usually a continuation of the information on page 1 of the brochure), panel 5 (the back panel), and panel 6 (the front panel). For example, you could include a price list on panel 4, contact information on panel 5, and just the company name and one or two enhancements on panel 6. Note that the readers of your brochure see panel 6 first. Therefore, you want to make it as attractive as possible to encourage readers to open the brochure and read the contents.

5. Before you start creating the brochure in Word, sketch the brochure layout on two blank pieces of paper. Put the sketch back-to-back and fold the brochure so that you can see how it will appear to readers. The more time you spend planning your brochure, the fewer problems you will encounter when you start creating your brochure in Word.

6. Refer to the brochure you created in Project 2. If you wish, you can adapt this brochure to advertise a tour that would interest you.

7. In Word, set the page orientation to Landscape and the four margins to .5, create an attractive header or footer for page 1 of the brochure, then save the brochure as **My Brochure** to the location where you are storing the files for this book.

8. Set the number of columns for page 1, then enter the text and enhancements for panels 1, 2, and 3. Include attractively formatted section headings and use drop caps to emphasize the first letter of several paragraphs. Alternatively, you can use drop caps to spell a word and then add appropriate text next to each letter. For ideas, refer to the "Moments to Remember" section of the brochure you created for Project 2.

9. Insert a column break at the end of page 1, then format the columns for page 2 of the brochure. Note that page 2 must display the information in three columns of equal width because readers will usually see only one panel at a time.

10. Enter the text and enhancements for page 2 of the brochure.

11. Add at least one piece of clip art and one piece of WordArt. You can add more pictures if you want, but be careful not to enhance your brochure with too many graphics. You want the finished brochure to have a clean, easy-to-read look.

12. View the brochure in Two Pages view, check the spelling and grammar, make any spacing adjustments required, save the brochure, then print a copy and close the document.

INDEPENDENT CHALLENGE 3

Create or modify your own resume. To help you determine the information required for your resume, fill in the boxes below and then create the resume in Word as directed.

1. Determine your objective. What kinds of positions are you looking for that will match your qualifications and experience? Enter your objective in the box below:

Resume Objective:

2. In the table below, list the components related to your educational background, starting with your most recent school or college. Note the name of the institution, the certificate or degree you received, and a selection of the courses relevant to the type of work you are seeking.

Year(s):	Institution:	Certificate/Degree:	Courses:

3. In the table below, list the details related to your work experience. Use parallel structure when listing your responsibilities; that is, make sure that each element uses the same grammatical structure. For example, you can start each point with a verb, such as "maintain," "manage," or "use," and then follow it with the relevant object, for example, "maintain company records" and "use Microsoft Word 2003 to create promotional materials." Make sure you use the appropriate tense: present tense for your current position and past tense for former positions.

Year(s):	Company or Institution:	Responsibilities:

4. In the table below, describe any volunteer experience you have, awards you have received and, if you wish, your hobbies and interests:

Year(s)	Focus of Additional Information	Examples
	Volunteer Experience	
	Awards	
	Hobbies/Interests	

5. Set up your resume in Word as follows:

   a. Type your name and format it attractively, then enter and enhance the appropriate contact information. Don't forget to include your e-mail address and your Web site address, if you have them.

   b. Save the resume as **My Resume** to the location where you are storing the files for this book.

   c. Create a new style called Resume Heading Style based on the Normal style with formatting you choose.

   d. Enter **Objective** formatted with the new Resume Heading Style, then type your objective.

   e. Create a table consisting of two columns, then enter the headings and text required for your resume. Refer to Project 3 for ideas.

   f. Fit the resume to one page, check spelling and grammar, print a copy, then save and close the document.

INDEPENDENT CHALLENGE 4

You have been asked to create a six-panel brochure to advertise a two-year intensive training program in drama and theatrical production offered by the Tulsa School of Drama. The information you need to include in the brochure is provided in a Word document. The completed brochure is shown in Figure B-14. Following are the directions required to complete the brochure:

1. Open Tulsa Brochure.doc from the location where you are storing the files for this book, then save it as **Tulsa School of Drama Brochure** to the same location.

2. Change the orientation of the document to Landscape orientation with .5" margins.

3. Create a header on the first page only that contains a green line filled with the wide upward diagonal pattern.

4. Format the text in three evenly spaced columns.

5. Modify the Heading 1 style so that it enhances text with an 18-point, green font.

6. Apply the Heading 1 style and format the text as shown in Figure B-14.

7. Format the table in panel 2 attractively as shown in Figure B-14.

8. Format the text on panel 5 and draw the rounded rectangle as shown in Figure B-14.

9. On panel 6, enter **Tulsa School of Drama**, enhance it so that it appears similar to Figure B-14, then insert an appropriate clip art picture. (*Hint*: Search for "drama" or "theater" in the Clip Art task pane.)

10. View the brochure over two pages, adjust the formatting where required, check the spelling and grammar, print a copy, then save and close the brochure.

PROGRAM OBJECTIVES

The Tulsa School of Drama offers students a wide range of courses in acting, directing, and stagecraft.

This two-year intensive program provides students with the training required to develop professional-level skills in all areas of theatrical production.

Upon successful completion of the Tulsa School of Drama program, graduates receive a certificate recognized as equivalent to 36 credits at the university level. Students may then enter university in the Junior year where they can fulfill the requirements for a Bachelor of Fine Arts in Drama.

ADMISSION PROCEDURES

Auditions for the Tulsa School of Drama are held at the school in January and February of each year for admission to the school in September. Candidates may apply for an audition by calling the School Registrar at (918) 555-3321.

The following materials must be provided to the Audition Committee six months prior to the audition date:

- Resume detailing performance experience and drama-theater education
- Transcript from the last educational institution attended
- Reference letter from two or more instructors (one of which should be a drama instructor)

- Video of a recent performance (acting students only)
- Directing script of a recent production (directing students only)
- Costume, lighting, or set designs of a recent production (stagecraft students only)

The audition will consist of the following elements:

- Sight analysis of a selection from a contemporary play chosen by the audition committee.
- Thirty-minute interview

In addition, acting students must present two prepared speeches and perform one sight reading of a role chosen by the audition committee.

PROGRAM CONTENT

The Tulsa School of Drama program is divided into two 8-month terms.

Year 1:	
DRA 100	History of Theater 1
DRA 101	Dramatic Theory 1
DRA 102	Elective 1
DRA 103	Elective 2
DRA 104	Year 1 Production
Year 2:	
DRA 200	History of Theater 2
DRA 201	Dramatic Theory 2
DRA 202	Elective 3
DRA 203	Career Choices
DRA 204	Year 2 Production

COURSE DESCRIPTIONS

DRA 100: History of Theater 1
Evolution of theater from the Greeks to the English Restoration. Special emphasis on Shakespearean drama.

DRA 101: Dramatic Theory 1
The fundamentals of dramatic theory, including techniques for dramatic criticism.

DRA 102: Elective 1
Choice of Acting 1, Directing 1, or Stagecraft 1.

DRA 103: Elective 2
Choice of Improvisation 1, Production 1, or Graphic Design 1

DRA 104: Year 1 Production
Participation in a full-length production of a play selected by the students

DRA 200: History of Theater 2
Development of the theater from the 19th century in England and the United States with special emphasis on contemporary US playwrights

DRA 201: Dramatic Theory 2
In-depth analysis of selected plays from a variety of genres and historical periods.

DRA 202: Elective 3
Choice of Acting 2, Directing 2, or Stagecraft 2

DRA 203: Career Choices
Development of job search skills to obtain employment in theater or film.

DRA 204: Year 2 Production
Participation in a full-length production of a musical selected by the students.

FACULTY

All the instructors at the Tulsa School of Drama continue to work professionally in theaters throughout North America. In addition to our regular faculty, we are proud to welcome the following artists-in-residence for the 2007 program:

Merilee Montcalm: Acting
Ms. Montcalm has won acclaim for her performances on and off Broadway. Her most recent triumph was playing Lady Macbeth in the recent production staged by the New York Theater.

Mark Levine: Directing
In 2006, Mr. Levine won the coveted Players Trophy for his production of *A Streetcar Named Desire* at the Old Vic Theater in London, England.

Rachel Goldblum: Stagecraft
Ms. Goldblum has won numerous awards for her costumer and set designs. Recently, she designed the costumes for the Oscar-winning film adaptation of *Wuthering Heights*.

*Tulsa
School of Drama*

180 Lakeview Road
Tulsa, OK 74104
Phone: (918) 555-3321
www.TulsaDrama.com

*Tulsa
School
Of
Drama*

Visual Workshop

As part of a report you've prepared for Azalea Designs about the development of their new e-business initiative, you need to create the Target diagram shown in Figure B-15. Match the diagram by experimenting with inserting shapes and applying AutoFormats. Save the diagram as **Azalea Designs Web Site Target Diagram** to the location where you are storing the files for this book, print a copy, then close the document.

FIGURE B-15: Target diagram

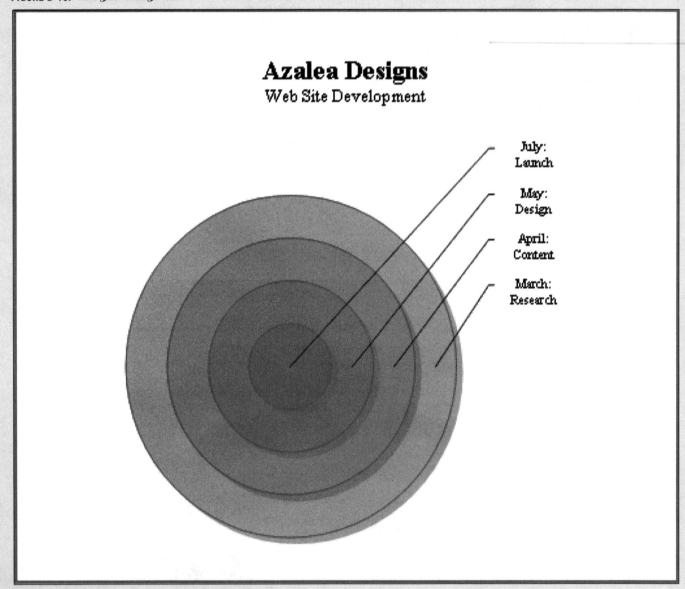

Microsoft
► Excel
Projects

Unit C

Excel Projects I

In this Unit You Will Create the Following:

► Projected Budget

► Expense Report

► Trip Planning Budget

Microsoft Excel provides the tools you need to make effective planning decisions. For example, suppose you plan to take a two-week vacation to Cancun and you have allocated $2,500 to cover all trip expenses. To find out if you have allocated enough money to cover expenses, you can set up a simple worksheet that lists anticipated expenses for airfare, accommodations, food, and entertainment. Once you total the expenses, you may find that they exceed the budgeted amount of $2,500. Rather than cancel your trip, you can try to determine which expenses you can decrease. For example, you could decide to decrease the cost of accommodations by staying at a less expensive hotel or you could allocate a reduced amount for shopping. In this unit, you will create and format a worksheet, build arithmetic formulas, use functions in calculations, and ask relevant "What if?" questions.

Projected Budget for Fire Mountain Camp

You need to create the Fire Mountain Camp's budget for the 2007 summer season, and then ask a series of "What if?" questions to determine realistic goals. To create the camp's budget, you Enter and Enhance Labels, Calculate Totals, Ask "What if?" Questions, and Format and Print the Budget. The completed budget appears in Figure C-8 on page 59.

activity:

Enter and Enhance Labels

You need to enter and enhance the name and address of the organization, the worksheet title, the current date, and the first series of labels.

steps:

1. Start Excel, close the Getting Started task pane, click the Select All button to the left of the A at the upper-left corner of the worksheet frame to select the entire worksheet, click the Font Size list arrow 10 ▾ on the Formatting toolbar, then click 12

2. Click cell A1, type Fire Mountain Summer Camp, press [Enter], type the remaining labels as shown in Figure C-1, then save your workbook as Projected Budget for Fire Mountain Summer Camp to the location where you are storing the files for this book

3. Click cell A1, click the Font list arrow Arial ▾ on the Formatting toolbar, click Bodoni MT Black (or a different font such as Britannic Bold), then change the font size to 20

Hint

Although the text extends into columns B and C, you need to select only cells A4 and A5—the place where the text originated.

4. Select cells A4 and A5, then change the font size to 16

5. Select cells A1:G5, right-click the selection, click Format Cells, click the Alignment tab, click the Horizontal list arrow, click Center Across Selection, then click OK

6. Select cells A4:G5, click the Fill Color list arrow 🖋▾ on the Formatting toolbar, click the Black box, click the Font Color list arrow 🅰▾ on the Formatting toolbar, then click the White box

7. Click cell B7, type May, then press [Enter]

Trouble

If "May" is moved to cell F7, click the Undo button, then make sure the Fill Handle pointer ➕ appears before you drag to the right.

8. Click cell B7 again, position the pointer over the lower-right corner to show the Fill Handle pointer ➕, drag the ➕ pointer to cell F7, then click the Center button 🖹 on the Formatting toolbar
The five months from May to September are added and centered.

9. Click cell G7, enter Totals and center it, click cell A8, enter the labels required for cells A8:A23 as shown in Figure C-2, click the Spelling button 🗸, correct any spelling errors, then save your workbook

FIGURE C-1: Labels for cells A1 through A5

Font list arrow

Font Size list arrow

Select All button, click to select the entire worksheet

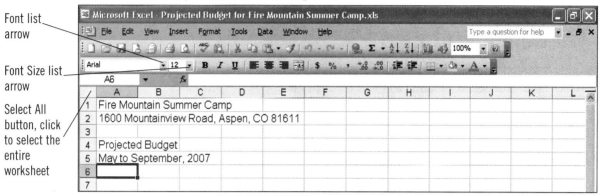

FIGURE C-2: Labels for budget categories

Enter "Totals" in cell G7

Labels for cells A8 through A23

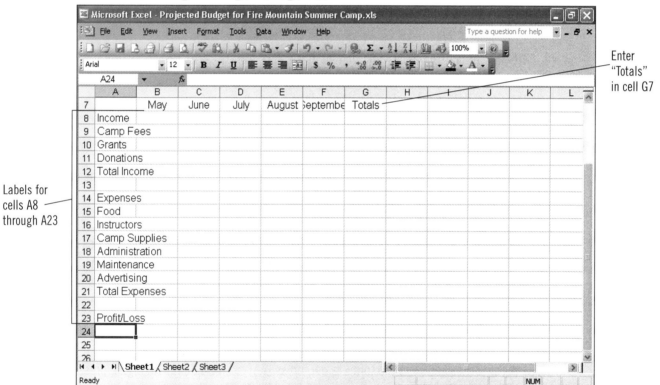

Clues to Use

Merging Cells

A merged cell is created by combining two or more cells into a single cell. The cell reference for the merged cell is the upper-left cell of the originally selected range. When you merge a range of cells containing data, only the data in the upper-left cell of the range is included in the merged cell. If you want to merge cells in a single row quickly, use the Merge and Center button on the Formatting toolbar and then adjust the alignment as needed. If you want to merge cells in several consecutive rows, use the Alignment tab in the Format Cells dialog box.

PROJECT 1

PROJECTED BUDGET FOR FIRE MOUNTAIN CAMP

activity:

Calculate Totals

You need to enter the income and expenses that Fire Mountain Camp anticipates in 2007. Then, you need to calculate the camp fees and the total income and expenses.

steps:

Hint

You use a new worksheet to avoid cluttering the first worksheet with data that will not be printed.

1. Position the pointer on the **column divider** between **A** and **B** on the worksheet frame so it changes to ↔, then double-click to increase the width of column A to fit all the labels

2. Click cell **B10**, enter the values for May as shown in Figure C-3, select cells **B10:B20**, position the pointer over the lower-right corner of cell **B20**, then drag the ✚ pointer to cell **F20**

3. Double-click the **Sheet1 tab** at the bottom of the worksheet, type **Budget**, press **[Enter]**, double-click the **Sheet2 tab**, type **Fees**, then press **[Enter]**

   In 2006, you know that approximately 100 teens attended camp each month in three payment categories: one-week, two-week, and three-week.

4. Enter and format the labels and values in the Fees worksheet as shown in Figure C-4

   Double-click or drag the column divider to widen column A so that the labels are clearly visible and then center and bold the labels in cells A1:D1.

5. Click cell **D2**, enter the formula **=B2*C2**, then press **[Enter]**

   You should see 45000 in cell D2. If not, check your formula and try again.

Hint

The exclamation mark (!) following Fees indicates that the formula comes from a worksheet other than the active worksheet.

6. Click cell **D2** again, drag the ✚ pointer down to cell **D4** to copy the formula into the next two cells, click cell **D5**, then double-click the **AutoSum button** Σ on the Standard toolbar

   The camp fees collected should be 149000.

7. Click the **Budget tab**, click cell **B9**, enter the formula **=Fees!D5**, press **[Enter]**, click cell **B9** again, then drag the ✚ pointer across to cell **F9** to copy the formula to the other months

   Oooops! Cells C9 through F9 contain zeroes. Why? Excel changed the copied formula because it uses relative references by default. However, you need to enter a formula that designates cell D5 as an absolute value to ensure that the formula always contains a reference to cell D5, no matter where in the worksheet the formula is copied.

8. Click cell **B9**, select **D5** in the formula bar, press **[F4]** to insert dollar ($) signs, press **[Enter]**, click cell **B9** again, then drag the ✚ pointer to fill cells **C9:F9** with the new formula

9. Select cells **B9:G12**, click Σ, select cells **B15:G21**, click Σ again, then click cell **G22**

   The total income displayed is 782500, and the total for expenses shown is 523500 as shown in Figure C-5.

Clues to Use

Relative and Absolute References

By default, Microsoft Excel considers all values entered in formulas as relative values. That is, Excel automatically changes all cell addresses in a formula when you copy the formula to a new location. If you do not want Excel to change the cell address of a value when you copy it, you must make the value absolute. To do this, you enter a dollar sign ($) before both the column and the row designation in the address. You can also press [F4] to insert the $ symbol. For example, $C$26 tells Excel that the reference to cell C26 must not change, even if you copy the formula to a new location in the worksheet.

FIGURE C-3: Values for cells B10 through B20

Microsoft Excel - Projected Budget for Fire Mountain Summer Camp.xls

File   Edit   View   Insert   Format   Tools   Data   Window   Help   Type a question for help

Arial   12   B I U $ %

A7

	A	B	C	D	E	F	G	H	I	J	K
7		May	June	July	August	Septembe	Totals				
8	Income										
9	Camp Fees										
10	Grants	5000									
11	Donations	2500									
12	Total Income										
13											
14	Expenses										
15	Food	75000									
16	Instructors	22000									
17	Camp Supplies	5500									
18	Administration	1200									
19	Maintenance	500									
20	Advertising	500									
21	Total Expenses										
22											
23	Profit/Loss										
24											

FIGURE C-4: Fees sheet labels and values

Column A widened

Labels centered and bold

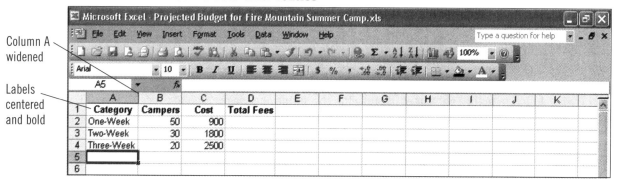

Microsoft Excel - Projected Budget for Fire Mountain Summer Camp.xls

File   Edit   View   Insert   Format   Tools   Data   Window   Help   Type a question for help

Arial   10   B I U $ %

A5

	A	B	C	D	E	F	G	H	I	J	K
1	**Category**	**Campers**	**Cost**	**Total Fees**							
2	One-Week	50	900								
3	Two-Week	30	1800								
4	Three-Week	20	2500								
5											
6											

FIGURE C-5: Worksheet completed with totals

Microsoft Excel - Projected Budget for Fire Mountain Summer Camp.xls

File   Edit   View   Insert   Format   Tools   Data   Window   Help   Type a question for help

Arial   12   B I U $ %

G22

	A	B	C	D	E	F	G	H	I	J	K
7		May	June	July	August	Septembe	Totals				
8	Income										
9	Camp Fees	149000	149000	149000	149000	149000	745000				
10	Grants	5000	5000	5000	5000	5000	25000				
11	Donations	2500	2500	2500	2500	2500	12500				
12	Total Income	156500	156500	156500	156500	156500	782500				
13											
14	Expenses										
15	Food	75000	75000	75000	75000	75000	375000				
16	Instructors	22000	22000	22000	22000	22000	110000				
17	Camp Supplies	5500	5500	5500	5500	5500	27500				
18	Administration	1200	1200	1200	1200	1200	6000				
19	Maintenance	500	500	500	500	500	2500				
20	Advertising	500	500	500	500	500	2500				
21	Total Expenses	104700	104700	104700	104700	104700	523500				
22											
23	Profit/Loss										
24											

Total income

Total expenses

PROJECTED BUDGET FOR FIRE MOUNTAIN CAMP

activity:

Ask "What if?" Questions

You need to calculate the profit you expect to make in each of the five months of the 2007 season, and then perform the calculations required to answer several "What if?" questions.

steps:

1. Click cell **B23**, enter the formula **=B12-B21**, press **[Enter]**, copy the formula across to cell **G23**, then click cell **G23** to deselect the range

The total projected profit for the 2007 camp season is 259000. The first "What if" question is: "What if you raise the one-week course fee to $1000?"

2. Click the **Fees tab**, click cell **C2**, type **1000**, press **[Enter]**, then click the **Budget tab**

By changing the value in C2, you answer the "What if" question and see that your total profit in cell G23 increases to 284000. Next, you want to know, "What if an increase in the one-week camp fee results in a 30% drop in the number of campers you can expect in 2007?"

3. Click the **Fees tab**, click cell **B2**, replace 50 with the formula **=50-(50*.3)** as shown in Figure C-6, press **[Enter]**, then click the **Budget tab**

The formula you entered in the Fees sheet subtracts 30% of 50 from the number of teens expected to take a one-week course (50). The new profit in cell G23 is 209000 — quite a reduction from 284000! Perhaps you shouldn't raise the one-week camp fee to $1000 if the result is a 30% drop in the number of teens who enroll!

4. Return to the **Fees sheet**, change the cost of the one-week camp fee in cell **C2** to **900** and the number of campers in cell **B2** to **50**, then return to the Budget sheet

The value in cell G23 is again 259000. Next, you want to know, "What if you launch a $5,000 advertising campaign in May?"

5. Click cell **B20** in the Budget sheet, type **5000**, then press **[Enter]**

If you increase your advertising cost, you reduce your total profit for the summer season (cell G23) to 254500. Next, you want to know, "What if the May advertising campaign leads to a 30% increase in revenue from camp fees in August and September?" You edit the formula in cells E9 and F9 to reflect a potential increase.

Trouble

A green triangle appears in cell E9. Move the pointer over the triangle to read the comment. When you copy the formula, the triangle disappears.

6. Click cell **E9**, click at the end of the formula entered on the formula bar, type ***1.3**, press **[Enter]**, then copy the formula to cell **F9**

The new total profit shown in cell G23 is 343900, a significant increase. As a result of this "What if" analysis, you decide to keep the advertising campaign in place. Finally, you want to know, "What if you hire a full-time executive assistant for $22,000?" You divide this amount by 5 to determine the monthly rate for the five months the camp is open and then you add the total to the values entered in the Administration row.

7. Click cell **B18**, enter the formula **=(22000/5)+1200**, press **[Enter]**, then copy the formula across to cell **F18**

Based on this "What if" analysis, your total profit as shown in cell G23 is now 321900.

8. Click cell **A24**, compare your worksheet to Figure C-7, then save the workbook

FIGURE C-6: Decreasing campers by 30%

Formula in cell B2

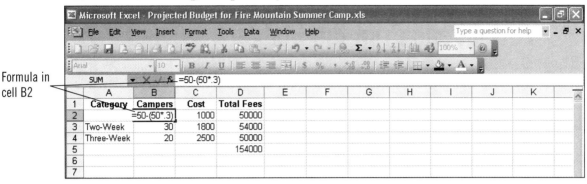

FIGURE C-7: Worksheet with completed budget

Advertising expense increased in May

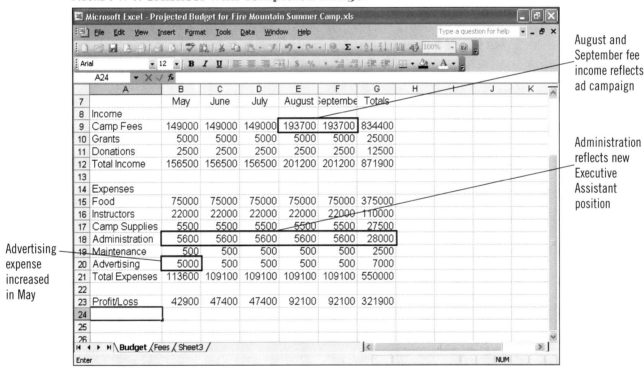

August and September fee income reflects ad campaign

Administration reflects new Executive Assistant position

activity:

Format and Print the Budget

To make the worksheet easier to read, you need to format values in the Currency Style or the Comma Style (depending on their location in the worksheet), add border lines to selected cells, and use a variety of Page Setup features. Then you need to print a copy of your budget.

Trouble

If ##'s appear in any cell, double-click the column divider to increase the column width automatically.

steps:

1. Select cells **B9:G9**, then click the **Currency Style button** $ on the Formatting toolbar
   The widths of columns B through G automatically increase to make room for the formatting.

2. Select cells **B12:G12**, press and hold **[Ctrl]**, then select cells **B15:G15**, cells **B21:G21**, and cells **B23:G23**, click $, then click cell **A24** to deselect the cells
   You use the [Ctrl] key to select a series of non-adjacent cells.

3. Use **[Ctrl]** to select cells **B10:G11** and cells **B16:G20**, then click the **Comma Style button** , on the Formatting toolbar, then click cell **A24** to deselect the cells
   Refer to Figure C-8 as you work.

4. Select cells **B12:G12**, click the **Borders list arrow** ⊞▾ on the Formatting toolbar, select the **Top and Double Bottom Border** style, then click outside the selected cells to see the change
   A single line appears above cells B12 through G12 and a double line appears below them.

5. Add the **Top and Double Bottom Border** style to cells **B21:G21**, then add the **Bottom Double Border** style to cells **B23:G23**

6. Select cells **B7:G7** and click the **Center button** ≡ on the Formatting toolbar

7. Press and hold **[Ctrl]**, select cells **A8**, **A12**, **A14**, **A21**, and **A23:G23**, then click the **Bold button** **B** on the Formatting toolbar to format all the cells at once

8. Click the **Print Preview button** 🔍 on the Standard toolbar, click **Setup**, click the **Landscape option button**, then click the **Fit to option button**

9. Click the **Margins tab**, click the **Horizontally** and **Vertically check boxes**, click the **Header/Footer tab**, click **Custom Header**, type **Fire Mountain Camp Budget** in the Left section, press **[Tab]** twice, type your name in the Right section, click **OK**, then click **OK** again

Additional Practice

For additional practice with the skills presented in this project, complete Independent Challenge 1.

10. Click **Print**, click **Close** to return to the workbook, then save and close the workbook
    The printed budget for Fire Mountain Camp is shown in Figure C-8.

FIGURE C-8: Completed budget

Excel

Your Name

Fire Mountain Camp Budget

Fire Mountain Camp

1600 Mountainview Road, Aspen, CO 81611

Projected Budget
May to September, 2007

	May	June	July	August	September	Totals
Income						
Camp Fees	$ 149,000.00	$ 149,000.00	$ 149,000.00	$ 193,700.00	$ 193,700.00	$ 834,400.00
Grants	5,000.00	5,000.00	5,000.00	5,000.00	5,000.00	25,000.00
Donations	2,500.00	2,500.00	2,500.00	2,500.00	2,500.00	12,500.00
Total Income	$ 156,500.00	$ 156,500.00	$ 156,500.00	$ 201,200.00	$ 201,200.00	$ 871,900.00
Expenses						
Food	$ 75,000.00	$ 75,000.00	$ 75,000.00	$ 75,000.00	$ 75,000.00	$ 375,000.00
Instructors	22,000.00	22,000.00	22,000.00	22,000.00	22,000.00	110,000.00
Camp Supplies	5,500.00	5,500.00	5,500.00	5,500.00	5,500.00	27,500.00
Administration	5,600.00	5,600.00	5,600.00	5,600.00	5,600.00	28,000.00
Maintenance	500.00	500.00	500.00	500.00	500.00	2,500.00
Advertising	5,000.00	500.00	500.00	500.00	500.00	7,000.00
Total Expenses	$ 113,600.00	$ 109,100.00	$ 109,100.00	$ 109,100.00	$ 109,100.00	$ 550,000.00
Profit/Loss	$ 42,900.00	$ 47,400.00	$ 47,400.00	$ 92,100.00	$ 92,100.00	$ 321,900.00

Travel Expense Report for E-Learning Associates

The three sales representatives at E-Learning Associates, a company that develops course materials for delivery online, have each submitted their travel expenses for the month of April. As the office administrator, you've been asked to record these expenses and prepare an expense report that summarizes the travel expenses incurred in April. To create the travel expense report, you Create the Expenses Form, Calculate Expenses, and Prepare the Expense Report. The completed report is shown in Figure C-15 on page 65.

activity:

Create the Expenses Form

You need to create a form to record expenses in Sheet1 of a new workbook and then copy the form to Sheet2 and Sheet3. The completed form is shown in Figure C-11.

Hint

The address is Suite 250–1800 Pacific Crest Road, San Francisco, CA 94171.

steps:

1. Start Excel, enter and format the labels as shown in Figure C-9, click cell **A30**, type **Note that the current mileage reimbursement rate is $.25 per mile.**, press **[Enter]**, then save the workbook as **Expense Statements for E-Learning Associates** to the location where you are storing files for this book
   Note the formatting directions in Figure C-9. If you do not have the Impact font, choose a different font.

2. Click cell **H12**, enter the formula: **=SUM(B12:G12)**, press **[Enter]**, copy the formula down through cell **H25**, click cell **B26**, enter the formula: **=SUM(B12:B25)**, press **[Enter]**, then copy the formula across through cell **G26**
   Note that zeroes appear in the cells that contain formulas.

3. Click cell **H27**, enter the formula **=SUM(H12:H25)**, press **[Enter]**, click cell **H29**, enter the formula **=H27-H28**, press **[Enter]**, select cells **B12:H29**, then click the Currency Style button **$** on the Formatting toolbar

4. Select rows **6, 7,** and **8**, click **Format** on the menu bar, point to **Row**, click **Height**, type **20**, click **OK**, select columns **B** through **H**, click **Format** on the menu bar, point to **Column**, click **Width**, type **12**, click **OK**, then increase the width of column A to **18**

5. Select cells **B6:F6**, click the Borders list arrow on the Formatting toolbar, click the **Bottom Border** button, then add a bottom border to cells **B7:F7**, cells **C8:D8**, and cells **F8:G8**

6. Select cells **A11:H26**, click the Borders list arrow, click the **All Borders** button, then enter and format text and add borders to cells **G27:H29** as shown in Figure C-10

7. Double-click the **Sheet1** tab, type **Chow**, press **[Enter]**, name the Sheet2 tab **Wilson**, then name the Sheet3 tab **Ramirez**

8. Go to the **Chow** sheet, click the **Select All** button in the upper-left of the worksheet frame (to the left of the A) to select the entire worksheet, click the **Copy button** on the Standard toolbar, show the **Wilson** worksheet, then click the **Paste button**

9. Show the **Ramirez** worksheet, click , click cell **A1** in the Ramirez worksheet, then save the workbook
   The Ramirez worksheet appears as shown in Figure C-11.

FIGURE C-9: Labels entered and enhanced

Impact font, 26-point, italic

Impact font, italic

22-point, bold, merged, and centered across cells A4 through H4

Bold all labels

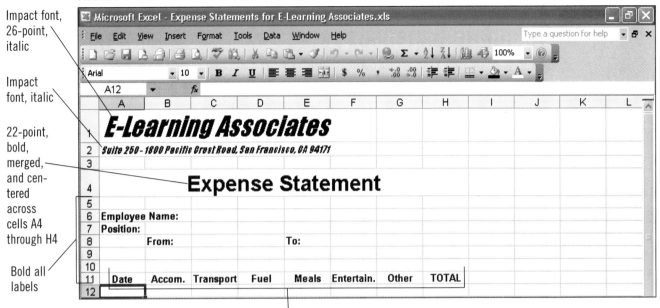

Center labels in cells A11 through H11

FIGURE C-10: Formatting for cells G27 through H29

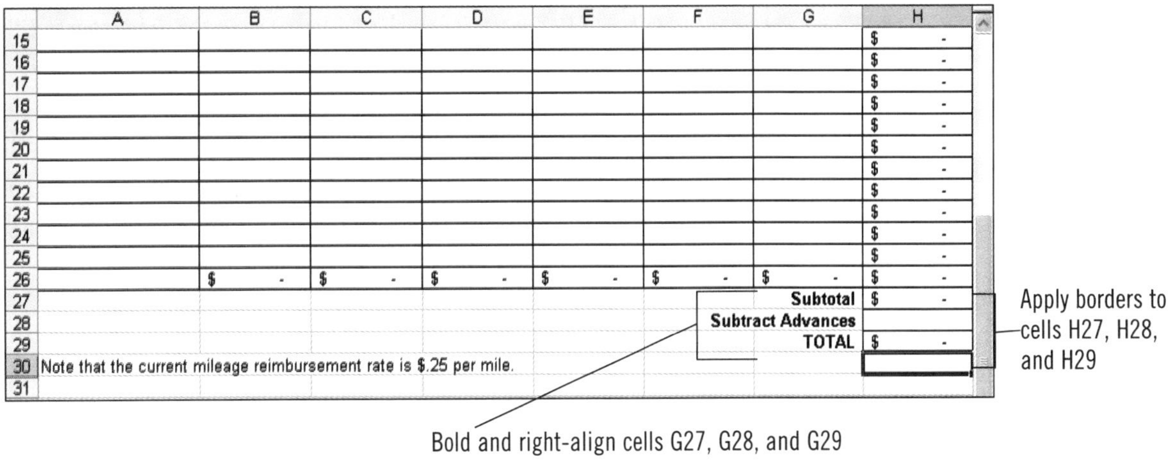

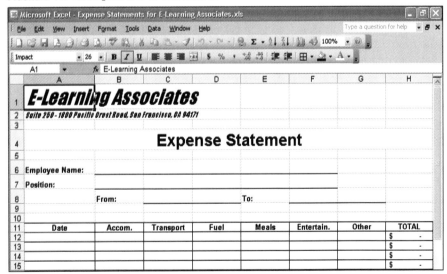

Apply borders to cells H27, H28, and H29

Bold and right-align cells G27, G28, and G29

FIGURE C-11: Completed worksheet

activity:

Calculate Expenses

The three associates have provided you with receipts from the various business trips they took in April. You need to enter these expenses in the expense form.

steps:

1. Click the **Chow tab**, click cell **B6**, type **Grace Chow**, click cell **B7**, then type **Sales Representative**

2. Click cell **C8**, type **April 2, 2006**, press **[Tab]** three times, type **April 5, 2006**, then press **[Enter]**
   When you enter the dates, Excel automatically changes the format to 2-Apr-06.

3. Click cell **C8**, press and hold **[Ctrl]**, click cell **F8**, click **Format** on the menu bar, click **Cells**, click the **Number tab**, click **Date** in the Category list box, select the date format **March 14, 2001** (you'll need to scroll down) in the Type section, then click **OK**

4. Click cell **A12**, type **April 2**, press **[Tab]**, type **=420/3**, press **[Tab]**, type **=194*1.09**, press **[Tab]**, type **=12*0.25**, press **[Tab]**, type **=12.5+45**, then press **[Enter]**
   *You've entered the expenses that Grace incurred on April 2. She stayed one of three nights in Dallas ($420/3), she flew to Dallas ($194 + 9% tax), she drove 12 miles to the airport (12*$0.25), and she bought lunch and dinner ($12.50 + $45.00). The total in cell H12 should be $411.96.*

5. Enter the remaining expenses for Grace Chow according to the following information:

   On April 3 and 4, Grace stayed two more nights at the Dallas Hilton Hotel @ the same rate she paid on April 2. From April 3 to 4, she rented a car @ $32.50/day + $4.30/day for insurance. On April 3, she drove 25 miles; she spent $10 on breakfast, $25 on lunch, and $50 on dinner; in the evening she spent $72 on a theater ticket. On April 4, she drove 35 miles, she spent $105 on meals, and she spent $12 on other expenses. On April 5, she paid $15 for breakfast, she drove 12 miles from the airport back to her home, and she spent $13 on other expenses.

6. Refer to Figure C-12 as you enter the expenses and then verify that the total in cell H29 is **$1,085.56**

7. Click the **Wilson tab**, then refer to Figure C-13 to enter the information and expenses for Mark Wilson

8. Verify that Mark's total expenses (less his advance) are **$530.36** in cell H29

9. Click the **Ramirez tab**, refer to Figure C-13 to enter the information and expenses for Maria Ramirez, verify that Maria's total expenses (less her advance) are **$628.25** in cell H29, then save the workbook

FIGURE C-12: Expenses for Grace Chow

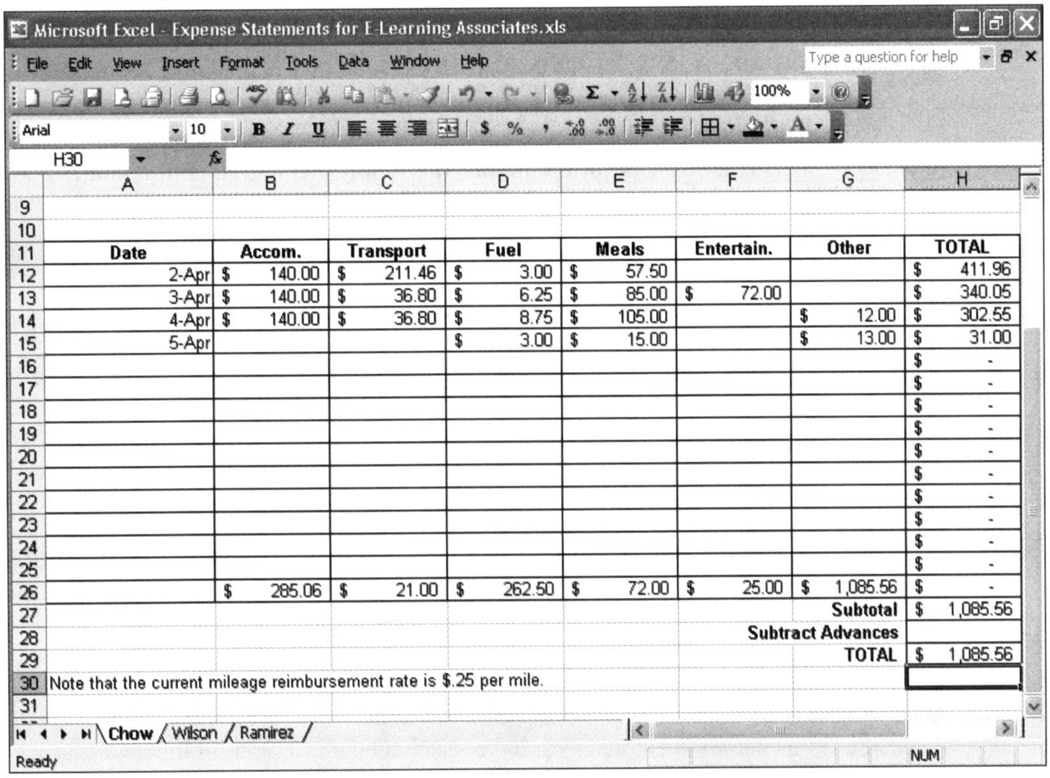

	A	B	C	D	E	F	G	H
9								
10								
11	Date	Accom.	Transport	Fuel	Meals	Entertain.	Other	TOTAL
12	2-Apr	$ 140.00	$ 211.46	$ 3.00	$ 57.50			$ 411.96
13	3-Apr	$ 140.00	$ 36.80	$ 6.25	$ 85.00	$ 72.00		$ 340.05
14	4-Apr	$ 140.00	$ 36.80	$ 8.75	$ 105.00		$ 12.00	$ 302.55
15	5-Apr			$ 3.00	$ 15.00		$ 13.00	$ 31.00
16								$ -
17								$ -
18								$ -
19								$ -
20								$ -
21								$ -
22								$ -
23								$ -
24								$ -
25								$ -
26		$ 285.06	$ 21.00	$ 262.50	$ 72.00	$ 25.00	$ 1,085.56	$ -
27							Subtotal	$ 1,085.56
28							Subtract Advances	
29							TOTAL	$ 1,085.56
30	Note that the current mileage reimbursement rate is $.25 per mile.							
31								

FIGURE C-13: Expenses for Mark and Maria

Mark Wilson

Mark Wilson, Sales Representative, incurred his expenses from April 8 to April 16, 2006, and has already been advanced $150. On April 8, Mark drove 30 miles, flew to Seattle for $90 + 9% tax, stayed overnight at the Baker Mountain Inn for $80 + 7% tax, and spent $52 on meals. On April 9, he took a ferry ride for $60, drove 30 miles, spent $45 on meals, and spent $22 on other expenses. On April 15, he drove 30 miles, flew to Phoenix for $110 + 9% tax, stayed overnight at the Sagebrush Motel for $72 + 8% tax, and spent $40 on meals. On April 16, he drove 30 miles, spent $35 on meals, and spent $15 on other expenses.

Maria Ramirez

Maria Ramirez, Sales Representative, incurred her expenses from April 5 to April 11, 2006, and has already been advanced $200. On April 5, Maria drove 28 miles and spent $55 on meals. On April 9, she flew to Chicago for $225.00 + 9% tax, spent $72 on meals, and drove 18 miles. On April 9 and April 10, she stayed at the Lakeside Hotel for $125/night + 11% tax. On April 10, she spent $88 on meals and $42.50 on other expenses. On April 11, she drove 18 miles and spent $32 on meals.

PROJECT **1**

activity:

Prepare the Expense Report

You need to consolidate data from the Chow, Wilson, and Ramirez worksheets to create the April Expense Report. Then, you need to enhance the report attractively and add a clip art picture. The completed expense report is shown in Figure C-15.

steps:

1. Click **Insert** on the menu bar, click **Worksheet**, double-click the **Sheet4** tab, type **Report**, press **[Enter]**, click the **Report tab**, then drag the Report tab to the right so that it appears after the Ramirez tab as shown in Figure C-14
   As you drag the tab, the sheet pointer ₪ appears.

2. Click the **Chow tab**, copy cells **A1:A4**, click the **Report tab**, click the **Paste button** ▣ on the Standard toolbar, click cell **A4**, then change Expense Statement to **April Expense Report**

3. Enter and format the names of the three employees in cells **A7, A8,** and **A9** as shown in Figure C-15, adjust the column A width to fit the names, enter and format the expense labels (**Accom.** to **Total**) in cells **B6:H6** as shown in Figure C-15, then select cells **B6:H6** and fill them with **Gray-25% shading**

4. Click cell **B7**, type **=**, click the **Chow tab**, click cell **B26**, press **[Enter]**, then copy the formula through cell **G7**

5. Click cell **B8**, type **=**, click the **Wilson tab**, click cell **B26**, press **[Enter]**, copy the formula through cell **G8**, then repeat the process to enter the amounts for Maria Ramirez in cells **B9:G9**

Hint

To calculate the advances, click cell H11, type =, then add cell H28 from the Wilson sheet to cell H28 from the Ramirez sheet.

6. Select cells **B7:H9**, click the **AutoSum button** Σ on the Standard toolbar, then calculate the total advances in cell **H11**

7. Enter and format the labels for cells **G10, G11,** and **G12** as shown in Figure C-15, calculate the subtotal and total April expenses, verify that the total April expenses are **$2,244.17**, click the **Wilson tab**, change the advance he received to **$300**, then verify that the total expenses in the Report tab are now **$2,094.17**

8. Click cell **A1**, click **Insert** on the menu bar, point to **Picture**, click **Clip Art**, type **computer** in the Search for text box in the Clip Art task pane, find and insert the clip art picture shown in Figure C-15, then size and position it as shown in Figure C-15

Additional Practice

For additional practice with the skills presented in this project, complete Independent Challenge 2.

9. Increase the height of rows 6 through 12 to **20**, click the **Print Preview button** ▣ on the Standard toolbar, click the **Setup tab**, center horizontally and enter header text as shown in Figure C-15, save the workbook, print a copy of the report, then close the workbook

FIGURE C-14: Repositioning the Report tab

12						
13						
14						
15						
16						
17						
18						
19						
20						
21						
22						
23						

ꓤ ◀ ▶ ꓕ \ Chow / Wilson / Ramirez / Report /

Ready   NUM

Sheet pointer appears when you drag a sheet tab

Report tab moved to the right of the Ramirez tab

FIGURE C-15: Completed Expense Report

April Expense Report   Your Name

E-Learning Associates
Suite 250 - 1800 Pacific Crest Road, San Francisco, CA 94171

April Expense Report

	Accom.	Transport	Fuel	Meals	Entertain.	Other	Total
Grace Chow	$ 420.00	$ 285.06	$ 21.00	$ 262.50	$ 72.00	$ 25.00	$ 1,085.56
Mark Wilson	$ 163.36	$ 278.00	$ 30.00	$ 172.00	$ -	$ 37.00	$ 680.36
Maria Ramirez	$ 277.50	$ 245.25	$ 16.00	$ 247.00	$ -	$ 42.50	$ 828.25

Subtotal	$	2,594.17
Less Advances	$	500.00
Total April Expenses	$	2,094.17

Planning Budget for a Japan Vacation

You hope to take a three-week trip to Japan with a friend. Your budget for the trip is $5,000. Before you buy your plane ticket, you need to determine how much you can spend on airfare, accommodations, food, entertainment, and transportation. You may *want* to stay in first-class hotels, but your $5,000 budget may not extend that far. What kind of trip can you really afford? For this project you need to **Set up the Budget** and then **Calculate Options**. The completed budget appears in Figure C-19 on page 69.

activity:

Set Up the Budget

steps:

1. Start Excel, set up Sheet1 so that it appears as shown in Figure C-16, then save the workbook as **Japan Trip Budget** to the location where you are storing the files for this book

2. Select cells **B4:E4**, right-click the selected cells, click **Format Cells**, then click the **Alignment tab**

3. Click the **Vertical list arrow**, click **Top**, drag the **red diamond** in the Orientation section down so the spin box shows **-90 Degrees** as shown in Figure C-17, then click **OK**
The labels in cells B4:E4 are rotated 90 degrees.

4. Click cell **E5**, enter the formula **=C5*D5**, press **[Enter]**, then copy the formula through cell **E10**

5. Click cell **E12**, then double-click the **AutoSum button** Σ on the Standard toolbar to calculate the subtotal
The expense subtotal is $7,345.00.

6. Click cell **E13**, calculate a 10% contingency on the subtotal, then press **[Enter]**
The value in the Contingency cell is $734.50.

7. Enter a formula in cell **E14** to add the **subtotal** to the **contingency** to determine your **total expenses**
Your total expenses in cell E14 are $8,079.50. You are $3,079.50 over your budget of $5,000.

8. As shown in Figure C-18, change the font size to **14** for cells **A4:E14**, then adjust column widths as needed

9. Save the workbook

Trouble

The required formula is =E12*.1.

FIGURE C-16: **Worksheet setup**

14-point, bold, cells merged and centered

24-point, bold, cells merged and centered

Currency

Bold and centered

Right-aligned

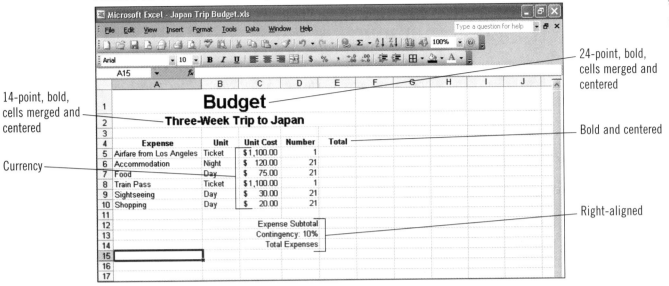

FIGURE C-17: **Format Cells dialog box**

Red diamond moved to −90 degrees

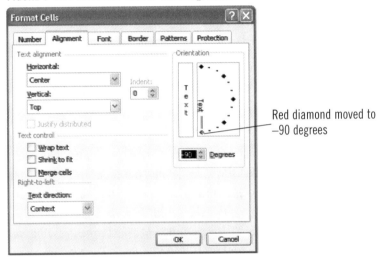

FIGURE C-18: **Worksheet with expenses**

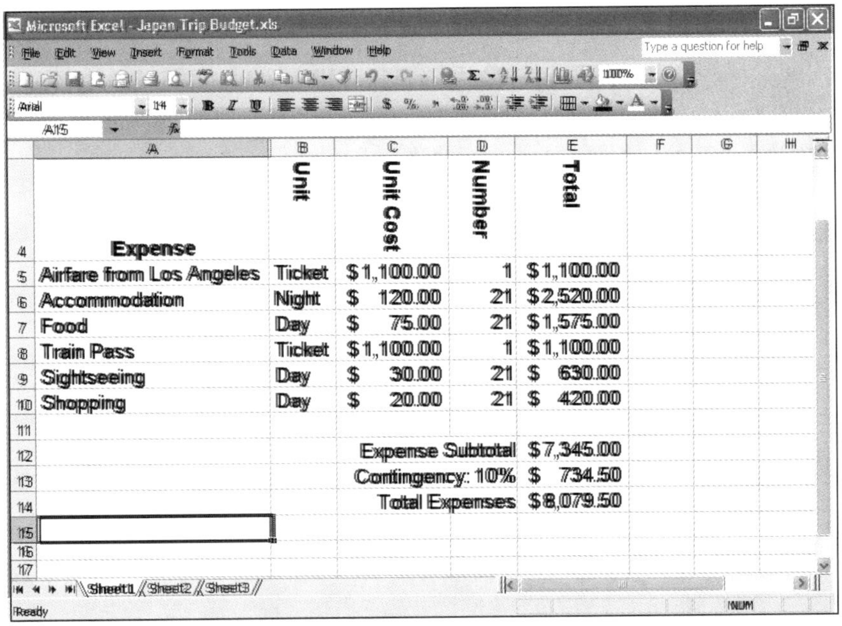

PLANNING BUDGET FOR A JAPAN VACATION

activity:

Calculate Options

You need to reduce the trip cost to $5,000. You decide to perform a variety of calculations to answer several "What if?" questions. As you enter data to answer the "What if?" questions in Steps 2 through 7, check the value in the Total Expenses cell against the total expenses value provided in the text. You will need to think carefully about the calculations required. For some steps, you need to insert new rows. The completed budget is shown in Figure C-19.

steps:

1. Rename the Sheet1 tab **Budget 1** and rename the Sheet2 tab **Budget 2**, return to the **Budget 1** sheet, click the **Select All button** in the upper-left corner of the worksheet frame, click the **Copy button** on the Standard toolbar, click the **Budget 2 tab**, then click the **Paste button** on the Standard toolbar

   Now you have two copies of the budget—your original copy and a new copy that you can modify by changing values to calculate responses to "What if?" questions.

2. Perform the calculation required to answer the question "What if you reduce your sightseeing allowance to $20 a day?"

   The total for sightseeing is $420, and the total expenses are now $7,848.50.

Hint

Replace the label Train Pass with Car Lease, and then change the values per the "What if?" question in Step 3.

3. What if you do not buy a train pass but instead lease a car for two weeks at a cost of $735 per week and share the cost of the car lease with a friend?

   Total expenses are now $7,447. Remember to divide the weekly car lease cost by two because you are sharing the expense with a friend.

4. What if you stay at youth hostels for 12 days ($30/night for one), stay in small inns for 6 days ($75.00/night for one), and then stay in moderately priced hotels for the remaining 3 days ($200/night for two)?

   You will need to insert two new rows for the various accommodation options. See Figure C-19 for the three labels that replace the Accommodations label. You will also need to copy the formula required to calculate the Youth Hostel, Inn, and Hotel expenses. You may need to adjust the cell references in the formula used to find the expense subtotal. The total expenses are now $5,896.00. Getting there!

5. What if you buy and cook your own food on the days that you stay in youth hostels, thereby reducing your food costs on those days to $20 a day?

   The total expenses are now $5,170.00.

6. If you lease a car, you will split gas costs with your friend during the two weeks that you have the car. You plan to drive approximately 2,000 kilometers; the car you plan to rent gets 13 kilometers to the liter; gas costs approximately $1.50 a liter

   The total expenses are now $5,296.92.

7. What if you book a charter flight that costs $200 less than the current airfare?

   Total expenses are now $5,076.92. You are still $76.92 over your budget of $5,000. You decide that you can just afford to pay the shortfall, but realize that you will need to stick very carefully to your budget.

8. Click cell **A1**, fill it with **Gray–25%**, then add border lines to cells as shown in Figure C-19

9. View the worksheet in Print Preview, center it **horizontally** (click the Margins tab in the Page Setup dialog box), add the **header text** shown in Figure C-19, save the workbook, print a copy, then close the workbook

Additional Practice

For additional practice with the skills presented in this project, complete Independent Challenge 3.

FIGURE C-19: Completed Trip Planning Budget

Excel

Japan Travel Budget   Your Name

Budget
Three-Week Trip to Japan

Expense	Unit		Unit Cost	Number		Total
Airfare from Los Angeles	Ticket	$	900.00	1	$	900.00
Accommodation: Youth Hostels	Night	$	30.00	12	$	360.00
Accommodation: Inns	Night	$	75.00	6	$	450.00
Accommodation: Hotels	Night	$	100.00	3	$	300.00
Food	Day	$	75.00	9	$	675.00
Food: Hostels	Day	$	20.00	12	$	240.00
Car Lease	Week	$	367.50	2	$	735.00
Gas	Kilometer	$	1.50	76.923	$	115.38
Sightseeing	Day	$	20.00	21	$	420.00
Shopping	Day	$	20.00	21	$	420.00

Expense Subtotal	$	4,615.38
Contingency: 10%	$	461.54
Total Expenses	$	5,076.92

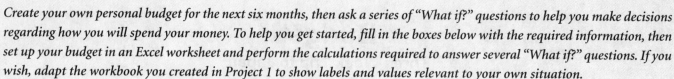

Independent Challenges

Create your own personal budget for the next six months, then ask a series of "What if?" questions to help you make decisions regarding how you will spend your money. To help you get started, fill in the boxes below with the required information, then set up your budget in an Excel worksheet and perform the calculations required to answer several "What if?" questions. If you wish, adapt the workbook you created in Project 1 to show labels and values relevant to your own situation.

1. You need to determine the goal of your budget. Even a personal budget should be created for a specific purpose. For example, you may wish to save for a vacation or to buy a car, or you may just want to live within a set income. Identify the goal of your budget in the box below:

Budget goal:

_____

_____

2. Determine your sources of income. You may receive money from a paycheck, from investment dividends, or from a student loan. Each income source requires a label and a row on your budget worksheet. In the box below, list the income labels you will require:

Income labels:

1. _____

2. _____

3. _____

4. _____

5. _____

3. Determine your expenses. At the very least, you will probably need to list your rent, food, utilities, phone, and transportation costs such as car payments, gas, insurance, and bus fares. In addition, include labels for entertainment, clothing, incidentals, and savings. In the box below, list the expense labels you have identified:

Expense labels:

1. _____   6. _____

2. _____   7. _____

3. _____   8. _____

4. _____   9. _____

5. _____   10. _____

4. Set up your budget in Excel as follows:

   a. Enter and enhance a title for your budget in cell A1.

   b. Enter the current date.

   c. Enter the **Income** and **Expenses** labels and appropriate subcategory labels in column A.

   d. Determine the time frame of your budget (e.g., monthly or weekly), then enter the appropriate labels starting in column B.

   e. Enter the values associated with your income and expenses categories. Adjust expenses according to the time of year. For example, your utilities costs will probably be less in the summer than in the winter, while your entertainment and travel expenses may occur mostly in the summer.

   f. Calculate your total income and expenses.

   g. Copy Sheet1 to Sheet2 of your budget, name Sheet1 **Budget** and Sheet2 **What If**, and then type at least five "What if?" questions at the bottom of the What If sheet. Try to formulate questions that will help you plan your finances to achieve the goal you set. Here are some sample "What if?" questions:

      1. What if I buy a car with payments of $250/month? (Remember to factor in costs for insurance and gas.)

      2. What if I move in March to a new apartment where my rent is 30% more than the current rent?

      3. What if I join a fitness club with monthly dues?

      4. What if I put 10% of my income in savings each month?

      5. What if I start taking violin lessons?

5. Make the necessary calculations and modifications to the copy of your budget to answer your five questions.

6. Add a row to the worksheet with a label and cells that calculate any surplus income remaining after expenses are subtracted.

7. Save your workbook as **My Personal Budget** to the location where you are storing the files for this book.

8. Format and print a copy of your budget.

INDEPENDENT CHALLENGE 2

You work for a company that requires you to travel frequently. Create expense records for three consecutive months. Then prepare an expense report that totals the expenses you incurred in each category for each month, the total for all expenses for each month, and the total for the three-month expenses minus the advances.

1. Set up Sheet1 with an attractive heading including the name and address of the company as well as labels for dates and each expense category. Categories include: accommodations, transportation, mileage (determine the mileage rate your company will pay; e.g., $.25/mile or $.16/kilometer), meals, entertainment, and miscellaneous (or other) expenses. If you wish, adapt the expense form you created for Project 2.

2. Copy your expense form to the next two sheets and then name the sheet tabs (e.g., March, April, May).

3. Enter your expenses for each month. Don't forget to include taxes in your calculations and to enter realistic expenses. For example, a flight from New York to Los Angeles should cost more than a flight from Montreal to Toronto. Assume that each time you fly, you drive your own car to the airport from your home town. Include the mileage calculation.

4. Save the workbook as **My Travel Expenses** to the location where you are storing the files for this book.

5. In a new worksheet, set up an attractive expense report for the three months. Include the name of the company for which you work and an appropriate picture.

6. Enter the formulas required to calculate your total expenses for each of the three months.

7. Format the worksheet containing the expense report attractively, include your name in the header, then print a copy of the report.

INDEPENDENT CHALLENGE 3

Create a planning budget to help you determine your expenses for a vacation of your choice. Adapt the budget you created for Project 3 if you wish. The following tasks will help you get started.

1. Before you create the worksheet in Excel, answer the questions listed below:
   a. Where do you plan to go for your vacation?
   b. What is your proposed budget?
   c. How long is your planned vacation?
   d. What kind of activities do you plan to do on your vacation (e.g., sightseeing, guided tours, horseback riding, skiing, etc.)?
2. Set up your worksheet with labels for transportation costs (airfare, car rental, train fares, etc.), accommodations, food, sightseeing, shopping, and any other expense categories appropriate to the kind of vacation you plan to take.
3. Include a contingency amount for emergency expenses that is 10% to 15% of your total expenses.
4. Try to make your budget as realistic as possible. You can choose to base your budget on a vacation you have already taken or on a vacation you hope to take.
5. Save your vacation planning budget as **My Vacation Budget** to the location where you are storing the files for this book, format it attractively, and print a copy.

INDEPENDENT CHALLENGE 4

You're planning a trip to Australia in May and decide to include your vacation budget with a personal budget for the six months from January to June. To make the budget as dynamic as possible, you include formulas that reference a Web query containing a table of currency exchange rates copied from a currency conversion Web site. You can then refresh the worksheet data periodically to see how the latest exchange rates are affecting your six-month budget.

1. Create the worksheet shown in Figure C-20, change the name of the Sheet1 tab to **Budget**, then save the workbook as **Australia Trip Budget** to the location where you are storing the files for this book.
2. Use AutoFill to fill in the months from February through June, then center the labels.
3. Copy the values for January through June.
4. Add a column labeled **Totals**, then calculate the row totals. Verify that all the values are formatted in the Comma style.
5. Calculate the monthly and total income, the monthly and total expenses, and the savings. Your total income is $30,649.68, your total expenses are $11,280.00, and your total savings are $19,369.68.
6. Click Data on the menu bar, point to Import External Data, click New Web Query, connect to the Internet if necessary, type the Web site address **www.xe.com** in the Address text box in the New Web Query dialog box, then click Go. The xe.com Currency Conversion Web site opens in the New Web Query dialog box.
   NOTE: If a warning appears related to running scripts, just click Yes and continue with the steps.
7. Scroll down the dialog box, then click the table select arrow button next to the XE.com Quick Cross Reference table as shown in Figure C-21. Note that the table select arrow button turns green and a check mark appears when you click it to indicate that the entire table has been selected.

FIGURE C-20:

	A	B	C
1		January	
2	**Income**		
3	Pay Check	4,548.28	
4	Investment Dividends	560.00	
5	**Total Income**		
6			
7	**Expenses**		
8	Rent	700.00	
9	Food	400.00	
10	Phone	100.00	
11	Utilities	150.00	
12	Car Payment	350.00	
13	Gas	80.00	
14	Car Insurance	100.00	
15	Vacation Hotels		
16	Vacation Food		
17	**Total Expenses**		
18			
19	**Total Savings**		
20			
21			

FIGURE C-21: New Web Query dialog box

Click table select arrow button to select the Quick Cross Reference table

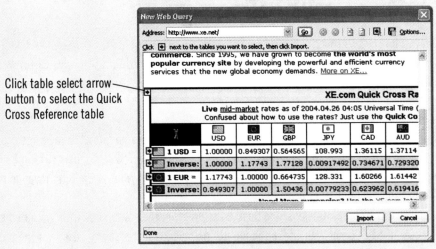

8. Click Options in the New Web Query dialog box, click the Full HTML formatting option button, click OK, then click Import.

9. Click the New worksheet option button, then click OK. The formatted data appears in a new worksheet. Note that image files are not included.

10. Rename the new worksheet **Currency**.

11. Return to the Budget worksheet, then click cell F15. You will be staying at hotels in Australia for eight days. You've checked out Australian hotels on the Internet and decided that 200 Australian dollars (AUD) per night is a reasonable amount to pay. You'd like to know what this amount converts to in U.S. dollars so you can include the hotel cost in your worksheet. You can also choose to convert the amount to euros or to another currency. However, the following steps relate to U.S. dollars.

12. In cell F15 of the Budget worksheet, enter the formula **=8*200*** and leave the insertion point in the cell. Switch to the Currency worksheet, click cell H8 (which contains the exchange rate for Australian dollars to U.S. dollars), then press **[Enter]** to add the value from cell H8 to your formula in the Budget worksheet. The value entered in cell F15 represents the cost of hotels for eight days in U.S. dollars, presuming you spend 200 AUD per night.

13. Click cell F16, enter the formula **=8*100*** and leave the insertion point in the cell. Switch to the Currency worksheet, click cell H8, and then press **[Enter]**. The amount entered in cell F16 represents the cost of food for eight days in U.S. dollars, presuming you spend 100 AUD per day. Note the total savings entered in cell H19.

14. Switch to the Currency worksheet, click cell H8, click Data on the menu bar, click Refresh Data, then click OK.

15. Return to the Budget worksheet, and note how the total savings in cell H19 has changed to reflect the updated exchange rate. On the xe.com Web site, the exchange rates are updated every minute. However, if the rates have not changed during this exercise, your savings value will not change either.

16. Format the worksheet attractively, include your name in the header, print a copy of the worksheet, then save and close the workbook.

Visual Workshop

Create the six-month budget shown in Figure C-22 for Kaleidoscope Designs, a new company that creates Web sites for small businesses. Enter the required formulas to calculate total revenue, expenses, and profit, then apply the Comma style to all the values. Save the budget as **Kaleidoscope Designs Budget** to the location where you are storing the files for this book, then answer the following questions:

1. In July, you estimate that 10 new businesses will contract Kaleidoscope Designs to create a Web site at an average cost of $1,200 per Web site. You project that the contract revenue generated in July will increase by 5% in August, 10% in September, then 20% for each of the remaining months. Calculate all increases based on July revenue. What is the total revenue for Web site design contracts in cell H6? Enter the value in cell B19.

2. In July, you estimate that 15 businesses will contract Kaleidoscope Designs to program their Web sites with animations and other interactive elements at an average cost of $1,500 per Web site. Each month the revenue increases by 10% over the previous month to December. (*Hint*: Enter =B7*1.1 in cell C7, then copy the formula through cell G7.) What is the total revenue in cell H8? Enter the value in cell B20.

3. Make the Salaries expense for both November and December $30,000. What is the total Salaries expense? Enter the value in cell B21.

4. Make the equipment leases for November and December four times the current equipment leases for October (e.g., $8,000). What is the total projected profit in cell H18? Enter the value in cell B22.

5. Format the values in rows 6 through 8, 11 through 16, 18, and cells B19:B22 with the Currency style and add border lines where appropriate.

6. Save the workbook, preview it, make sure the worksheet fits on one page in landscape orientation and is centered horizontally and vertically, add your name to the header, print a copy of the worksheet, then close the workbook and Excel.

FIGURE C-22: Kaleidoscope Designs worksheet

	A	B	C	D	E	F	G	H	I
1				**Kaleidoscope Designs**					
2				**Proposed Six-Month Budget: July to December, 2007**					
3									
4			**July**	**August**	**September**	**October**	**November**	**December**	**Totals**
5	REVENUE								
6	Web site design contracts								
7	Web animation contracts								
8	**Total Revenue**								
9									
10	EXPENSES								
11	Salaries		25000	25000	25000	25000	25000	25000	
12	Rent		6000	6000	6000	6000	6000	6000	
13	Equipment Leases		2000	2000	2000	2000	2000	2000	
14	Advertising		800	800	800	800	800	800	
15	Operating Costs		1500	1500	1500	1500	1500	1500	
16	**Total Expenses**								
17									
18	PROFIT/LOSS								
19	Question 1 Answer								
20	Question 2 Answer								
21	Question 3 Answer								
22	Question 4 Answer								

Microsoft
►Excel
Projects

Excel

Unit D

Excel Projects II

In this Unit You Will Create the Following:

 **Sales Forecast**

 **Course Grades Analysis**

 **Personal Investment Analysis**

With Microsoft Excel, you can analyze numerical data and identify patterns and trends. For example, you can use the powerful Scenario function to make predictions based on a current set of data. You can then use these predictions to plan business and sales ventures, analyze current sales patterns, and create sales forecasts. You can also display the results of an analysis visually in the form of a chart, such as a bar chart or a pie chart. In this unit, you will create scenarios to forecast sales, create a lookup table and use the Lookup function, build a pie chart from a PivotTable, and use various financial functions to analyze investments.

Sales Forecast for WorkEase

You own WorkEase, a small consulting firm that advises businesses about workplace safety issues and sells ergonomically correct workstations. You are considering moving from your home office to a commercial office space and hiring an executive assistant and a sales representative. To help you decide what course of action you should take, you use Excel to complete four activities: Set up the Workbook, Create Current Scenarios, Create Best and Worst Case Scenarios, and Format and Print the Scenarios. The completed printouts of the Best Case and Worst Case scenarios are shown in Figures D-8 and D-9 on page 83.

activity:

Set Up the Workbook

You need to enter the labels and values for the six-month revenue and expenses statement for WorkEase and calculate your total revenue, expenses, and net income.

Hint

The result of each calculation appears in parentheses in the text.

Trouble

Move the pointer over a green rectangle to see the Trace Error Tag.

steps:

1. Start Excel, set up and format the worksheet as shown in Figure D-1, then save the workbook as **Sales Forecasts for WorkEase** to the location where you are storing the files for this book

2. Click cell **B7**, enter a formula that calculates 3% of cell **B6** (450), then in cell **B8** enter a formula that subtracts cell **B7** from cell **B6** (14550)

The formula in cell B7 calculates the value of returned products as an average of 3% of total sales. The formula in cell B8 calculates the net sales after the returns have been subtracted.

3. In cell **B9**, enter a formula that calculates 60% of cell **B8** (8730), then enter a formula in cell **B10** that subtracts cell **B9** from cell **B8** (5820)

The formula in cell B9 calculates the cost of goods sold as 60% of the total sales. The formula in cell B10 calculates the gross profit on sales, which amounts to the cost of sales subtracted from the net sales. A green triangle appears in cell B9 because Excel has determined that the formula is inconsistent with formulas in adjacent cells. The formula in cell B9 multiplies values, while the formulas in cells B8 and B10 subtract values. You will remove the green triangle in a later step.

4. Select cells **B7:B10**, then fill cells **C7:G10** with the formulas

5. Select cells **B6:H10**, click the **AutoSum button** Σ on the Standard toolbar, select cells **B9:G9**, click the **Trace Error Tag** ⬦ ▾, then click **Ignore Error**

6. Select cells **B13:H17**, click Σ, click cell **B19**, then enter a formula that subtracts the total expenses in cell **B17** from the gross profit on sales in cell **B10** (920)

7. Fill cells **C19:H19** with the formula, then save the workbook

The total net profit for sales from July to December 2006 is 11728 as shown in cell H19 in Figure D-2.

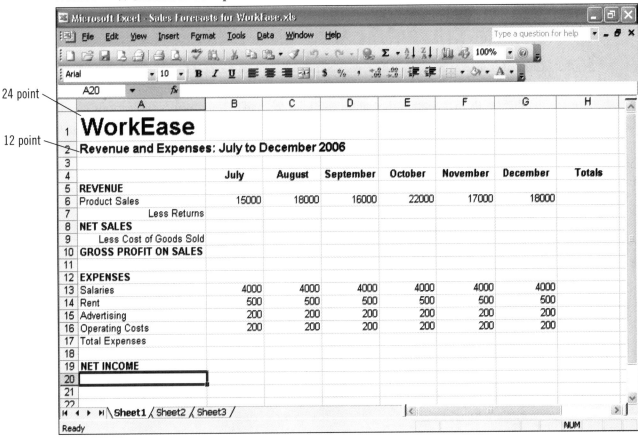

FIGURE D-1: Worksheet setup

24 point →

12 point →

(Excel window: Microsoft Excel - Sales Forecasts for WorkEase.xls)

	July	August	September	October	November	December	Totals
WorkEase							
Revenue and Expenses: July to December 2006							
	July	August	September	October	November	December	Totals
REVENUE							
Product Sales	15000	18000	16000	22000	17000	18000	
Less Returns							
NET SALES							
Less Cost of Goods Sold							
GROSS PROFIT ON SALES							
EXPENSES							
Salaries	4000	4000	4000	4000	4000	4000	
Rent	500	500	500	500	500	500	
Advertising	200	200	200	200	200	200	
Operating Costs	200	200	200	200	200	200	
Total Expenses							
NET INCOME							

FIGURE D-2: Worksheet with totals calculated

(Excel window)

	July	August	September	October	November	December	Totals
WorkEase							
Revenue and Expenses: July to December 2006							
	July	August	September	October	November	December	Totals
REVENUE							
Product Sales	15000	18000	16000	22000	17000	18000	106000
Less Returns	450	540	480	660	510	540	3180
NET SALES	14550	17460	15520	21340	16490	17460	102820
Less Cost of Goods Sold	8730	10476	9312	12804	9894	10476	61692
GROSS PROFIT ON SALES	5820	6984	6208	8536	6596	6984	41128
EXPENSES							
Salaries	4000	4000	4000	4000	4000	4000	24000
Rent	500	500	500	500	500	500	3000
Advertising	200	200	200	200	200	200	1200
Operating Costs	200	200	200	200	200	200	1200
Total Expenses	4900	4900	4900	4900	4900	4900	29400
NET INCOME	920	2084	1308	3636	1696	2084	11728

activity:

Create Current Scenarios

Current scenarios represent the revenue and expenses you expect to generate from July to December 2006 if you continue to manage WorkEase on your own from your home office. First, you need to highlight cells that contain the values you plan to change when you create various scenarios. Then, you need to use the Scenario Manager to create current scenarios from the values for the current product sales and the expenses for rent, salaries, and operating costs.

steps:

1. Click cell **B6**, press and hold [Ctrl], then select cells **B6:H6**, cells **B13:H14**, and cells **B16:H16**

2. Click the **Fill Color list arrow** 🎨 ▾ on the Formatting toolbar, click the **Yellow** color, format cells in the **Comma** or **Currency** style as shown in Figure D-3, then widen the columns if necessary
The cells for Product Sales, Salaries, Rent, and Operating Costs are filled with yellow because they contain values you need to change when you create different scenarios.

3. Select cells **B6:G6**, click **Tools** on the menu bar, click **Scenarios**, then click **Add**

4. Type **Current Sales**, click **OK**, then click **OK** again to accept the values currently entered in cells **B6:G6**
The Current Sales scenario consists of the values currently entered in cells B6:G6.

5. Click **Add**, type **Current Salaries**, click the **Collapse Dialog Box button** 📑, select cells **B13:G13**, click the **Restore Dialog Box button** 📖, click **OK**, then click **OK**

6. Add a scenario called **Current Rent** based on cells **B14:G14**, then add a scenario called **Current Operating Costs** based on cells **B16:G16**

7. Compare the Scenario Manager dialog box to Figure D-4

8. Click **Close** to exit the Scenario Manager dialog box, then save the workbook

FIGURE D-3: Formatted worksheet

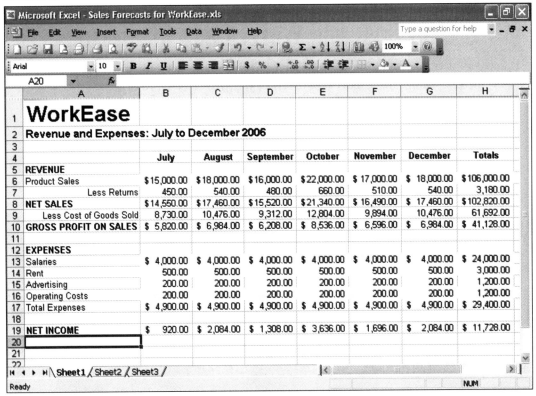

FIGURE D-4: Scenario Manager dialog box

PROJECT 1

activity:

Create Best and Worst Case Scenarios

You need to change the values in the worksheet to reflect your Best Case projections, and then you need to change the values again to reflect your Worst Case projections.

steps:

1. Click **Tools** on the menu bar, click **Scenarios**, click **Current Sales**, click **Add**, type **Best Case Sales**, then click **OK**

2. Type **45000**, press **[Tab]**, enter the values for cells **C6:G6** of Best Case Sales as shown in Figure D-5, then click **OK**

These values represent the sales you hope to generate by moving to a commercial space and hiring additional help.

3. Click **Current Salaries**, click **Add**, type **Best Case Salaries**, click **OK**, type **9000**, press **[Tab]**, enter **9000** for cells **C13:G13**, then click **OK**

You estimate that your salaries expense will more than double when you hire a new sales representative and an assistant.

4. Click **Current Rent**, add a scenario called **Best Case Rent** that changes all the values in cells **B14:G14** to **1500**, click **Current Operating Costs**, then add a scenario called **Best Case Operating Costs** that changes all the values in cells **B16:G16** to **800**

You hope to obtain office space for $1,500 a month and generate operating costs of no more than $800 a month.

Trouble

If cell H19 contains a different value, open the Scenario Manager dialog box and review the values you've entered for each of the four Best Case scenarios.

5. Click **Best Case Sales**, click **Show**, click **Best Case Salaries**, click **Show**, show the remaining **Best Case scenarios**, then click **Close**

The value in cell H19 is $72,620.00. If all goes as you have planned, you should do very well if you move to a commercial space and hire new personnel to help you sell WorkEase products. But what if things don't go as planned?

6. Click **Tools**, click **Scenarios**, click **Current Sales**, click **Add**, type **Worst Case Sales**, click **OK**, type **30000**, press **[Tab]**, enter the values for cells **C6:G6** of Worst Case Sales as shown in Figure D-6, then click **OK**

7. Add the Worst Case Salaries, Worst Case Rent, and Worst Case Operating Costs scenarios based on the values displayed below:

Worst Case Salaries	10000
Worst Case Rent	4000
Worst Case Operating Costs	1000

8. Show all the Worst Case scenarios, then close the Scenario Manager dialog box

The total net income displayed in cell H19 is now $(13,600.00) as shown in Figure D-7. The Worst Case scenarios are based on your projection of lower sales paired with higher expenses for salaries, rent, and operating costs.

9. Click **Tools** on the menu bar, click **Scenarios**, click **Current Sales** (you will need to scroll up), click **Show**, show all the remaining Current scenarios, click **Close**, then fill cell H19 with **yellow** and apply **Bold**

You should see $11,728.00 in cell H19.

FIGURE D-5: Best Case Sales values

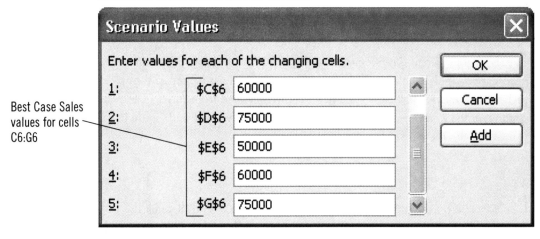

Best Case Sales values for cells C6:G6

FIGURE D-6: Worst Case Sales values

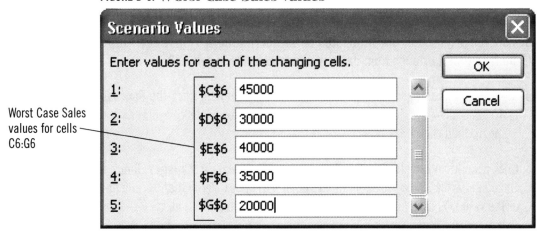

Worst Case Sales values for cells C6:G6

FIGURE D-7: Worksheet with Worst Case scenarios shown

Microsoft Excel - Sales Forecasts for WorkEase.xls

	A	B	C	D	E	F	G	H
1	**WorkEase**							
2	**Revenue and Expenses: July to December 2006**							
3								
4		July	August	September	October	November	December	Totals
5	REVENUE							
6	Product Sales	$30,000.00	$45,000.00	$30,000.00	$40,000.00	$35,000.00	$ 20,000.00	$200,000.00
7	Less Returns	900.00	1,350.00	900.00	1,200.00	1,050.00	600.00	6,000.00
8	NET SALES	$29,100.00	$43,650.00	$29,100.00	$38,800.00	$ 33,950.00	$ 19,400.00	$194,000.00
9	Less Cost of Goods Sold	17,460.00	26,190.00	17,460.00	23,280.00	20,370.00	11,640.00	116,400.00
10	GROSS PROFIT ON SALES	$11,640.00	$17,460.00	$11,640.00	$15,520.00	$ 13,580.00	$ 7,760.00	$ 77,600.00
11								
12	EXPENSES							
13	Salaries	$10,000.00	$10,000.00	$10,000.00	$10,000.00	$ 10,000.00	$ 10,000.00	$ 60,000.00
14	Rent	4,000.00	4,000.00	4,000.00	4,000.00	4,000.00	4,000.00	24,000.00
15	Advertising	200.00	200.00	200.00	200.00	200.00	200.00	1,200.00
16	Operating Costs	1,000.00	1,000.00	1,000.00	1,000.00	1,000.00	1,000.00	6,000.00
17	Total Expenses	$15,200.00	$15,200.00	$15,200.00	$15,200.00	$ 15,200.00	$ 15,200.00	$ 91,200.00
18								
19	NET INCOME	$ (3,560.00)	$ 2,260.00	$ (3,560.00)	$ 320.00	$ (1,620.00)	$ (7,440.00)	$ (13,600.00)
20								
21								
22								

PROJECT 1

SALES FORECAST FOR WORKEASE

activity:

Format and Print the Scenarios

At present, the Current Case scenarios are displayed. You decide to print worksheets to show the three sets of scenarios. To highlight the differences among the three sets of scenarios, you create a column chart for each set of scenarios that shows the net income generated from July to December. Figure D-8 shows a printout of the worksheet with the Best Case scenarios displayed, and Figure D-9 shows a printout of the worksheet with the Worst Case scenarios displayed.

steps:

1. Select cells **B4:G4**, press and hold **[Ctrl]**, select cells **B19:G19**, click the **Chart Wizard button** 📖 on the Standard toolbar, then click **Next** to accept the default column chart

2. Click **Next** to accept the range you selected, enter **Current Monthly Net Income** as the chart title, click the **Legend tab**, click the **Show legend check** box to deselect it, then click **Finish**

3. Move the pointer over any white area of the chart, drag the chart down to **row 22**, then resize the chart so that it extends from halfway across cell **A22** to cell **G40**

4. Right-click the **category axis** (the x-axis), click **Format Axis**, click the **Font tab**, change the font size to **10 point**, click **OK**, right-click the **value axis** (the y-axis), click **Format Axis**, change the font size to **10 point**, then click **OK**

5. Click away from the chart to deselect it, open the **Scenario Manager dialog box**, show all the **Best Case scenarios**, close the Scenario Manager dialog box, verify that **20,000** appears as the top value of the value (Y) axis, show all the **Current scenarios** again, right-click the **value axis**, click **Format Axis**, click the **Scale tab**, select the contents of the **Maximum text box**, type **20000**, then click **OK**
You change the top value of the value axis to match the top value of the value axis when the Best Case scenarios are active. By so doing, you ensure that the column charts provide a meaningful comparison among the three sets of scenarios.

6. Click away from the chart to deselect it, click the **Print Preview button** 🔍 on the Standard toolbar, click **Setup**, format the worksheet so that it fits on one page, is horizontally centered, and includes a custom header that displays **Current Scenarios** at the left and **your name** at the right, click **OK**, click **OK**, click **Print**, then click **OK**

7. Click **Tools** on the menu bar, click **Scenarios**, show all the **Best Case scenarios**, then verify that **$72,620.00** appears in cell H19

8. Click the **chart title**, change the chart title to **Best Case Forecast**, click outside the chart, click 🔍, click **Setup**, change the custom header text to **Best Case Scenarios**, then print a copy
Figure D-8 shows a printout of the worksheet with the Best Case scenarios active.

Additional Practice

For additional practice with the skills presented in this project, complete Independent Challenge 1.

9. Click **Tools**, click **Scenarios**, show all the **Worst Case scenarios**, verify that **$(13,600.00)** appears in cell H19, click **Close**, change the chart title to **Worst Case Forecast**, change the custom header to show **Worst Case Scenarios**, print a copy, then save and close the workbook
Figure D-9 shows a printout of the worksheet with the Worst Case scenarios active. Now that you have printed copies of all three worksheets you can mix and match scenarios to try out new predictions. For example, you could show the Current Salaries and Current Operating Costs scenarios along with the Best Case Rent scenario and the Worst Case Sales scenario. The net income in cell H19 changes with each combination.

FIGURE D-8: Best Case scenarios

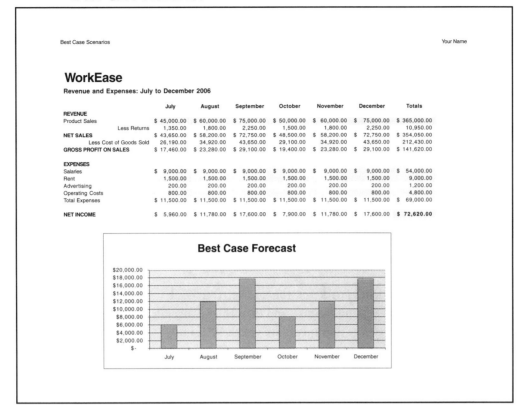

Best Case Scenarios   Your Name

WorkEase

Revenue and Expenses: July to December 2006

	July	August	September	October	November	December	Totals
REVENUE							
Product Sales	$ 45,000.00	$ 60,000.00	$ 75,000.00	$ 50,000.00	$ 60,000.00	$ 75,000.00	$ 365,000.00
Less Returns	1,350.00	1,800.00	2,250.00	1,500.00	1,800.00	2,250.00	10,950.00
NET SALES	$ 43,650.00	$ 58,200.00	$ 72,750.00	$ 48,500.00	$ 58,200.00	$ 72,750.00	$ 354,050.00
Less Cost of Goods Sold	26,190.00	34,920.00	43,650.00	29,100.00	34,920.00	43,650.00	212,430.00
GROSS PROFIT ON SALES	$ 17,460.00	$ 23,280.00	$ 29,100.00	$ 19,400.00	$ 23,280.00	$ 29,100.00	$ 141,620.00
EXPENSES							
Salaries	$ 9,000.00	$ 9,000.00	$ 9,000.00	$ 9,000.00	$ 9,000.00	$ 9,000.00	$ 54,000.00
Rent	1,500.00	1,500.00	1,500.00	1,500.00	1,500.00	1,500.00	9,000.00
Advertising	200.00	200.00	200.00	200.00	200.00	200.00	1,200.00
Operating Costs	800.00	800.00	800.00	800.00	800.00	800.00	4,800.00
Total Expenses	$ 11,500.00	$ 11,500.00	$ 11,500.00	$ 11,500.00	$ 11,500.00	$ 11,500.00	$ 69,000.00
NET INCOME	$ 5,960.00	$ 11,780.00	$ 17,600.00	$ 7,900.00	$ 11,780.00	$ 17,600.00	**$ 72,620.00**

Best Case Forecast

FIGURE D-9: Worst Case scenarios

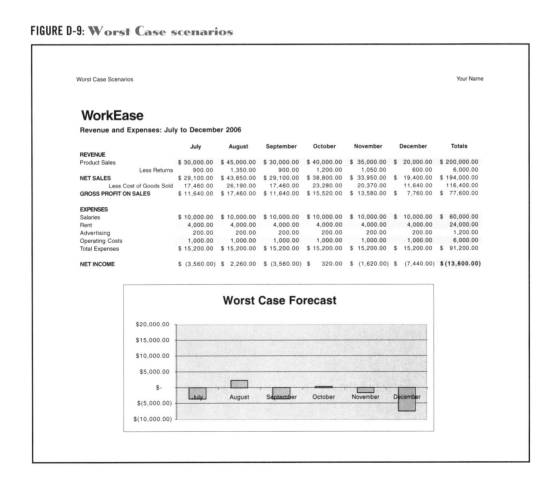

Worst Case Scenarios   Your Name

WorkEase

Revenue and Expenses: July to December 2006

	July	August	September	October	November	December	Totals
REVENUE							
Product Sales	$ 30,000.00	$ 45,000.00	$ 30,000.00	$ 40,000.00	$ 35,000.00	$ 20,000.00	$ 200,000.00
Less Returns	900.00	1,350.00	900.00	1,200.00	1,050.00	600.00	6,000.00
NET SALES	$ 29,100.00	$ 43,650.00	$ 29,100.00	$ 38,800.00	$ 33,950.00	$ 19,400.00	$ 194,000.00
Less Cost of Goods Sold	17,460.00	26,190.00	17,460.00	23,280.00	20,370.00	11,640.00	116,400.00
GROSS PROFIT ON SALES	$ 11,640.00	$ 17,460.00	$ 11,640.00	$ 15,520.00	$ 13,580.00	$ 7,760.00	$ 77,600.00
EXPENSES							
Salaries	$ 10,000.00	$ 10,000.00	$ 10,000.00	$ 10,000.00	$ 10,000.00	$ 10,000.00	$ 60,000.00
Rent	4,000.00	4,000.00	4,000.00	4,000.00	4,000.00	4,000.00	24,000.00
Advertising	200.00	200.00	200.00	200.00	200.00	200.00	1,200.00
Operating Costs	1,000.00	1,000.00	1,000.00	1,000.00	1,000.00	1,000.00	6,000.00
Total Expenses	$ 15,200.00	$ 15,200.00	$ 15,200.00	$ 15,200.00	$ 15,200.00	$ 15,200.00	$ 91,200.00
NET INCOME	$ (3,560.00)	$ 2,260.00	$ (3,560.00)	$ 320.00	$ (1,620.00)	$ (7,440.00)	**$ (13,600.00)**

Worst Case Forecast

Course Grades Analysis for Management 100

As the instructor of Management 100, you need to calculate a final grade for each student and then create a chart to help you analyze how well your students performed. To complete the course grades analysis, you need to Calculate Totals and Grades, Create a PivotTable and Chart, and then Format the Course Grades Analysis. The completed course grades analysis is shown in Figure D-15 on page 89.

activity:

Calculate Totals and Grades

To calculate a student's mark for the course, you need to enter totals for each grade category (Assignments, Quizzes, and Exams), and then enter a formula to *weigh* the grades earned by the students according to type. Assignments are worth 50%, quizzes 15%, and exams 35%.

steps:

Trouble
Type "I" as in Irene followed by "21".

1. Start Excel, set up and format the worksheet so that it appears as shown in Figure D-10, then save the workbook as Course Grades Analysis to the location where you are storing the files for this book

2. Click cell I4, type =(B4+C4+D4)/(B20+C20+D20)*I21, press [Enter], then verify that 29.75 appears in cell I4

3. Click cell I4, click B20 in the formula on the formula bar, press [F4] to make the value absolute, click C20, press [F4], click D20, press [F4], click I21, then press [F4]
   You use the [F4] command to insert the dollar signs ($) because you want to make the values in cells B20, C20, D20, and I21 absolute. When you copy the formula for the rest of the students, you want each formula to divide the total assignment score by the value in row 21.

4. Press [Enter], copy the formula through cell I18, then click the Comma Style button ⟨,⟩ on the Formatting toolbar

Trouble
The formula required is =(G4+H4)/($G$20+$H$20) *$K$21.

5. Click cell J4, enter the formula =(E4+F4)/(E20+F20)*J21, make cells E20, F20, and J21 absolute, press [Enter], copy the formula through cell J18, then click ⟨,⟩

6. Click cell K4, enter the formula that calculates the weighted score for exams, copy the formula through cell K18, then click ⟨,⟩
   Marta earned 24.00 out of 25 for quizzes and 33.60 out of 40 for exams.

7. Select cells I4:L18, click the AutoSum button ⟨Σ⟩, then widen the column if necessary
   Marta's total score is 87.35.

8. Double-click the Sheet1 tab, type Grades, press [Enter], double-click the Sheet2 tab, type Lookup, press [Enter], set up the Lookup worksheet so that it appears as shown in Figure D-11, then save the workbook

FIGURE D-10: Course Grades worksheet

Width of columns
B to M set at 6

20 point and
centered across
columns A to M

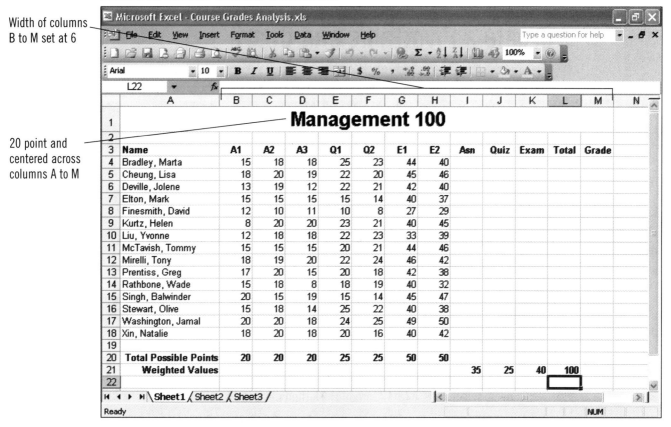

	A	B	C	D	E	F	G	H	I	J	K	L	M	N
1				**Management 100**										
2														
3	**Name**	**A1**	**A2**	**A3**	**Q1**	**Q2**	**E1**	**E2**	**Asn**	**Quiz**	**Exam**	**Total**	**Grade**	
4	Bradley, Marta	15	18	18	25	23	44	40						
5	Cheung, Lisa	18	20	19	22	20	45	46						
6	Deville, Jolene	13	19	12	22	21	42	40						
7	Elton, Mark	15	15	15	15	14	40	37						
8	Finesmith, David	12	10	11	10	8	27	29						
9	Kurtz, Helen	8	20	20	23	21	40	45						
10	Liu, Yvonne	12	18	18	22	23	33	39						
11	McTavish, Tommy	15	15	15	20	21	44	46						
12	Mirelli, Tony	18	19	20	22	24	46	42						
13	Prentiss, Greg	17	20	15	20	18	42	38						
14	Rathbone, Wade	15	18	8	18	19	40	32						
15	Singh, Balwinder	20	15	19	15	14	45	47						
16	Stewart, Olive	15	18	14	25	22	40	38						
17	Washington, Jamal	20	20	18	24	25	49	50						
18	Xin, Natalie	18	20	18	20	16	40	42						
19														
20	**Total Possible Points**	**20**	**20**	**20**	**25**	**25**	**50**	**50**						
21	**Weighted Values**									35	25	40	100	
22														

FIGURE D-11: Lookup Table

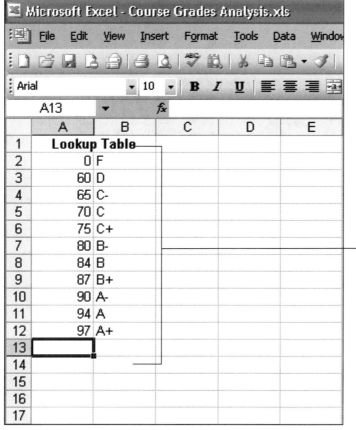

	A	B	C	D	E
1	**Lookup Table**				
2	0	F			
3	60	D			
4	65	C-			
5	70	C			
6	75	C+			
7	80	B-			
8	84	B			
9	87	B+			
10	90	A-			
11	94	A			
12	97	A+			
13					

This lookup table lists the grades corresponding to score values. You use a lookup table to look up the letter grade earned by each student; the letter grade corresponds to the student's total score entered in column L of the Grades sheet (not shown here).

activity:

Create a PivotTable and Chart

First you need to enter a formula that refers to the lookup table you created in the Lookup sheet. Then you need to create a PivotTable that counts the number of times that each letter grade appears in column M of the Grades sheet. A PivotTable is an interactive table that quickly summarizes large amounts of data. You use a PivotTable when you want a quick way to sort, subtotal, and total a series of values. Once you have completed the PivotTable from the list of student grades, you need to create a pie chart that compares how many students earned each letter grade.

steps:

Trouble

An install warning appears if the Insert Function feature is being used for the first time.

1. Click the **Grades tab**, click cell **M4**, click the **Insert Function button** *fx* on the Formula bar, type **Lookup** in the Search for a function text box, click **Go**, then click **OK**

2. Click **lookup_value,array**, click **OK**, type **L4** in the Lookup_value text box, then press **[Tab]**

   You've entered the cell address of the value that the lookup table must use to assign a grade. This value represents Marta's total score out of 100 for the course.

3. Click the **Collapse Dialog Box button** next to **Array**, click the **Lookup tab** to show the Lookup worksheet, select cells **A2:B12**, press **[F4]**, then click the **Restore Dialog Box button**

   The Function Arguments dialog box appears as shown in Figure D-12. Marta will earn a B+ for Management 100.

4. Click **OK**, copy the formula in cell **M4** down through cell **M18**, then save the workbook

   You should save the workbook before you create a PivotChart.

5. With cells M4:M18 still selected, click **Data** on the menu bar, click **PivotTable and PivotChart Report**, click **Next**, click **Next**, then click **Finish**

   A new worksheet appears with the layout for a PivotTable.

6. Drag the PivotTable Field List dialog box and PivotTable toolbar to position them as shown in Figure D-13, drag **Grade** to the **Drop Row Fields Here** section of the table, then drag **Grade** again to the **Drop Data Items Here** area

   The PivotTable starts in cell A3 of Sheet4. As you can see, the "A+" entry appears below the "A-" entry and the "B+" and "C+" entries appear in the wrong positions. You need to reposition these entries so that the grades are listed in hierarchical order.

Trouble

Be sure to position the pointer just above cell A6 and not the row 6 indicator.

7. Click the **row 6** indicator to select all of row 6, point the pointer just above cell **A6**, then click and drag row 6 up to row 5 so that the "A+" entry appears above the "A-" entry

8. Repeat the process to move "B+" above "B" and "C+" above "C"

9. Click the **Chart Wizard button** on the PivotTable toolbar, click **Chart** on the menu bar, click **Chart Type**, click **Pie**, click **OK**, then save the document

   A pie chart appears in a new worksheet called Chart1 as shown in Figure D-14.

FIGURE D-12: **Function Arguments dialog box**

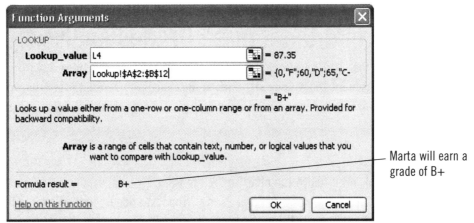

Marta will earn a grade of B+

FIGURE D-13: **PivotTable worksheet**

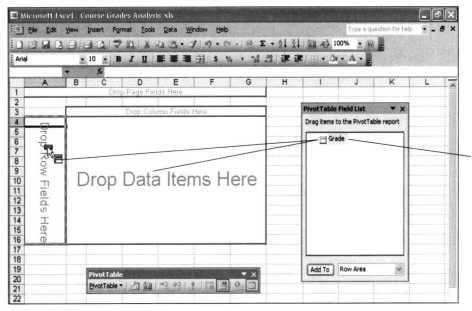

Drag Grade from the PivotTable Field List to the Drop Row Fields Here column and the Drop Data Items Here area

FIGURE D-14: **Pie chart created**

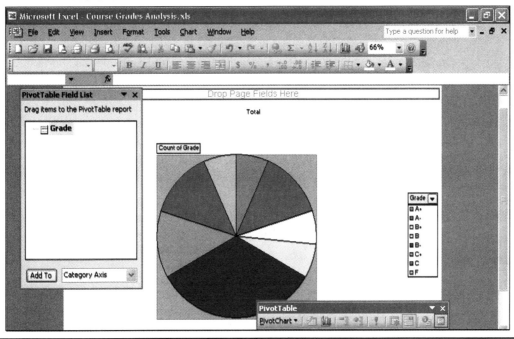

activity:

Format the Course Grades Analysis

Now that you have created a pie chart that shows the breakdown of grades for the students in Management 100, you need to format the chart, copy it into the Grades worksheet, and then format the worksheet for printing. Your completed course grades analysis will appear as shown in Figure D-15.

steps:

1. Click **Total** above the chart, click the **Font Size list arrow** [10 ▾] on the Formatting toolbar, click 24, type **Breakdown of Final Grades** (the text appears in the Formula bar), press [Enter], then click the **Bold button** [B] on the Formatting toolbar

2. Right-click the gray **Count of Grade button**, then click **Hide PivotChart Field Buttons**

3. Click **Chart** on the menu bar, click **Chart Options**, click the **Legend tab**, click the **Show Legend check box** to deselect it, click the **Data Labels tab**, click the **Category name check box** and the **Percentage check box**, then click **OK**

Trouble

If you delete another chart element by mistake, click the Undo button on the Standard toolbar and try again. You need to click only in the gray area behind the chart.

4. Click just the **gray plot area** behind the pie chart, press [Delete], move the pointer to a **white area** of the chart near the title until you see a Chart Area ScreenTip, right-click, click **Format Chart Area**, click the **Automatic option button** in both the Border section and the Area section of the Format Chart Area dialog box, click **OK**, then click away from the chart to deselect it
   When you select Automatic for the chart Border and chart Area, Excel applies a single-line border around the chart and fills the chart area with white.

5. Click the **Copy button** [📋] on the Standard toolbar, click the **Grades tab**, click cell **A24**, click the **Paste button** [📋 ▾] on the Standard toolbar, click away from the chart to deselect it, click **View** on the menu bar, click **Page Break Preview**, then click **OK** if necessary in the Welcome to Page Break Preview dialog box
   As you can see by the blue dotted lines, the worksheet will currently print over more than one page.

6. Click the **Print Preview button** [🔍] on the Standard toolbar, click **Setup**, click the **Page tab**, click the **Fit to option button**, click the **Margins tab**, click the **Horizontally check box**, click the **Header/Footer tab**, click **Custom Header**, enter text for the header as shown in Figure D-15, then exit the Page Setup dialog box
   Now all the data fits on one page.

7. Click the **Normal View button** on the Print Preview toolbar, select cells **A3:M21**, click **Format** on the menu bar, click **AutoFormat**, click the **Classic 3 format**, then click **OK**
   Your worksheet is looking readable and quite snazzy.

Trouble

Be sure to drag the lower-right corner of the chart area.

8. Click **View** on the menu bar, click **Zoom**, click the **50% option button**, click **OK**, click the **pie chart** to select it, scroll down to view the lower-right corner, then drag the lower-right corner handle up to cell **M46**

Additional Practice

For additional practice with the skills presented in this project, complete Independent Challenge 2.

9. Print a copy of the worksheet, then save and close the workbook
   Your printed worksheet should appear similar to Figure D-15.

Course Grades Analysis

Your Name

Management 100

Name	A1	A2	A3	Q1	Q2	E1	E2	Asn	Quiz	Exam	Total	Grade
Bradley, Marta	15	18	18	25	23	44	40	29.75	24.00	33.60	87.35	B+
Cheung, Lisa	18	20	19	22	20	45	46	33.25	21.00	36.40	90.65	A-
Deville, Jolene	13	19	12	22	21	42	40	25.67	21.50	32.80	79.97	C+
Elton, Mark	15	15	15	15	14	40	37	26.25	14.50	30.80	71.55	C
Finesmith, David	12	10	11	10	8	27	29	19.25	9.00	22.40	50.65	F
Kurtz, Helen	8	20	20	23	21	40	45	28.00	22.00	34.00	84.00	B
Liu, Yvonne	12	18	18	22	23	33	39	28.00	22.50	28.80	79.30	C+
McTavish, Tommy	15	15	15	20	21	44	46	26.25	20.50	36.00	82.75	B-
Mirelli, Tony	18	19	20	22	24	46	42	33.25	23.00	35.20	91.45	A-
Prentiss, Greg	17	20	15	20	18	42	38	30.33	19.00	32.00	81.33	B-
Rathbone, Wade	15	18	8	18	19	40	32	23.92	18.50	28.80	71.22	C
Singh, Balwinder	20	15	19	15	14	45	47	31.50	14.50	36.80	82.80	B-
Stewart, Olive	15	18	14	25	22	40	38	27.42	23.50	31.20	82.12	B-
Washington, Jamal	20	20	18	24	25	49	50	33.83	24.50	39.60	97.93	A+
Xin, Natalie	18	20	18	20	16	40	42	32.67	18.00	32.80	83.47	B-
Total Possible Points	20	20	20	25	25	50	50					
Weighted Values								35	25	40	100	

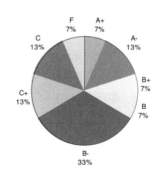

Breakdown of Final Grades

F 7%
A+ 7%
A- 13%
C 13%
B+ 7%
C+ 13%
B 7%
B- 33%

Excel

Personal Investment Analysis

You have decided to use Excel to analyze your investment options. The financial formulas you need to use are Future Value and Present Value. To analyze investment options, you need to **Ask Financial Questions** and **Chart Results**.

activity:

Ask Financial Questions

You need to use the Future Value and Present Value formulas to answer a series of financial questions.

steps:

1. Start Excel, type the following text in cell A1: **How much money will an investment of $15,000 be worth in 20 years if I invest at a 7.5% rate of return?**, then press **[Enter]**

2. In cell A2, type **Answer:**, right-align and apply bold as shown in Figure D-16, then save the workbook as **Investment Analysis** to the location where you are storing the files for this book

Trouble

The carat sign (^) is located above the "6" on your keyboard.

3. Click cell **B2**, enter the Future Value formula **=15000*(1+.075)^20**, then press **[Enter]**

    You use the Future Value formula to determine how much $15,000 will be worth in 20 years if you invest it at an interest rate of 7.5%. In words, the Future Value formula is =Present Value(1+Interest Rate)^Number of Years. In the formula you just entered, 15000 is the present value, .075 is the interest rate, and 20 is the number of years.*

4. Format cell **B2** with the **Currency style**

    In 20 years, $15,000 will be worth $63,717.77 if you invest it at an annual interest rate of 7.5% for 20 years.

5. Click cell **A4**, then enter the questions and enter and enhance **Answer:** where required as shown in Figure D-17

6. Click cell **B5**, enter the Present Value formula: **=40000/(1+0.065)^5**, press **[Enter]**, format the result in the **Currency style**, then verify that the amount is **$29,195.23**

    You use the Present Value formula to determine how much money you need to save now at an interest rate of 6.5% in order to have $40,000 in 5 years. In words, the Present Value formula is =Future Value/(1+Interest Rate)^Number of Years. In the formula you just entered, 40000 is the future value, .065 is the interest rate, and 5 is the number of years.

7. Use the Present Value or Future Value formulas where required to enter the correct answers in cells B8 and B11

8. Check your answers in cells B8 and B11 against the values displayed in Figure D-18, then save the workbook

    If your answers are not correct, check your formulas and try again.

FIGURE D-16: **Question 1**

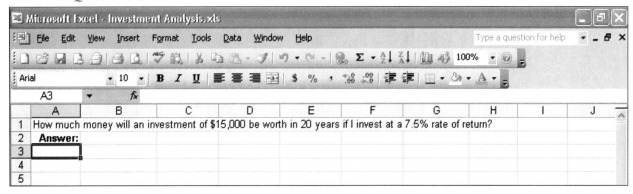

FIGURE D-17: **Questions 2 to 4**

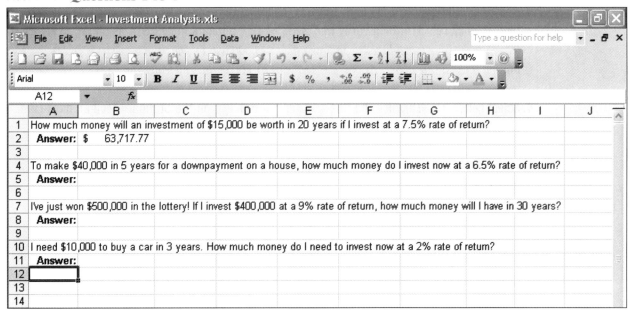

FIGURE D-18: **Investment analysis answers**

Use the
Future
Value
formula

Use the
Present
Value
formula

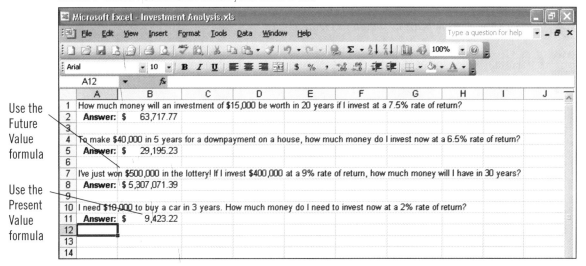

PROJECT 3

activity:

Chart Results

You need to create a chart to show how an investment of $25,000 can grow over a period of 30 years if invested at 5%.

steps:

1. Click cell **B14**, type **5**, press **[Tab]**, type **10**, select cells **B14:C14**, then drag the handle to cell **G14** to fill the cells

2. Click cell **B15**, enter the formula **=25000*(1+.05)^B14**, then press **[Enter]**

3. Copy the formula across through cell **G15**, click the **Currency Style button** $ on the Formatting toolbar, click cell **G16**, then verify that **$108,048.56** appears in cell **G14** as shown in Figure D-19
The Future Value formula tells you how much $25,000 will be worth in 30 years if you invest it at an annual interest rate of 5%. As you can see, your $15,000 grows by leaps and bounds over the 30 years.

4. Select cells **B15:G15**, click the **Chart Wizard button** on the Standard toolbar, click **Line**, then click **Next**

5. Click the **Series tab**, click the **Collapse Dialog Box button** to the right of the Category (X) axis labels text box, select cells **B14:G14**, then click the **Restore Dialog Box button**

6. Click **Next**, click the **Titles tab**, type **Investment Growth** as the chart title, click the **Legend tab**, click the **Show legend check box** to deselect it, then click **Finish**

7. Size and position the chart so that it extends from cells **B17:G34**, right-click the value axis (y-axis), click **Format Axis**, click the **Font tab**, select the **10 point** font size, then click **OK**

8. Right-click the category axis (x-axis), click **Format Axis**, change the font size to **10 point**, click the **Alignment tab**, click the **up arrow** to rotate the text by **20 degrees** as shown in Figure D-20, then click **OK**
The line chart appears as shown in Figure D-21.

9. Format the worksheet to fit on one page, create a custom header containing your name, print a copy of the worksheet, then save and close the workbook

Additional Practice

For additional practice with the skills presented in this project, complete Independent Challenge 3.

FIGURE D-19: Data for chart

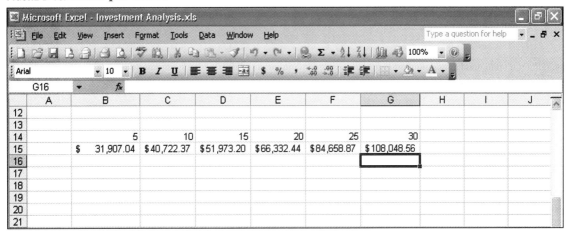

FIGURE D-20: Format Axis dialog box

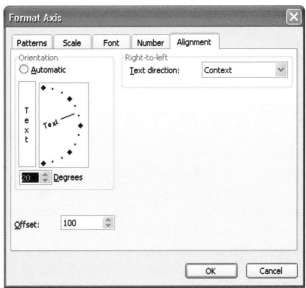

FIGURE D-21: Completed line chart

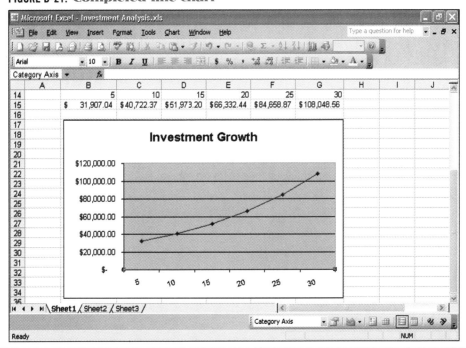

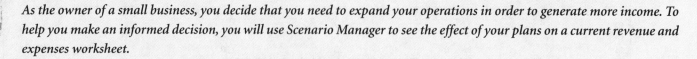

Independent Challenges

INDEPENDENT CHALLENGE 1

As the owner of a small business, you decide that you need to expand your operations in order to generate more income. To help you make an informed decision, you will use Scenario Manager to see the effect of your plans on a current revenue and expenses worksheet.

1. Determine the name of your company, the type of business it conducts, and your plans for expansion. For example, you could run a home-based catering service that has grown big enough to warrant moving the business out of your home and into a commercial location. Alternatively, you could run a snow removal business from a small commercial office and decide to move into a larger office and buy several new pieces of snow removal equipment. Write the name of your company and a short description of your expansion plans in the box below:

> **Company Name:** ....
>
> **Description of Expansion Plans:**

2. Create a worksheet that shows your revenue and expenses over a six-month period. Include labels for each of six months (e.g., January to June); labels for the various types of revenue you generate (e.g., Catering Sales and Consulting); and labels for your various expenses (e.g., Rent, Salaries, Advertising, Equipment, and Operating Costs). Note that returns and cost of goods sold are calculated as a percentage of your gross revenue (usually 3% for returns and 60% to 70% for cost of sales). Calculate your revenue and expenses both by month and by six-month total.

3. Save the workbook as **My Predictions** to the location where you are storing the files for this book.

4. Create Current scenarios from the data currently entered in the worksheet. Note that you only need to create scenarios for the rows that contain the values you will change when you create a Best Case and Worst Case scenario.

5. Change values in the worksheet to reflect your best case predictions should you carry out your expansion plans. For example, if you decide to relocate, your Rent expense may increase, and if you hire an assistant, your Salaries expense will increase. Make sure you also increase your income to reflect the increased revenue you expect after expanding.

6. Create Best Case scenarios from the new values you have entered in the worksheet.

7. Change the values again to reflect your worst case predictions, should your expansion plans fail to proceed as well as you hope, then create Worst Case scenarios from the values that represent your worst case predictions.

8. Show the Best Case scenarios, create a column chart that displays the Best Case monthly income, then format and print a copy of the worksheet. Make sure you include your name and **Best Case Forecast** in the header.

9. Note the upper limit of the value axis (x-axis) in the column chart. You want the printed column charts with the Current, Best, and Worst Case scenarios worksheets to display the same upper limit on the value axis so that the differences in the three charts are readily apparent.

10. Show the Current scenarios, change the title of the column chart, change the upper limit on the value axis to the same upper limit displayed in the Best Case column chart, change the header to reflect the worksheet content, then print a copy.

11. Show the Worst Case scenarios, change the title of the column chart, change the upper limit on the value axis to the same upper limit displayed in the Best Case column chart, change the header to reflect the worksheet content, then print a copy.

12. Save and close the workbook.

INDEPENDENT CHALLENGE 2

You have been working all term as a teaching assistant for a course of your choice. The instructor you work for has given you the grade sheet she has kept "by hand" and has asked you to transfer it to Excel and then calculate each student's grade. Complete the steps below to create a course grades analysis for a course of your choice.

1. Determine the name of the course. For example, the course could be English 100, Psychology 210, or International Business 301.
2. Determine the grade categories and the percentage of scores allocated to each category. Allocate at least three grade categories and make sure the percentages (weighted values) you assign add up to 100%. For example, you could allocate 40% of the total grade to Assignments, 30% to Exams, and 30% to Presentations.
3. Start Excel, set up a worksheet called **Grades** with the name of the course, a list of at least 15 students, and labels for the various assignments, exams, quizzes, etc. Make sure you include at least two items in each of the three grade categories you have selected.
4. Save the workbook as **My Grades Analysis** to the location where you are storing the files for this book.
5. Determine the total scores possible for each item in each grade category and enter the totals one row below the list of names. To check the setup of your course grades analysis, refer to the course grades analysis you created for Project 2.
6. Enter the points for each student. Make sure you refer to the totals you entered to ensure that each score you enter for each student is equal to or less than the total points possible.
7. Calculate the total points for each grade category, divide the total points by the total of the possible points, then multiply the result by the percentage you assigned to the mark category. The formula required is: Sum of Student's Points/Sum of Total Points*Weighted Value. Make sure you use absolute references so that you can copy the formula without errors. For example, if the Assignment points are entered in cells C4, D4, and F4, the total possible points are entered in cells C25, D25, and F25, and the weighted value of Assignments is 40%, the formula required is =(C4+D4+F4)/($C$25+$D$25+$F$25)*.4
8. Calculate the total points out of 100 earned by the first student on your list.
9. Copy the formulas you used to calculate the first student's weighted score in each category and the total score for the remaining students.
10. Create a Lookup table in a worksheet called **Lookup** that lists the letter grades and ranges you specify.
11. Enter the LOOKUP formula in the appropriate cell in the Grades worksheet, then copy the formula down for the remaining students.
12. Create a PivotTable that counts the number of times each letter grade appears.
13. Create a pie chart from the data in the PivotTable to show the scores by letter grade, then copy it to the Grades sheet.
14. Save the workbook, format the Grades sheet and pie chart so that it is readable and attractive, print a copy, then save and close the workbook.

INDEPENDENT CHALLENGE 3

You have just won $500,000 in the lottery! You can choose to accept the entire $500,000 right now or a monthly payment of $5,000 for 15 years. Complete the following steps to determine which option you should choose.

1. Start Excel, save a new workbook as **My Investments** to the location where you are storing the files for this book, then in cell A1, enter the formula to determine the future value of $500,000 in 15 years, presuming that you will invest the money at a 5% annual interest rate. Note that the Future Value formula required is =500000*(1+0.05)^15.
2. Format the result in the Currency style and verify that in 15 years, $500,000 is worth $1,039,464.09 if invested at 5%.
3. Click cell A2, then use the FV function to calculate how much $5,000 per month will be worth in 15 years if you invest it at 5% per year, compounded monthly. Here's how:
   a. Click the Insert Function button on the formula bar, type Future Value, then click Go.
   b. Select FV from the list of functions, then click OK.
   c. Complete the FV Function Arguments dialog box as shown in Figure D-22.
   d. Click OK, then verify that you will receive $1,336,444.72 if you invest $5,000 each month at 5%. Note that the monthly investment option yields a much higher return.

FIGURE D-22: FV function

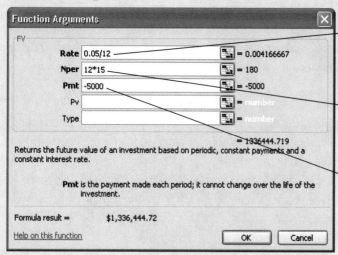

Rate is the current interest rate (5%) divided by 12 to determine the monthly interest rate

Function Arguments	
FV	
Rate	0.05/12 = 0.004166667
Nper	12*15 = 180
Pmt	-5000 = -5000
Pv	number
Type	number

= 1336444.719

Returns the future value of an investment based on periodic, constant payments and a constant interest rate.

Pmt is the payment made each period; it cannot change over the life of the investment.

Formula result = $1,336,444.72

Help on this function   OK   Cancel

Nper is the number of months in the year (12) multiplied by the number of years (15)

Pmt is the amount you plan to invest each month ($5000) at 5% annual interest. The Pmt amount is entered as a negative number

4. Create a line chart that compares the growth of the winnings, depending on which option is chosen: Lump sum of $500,000 now or $5,000 a month for 15 years. Set up the worksheet as follows:

a. Enter **Lump Sum** in cell B5 and **Monthly Payment** in cell C5. Bold and center the labels, then widen the columns as required.

b. Enter **1** in cell A6 and **2** in cell A7.

c. Select cells A6 and A7, then drag the fill handle to cell A20 to enter numbers from 1 to 15. These numbers represent the years over which you will invest your winnings.

d. Click cell A1, click the Copy button, click cell B6, then click the Paste button.

e. Modify the formula in cell B6 to change the number of years (currently 15) to cell A6 so that the formula is:
     =500000*(1+0.05)^A6, then copy the formula down through cell A20.

f. Click cell A2, click the Copy button, click cell C6, then click the Paste button.

g. Modify the formula in cell C6 to change the number of years (currently 15) to cell A6 so that the formula is as follows :
     =FV(0.05/12,12*A6,-5000), then copy the formula down through cell A20.

h. Select cells A5:C20, then create a line chart. Move the legend to the bottom and reduce the font size of chart labels.

i. Create a text box that includes the text: **Investment from monthly payments exceeds lump sum investment after 11 years**.

j. Draw an arrow from the text box to the point on the chart where the monthly payments line intersects the lump sum line.

5. Save the worksheet, print a copy, then close it.

INDEPENDENT CHALLENGE 4

You run a sailboat rental business in Antigua that caters to adventure-based travelers who rent sailboats for up to two weeks to explore the Caribbean Islands. During the previous summer, you failed to make a profit on the business. Now you want to project sales for the coming summer months based on your plan to acquire more sailboats, increase advertising costs, and move into an attractive new boathouse.

1. Create the worksheet shown in Figure D-23, then save the workbook as **Summer Sailboat Rentals**. Enhance the worksheet with a clip art picture of a sailboat. Fill cell A1 with light yellow.

FIGURE D-23: Revenue and expenses worksheet

	A	B	C	D	E	F
1	**Trade Wind Rentals**					
2	Summer Rentals					
3						
4		June	July	August	Totals	
5	**REVENUE**					
6	Rental Income	$54,000.00	$62,000.00	$75,000.00		
7	Less Returns: 4%					
8	**NET REVENUE**					
9	Less Cost of Rentals: 75%					
10	**GROSS PROFIT ON RENTALS**					
11						
12	**EXPENSES**					
13	Salaries	$ 8,200.00	$ 8,200.00	$ 8,200.00		
14	Rent	1,500.00	1,500.00	1,500.00		
15	Advertising	2,500.00	2,500.00	2,500.00		
16	Operating Costs	2,000.00	2,000.00	2,000.00		
17	Total Expenses					
18						
19	**NET INCOME**					
20						

Sheet1 / Sheet2 / Sheet3 /

2. Calculate the Returns, Net Revenue, Cost of Rentals (75% of Rental Income), Gross Profit on Rentals, Total Expenses, and Net Income.

3. Ensure that your total net income in cell E19 is (2,490.00). Note that you need to calculate the cost of rentals as 75% of the Rental Income, not the Net Revenue.

4. Create Current scenarios of the data for Rental Income, Rent, and Advertising. Call the scenarios **Current Rental Income**, **Current Rent**, and **Current Advertising**.

5. Create the following Expansion scenarios for the Rental Income, Rent, and Advertising data:

Expansion Rental Income:	June: 106,000; July: 135,500; August: 177,450
Expansion Rent:	$2,200 per month
Expansion Advertising:	$3,000 per month

6. Verify that your net income in cell E19 is $41,779.50 after you have created and then displayed the three Expansion scenarios.

7. With the Expansion scenarios still displayed, create a bar chart that displays the monthly net income. Note the upper limit of the value axis ($25,000). Format the bar chart attractively as shown in Figure D-24.

8. As shown in Figure D-24, apply shading to cells containing scenarios and the Net Income total, insert a custom header, then format and print a copy of the worksheet.

9. Display the Current scenarios, modify the header and chart title as shown in Figure D-25, then change the upper limit of the value axis to $25,000 so that it matches the bar chart that shows the Expansion net income.

10. Print a copy of the Current scenarios worksheet, then save and close the workbook.

FIGURE D-24: *Projected Summer Rentals worksheet*

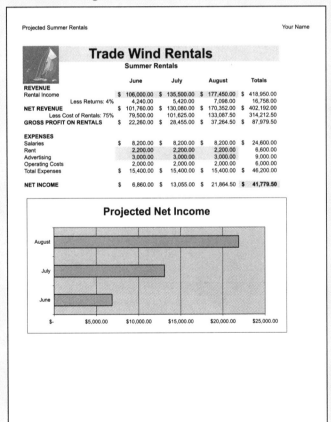

FIGURE D-25: *Current Summer Rentals worksheet*

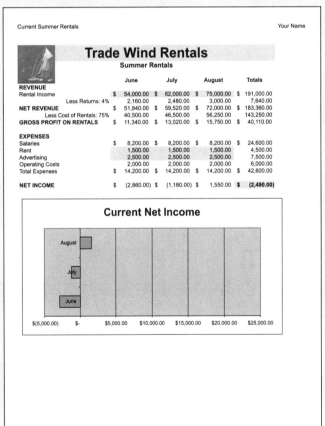

Visual Workshop

You have just completed a survey of the leisure activities most preferred by your classmates in the business program at Cape Cod College. Now you want to create a chart to display the results of your survey. Create the worksheet shown in Figure D-26, then create a PivotTable that counts the number of times each activity appears in column B of Sheet1. Note that you will need to drag the Activity field into the Drop Row Fields Here and the Drop Data Items Here sections of the PivotTable. Once you have created the PivotTable, create the pie chart shown in Figure D-26. Size and position the chart as shown in Figure D-26. Save your workbook as **Leisure Activities** to the location where you are saving the files for this book, print a copy of Sheet1, then save and close the workbook.

FIGURE D-26: Leisure Activities worksheet

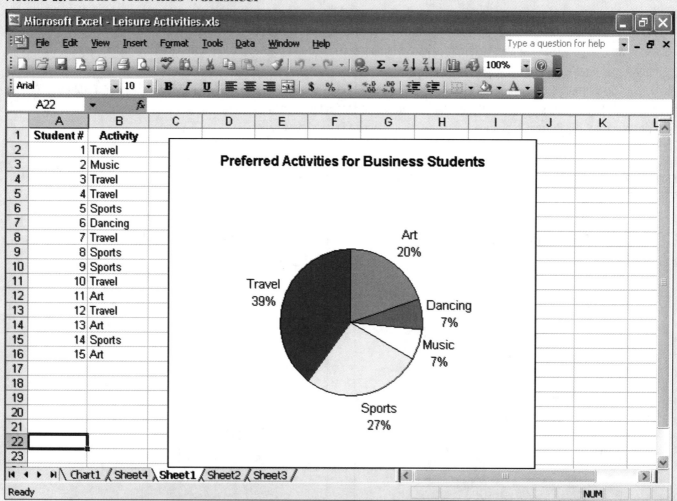

Microsoft
► Word and Excel
Projects

Unit E

Integration Projects I

In this Unit You Will Create the Following:

Job Performance Reviews

Sales Report

Marketing Update

You can use the integration capabilities of Office 2003 to combine text you create in Word with numerical data that you analyze in Excel. For example, suppose you have created a report in Word that references a variety of charts and other data created in Excel. You can copy selected data from Excel and paste it into the Word report as a link. Every time you make a change to the data in Excel, the changes are also made to the data you copied and pasted as a link into the Word report because the two files are linked. In this unit, you will learn how to link documents that combine elements created in both Word and Excel.

Job Performance Reviews

Kevin Moore and Danielle Shaw have worked for Vanguard Industries as service agents for one year. They are now due to be evaluated. As their supervisor, you need to create a form that you can use to compile the results of each employee's performance review. To complete the performance reviews, you **Create the Form in Word**, **Add Form Fields in Word**, **Compile Results in Excel**, and then **Link the Form and Results** for each employee. The completed performance review for Danielle is shown in Figure E-9 on page 107.

activity:

Create the Form in Word

You need to set up the performance review form in Word and then create a table to contain the data for the form.

steps:

1. Start Word, open the Page Setup dialog box, set the Top and Bottom margins at .6", set the Left and Right margins at 1", then click OK

2. Click the Styles and Formatting button ![A] on the Formatting toolbar, right-click Normal in the Pick formatting to apply list, click Modify, click the Font list arrow, select Arial Rounded MT Bold, click OK, close the Styles and Formatting task pane, then save the document as Performance Review Form to the location where you are storing the files for this book

3. Type Vanguard Industries, press [Enter], type Job Performance Review, press [Enter], center both lines of text, then enhance Vanguard Industries with 20 point

4. Click the blank line below Job Performance Review, click Table on the menu bar, point to Insert, click Table, type 4, press [Tab], type 14, click OK, then type the text for the table as shown in Figure E-1

5. Click View on the menu bar, point to Toolbars, click Tables and Borders, select all four cells in row 1, then click the Merge Cells button ![icon] on the Tables and Borders toolbar

6. With cell A1 still selected, click the Shading Color list arrow ![icon] on the Tables and Borders toolbar, click the Black color, click the Font Color list arrow ![A] on the Formatting toolbar, click the White color, then click the Center button ![icon] on the Formatting toolbar

Trouble

Click the Undo button on the Standard toolbar if the result of an action does not match Figure E-2.

7. Use Figure E-2 as your guide to merge cells, fill cells with black, change the font color of the text to white, then center the text

8. Click to the left of row 1, drag to select rows 1 through 6 (Rankings), press and hold [Ctrl], then click to the left of Ranking Summary, Ranking Chart, and Written Evaluation to select them also
   You can use the [Ctrl] key to select non-adjacent rows and cells in a table quickly so that you can apply formatting all at once.

9. Click Table on the menu bar, click Table Properties, click the Row tab, click the Specify Height check box, type .3, click the Cell tab, click the Center option in the Vertical alignment section, click OK, click the title to deselect the table, close the Tables and Borders toolbar, then save the document

FIGURE E-1: **Table text**

Vanguard·Industries¶
Job·Performance·Review¶

Employee· Information¤	¤	¤	¤
Employee·Name:¤	¤	Date:¤	¤
Job·Title:¤	¤	Employee·ID:¤	¤
Department:¤	¤	Manager:¤	¤
Review·Period:¤	¤	To:¤	¤
Rankings¤	¤	¤	¤
¤	¤	¤	¤
Ranking·Summary¤	¤	¤	¤
¤	¤	¤	¤
Ranking·Chart¤	¤	¤	¤
¤	¤	¤	¤
Written·Evaluation¤	¤	¤	¤
Supervisor· Comments:¤	¤	¤	¤
Goals·(as·agreed· upon·by·employee· and·manager):¤	¤	¤	¤

These rows are left blank

FIGURE E-2: **Table cells merged and formatted**

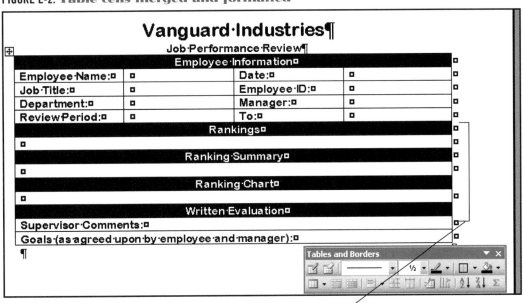

Merge cells in each of these rows, then fill four rows with black and change the font color to white as shown

activity:

Add Form Fields in Word

You plan to use the same performance review form to record the performance reviews of numerous employees. You want the form to be an electronic one that you can complete on the computer. To make the form reusable, you need to insert form fields.

steps:

1. Click **cell 2 in row 2** (to the right of Employee Name:), click **View** on the menu bar, point to **Toolbars**, then click **Forms** to show the Forms toolbar

You select form fields from the Forms toolbar.

2. Click the **Text Form Field button** on the Forms toolbar to insert a form field as shown in Figure E-3

3. Press **[Tab]** twice to move to the blank cell to the right of Date:, click , click the **Form Field Options button** on the Forms toolbar, click the **Type list arrow**, click **Date**, click the **Date format list arrow**, select the **MMMM d, yyyy** format as shown in Figure E-4, then click **OK**

In the Text Field Options dialog box you can specify how you want text entered into a field. When you fill in the form, you will only be able to enter a date in the cell to the right of Date:.

4. Click **cell 4 in row 3** (to the right of Employee ID:), click , click , click the **Type list arrow**, click **Number**, select the contents of the **Maximum Length text box**, type **4**, then click **OK**

When you fill in the form, you will only be able to enter up to four digits in the cell to the right of Employee ID:.

5. Insert text form fields in the cells to the right of **Job Title:**, **Department:**, and **Manager:**

6. Select the form field to the right of **Date:**, click the **Copy button** , click **cell 2 in row 5** (to the right of Review Period:), click the **Paste button** , click **cell 4 in row 5** (to the right of To:), then click

You can copy and paste fields that contain special formatting to save time.

7. Scroll down the form, click to the right of **Supervisor Comments:**, press **[Enter]**, insert a text form field, click to the right of the **Goals** statement, press **[Enter]**, then insert a text form field

8. Save the document, save the document again as **Performance Review_Kevin Moore**, then click the **Protect Form button** on the Forms toolbar

By selecting the Protect Form button, you "activate" the form fields so that you can enter only the preset data types.

9. Click **cell 2 in row 2** (to the right of Employee Name:), enter data related to Kevin Moore as shown in Figure E-5, press **[Tab]** to move from cell to cell, then save the document

FIGURE E-3: **Form field inserted**

Text Form Field button

Form field

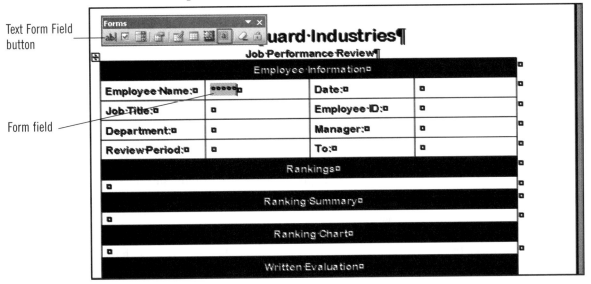

FIGURE E-4: **Text Form Field Options dialog box**

Date format

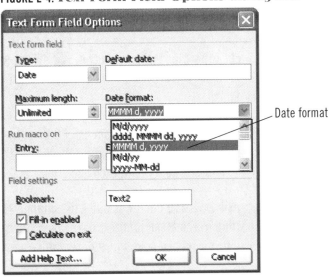

FIGURE E-5: **Form text for Kevin Moore**

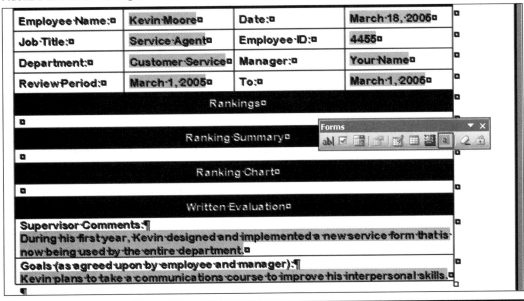

PROJECT 1

activity:

Compile Results in Excel

You need to create a worksheet in Excel into which you can enter the numerical results of the performance review. You also need to create a chart in Excel that summarizes the results.

steps:

1. Start Excel, type **Supervisor Rating** in cell A1, select cells **A1:B1**, click the **Merge and Center button** ⊞ on the Formatting toolbar, apply **Bold** formatting, enter and enhance the text as shown in Figure E-6, then save the workbook as **Job Performance Reviews** to the location where you are saving the files for this book

2. Double-click the **Sheet1** tab, type **Kevin**, press [Enter], click cell **B8**, click the **AutoSum button** Σ twice on the Standard toolbar, click cell **D8**, then click Σ twice

3. Click cell **B10**, type **=(B2+D2)/2**, press [Enter], click **cell B10**, then use the ✛ pointer to fill cells **B11:B15** with the formula in cell B10

   This formula determines the average score between the Supervisor Rating and the Peer Rating.

4. Select cells **A10:B15**, click the **Chart Wizard button** 📊 on the Standard toolbar, click **Column** if not selected, click **Next**, click **Next**, click the **Legend tab**, click the **Show Legend check** box to deselect it, then click **Finish**

5. Size and position the chart so that it extends from cell **C9** through cell **H26**, right-click the **category axis (x-axis)**, click **Format Axis**, click the **Alignment tab**, change the alignment to **45 degrees**, click the **Font tab**, change the font size to **9 point**, then click **OK**

Trouble

Even if the value in the Maximum text box is 5, you must select and retype 5.

6. Right-click the **value axis (y-axis)**, click **Format Axis**, change the font size to **9 point**, click the **Scale tab**, select the value in the Maximum text box, type **5**, then click **OK**

   You set the maximum scale for the value axis at 5 so that the scale remains the same regardless of the data entered in the chart.

7. Double-click the **Sheet2** tab, type **Danielle**, press [Enter], click the **Kevin tab**, click the **Select All button** to the left of the **A** at the upper-left corner of the worksheet frame to select the entire worksheet, click the **Copy button** 📋 on the Standard toolbar, click the **Danielle tab**, then click the **Paste button** 📋 on the Standard toolbar

8. Enter values for Danielle in cells **B2:B7** and cells **D2:D7** as shown in Figure E-7, then verify that the totals update as shown in Figure E-8

9. Right-click the **chart**, click **Source Data**, click the **Data Range tab** if it is not already selected, click the **Collapse Dialog Box button** 📲 next to Data Range, click the **Danielle tab**, select cells **A10:B15**, click the **Restore Dialog Box button** 📭, click **OK**, then save the workbook

   The chart appears as shown in Figure E-8. When you copied the chart from the Kevin worksheet to the Danielle worksheet, the chart still referenced the cells in the Kevin worksheet. You changed the reference so that the chart shows data related to Danielle's rankings.

FIGURE E-6: Worksheet labels and values

	A	B	C	D	E	F	G	H
1	**Supervisor Rating**		**Peer Rating**					
2	Job Knowledge	5	Job Knowledge	4				
3	Work Quality	5	Work Quality	3				
4	Attendance	4	Attendance	4				
5	Initiative	5	Initiative	4				
6	Communication Skills	3	Communication Skills	1				
7	Dependability	4	Dependability	4				
8								
9	**Average Rating**							
10	Job Knowledge							
11	Work Quality							
12	Attendance							
13	Initiative							
14	Communication Skills							
15	Dependability							
16								

FIGURE E-7: Values for Danielle

	A	B	C	D	E
1	**Supervisor Rating**		**Peer Rating**		
2	Job Knowledge	2	Job Knowledge	1	
3	Work Quality	3	Work Quality	1	
4	Attendance	1	Attendance	3	
5	Initiative	1	Initiative	2	
6	Communication Skills	2	Communication Skills	2	
7	Dependability	2	Dependability	1	
8		11		10	

Verify updated values

FIGURE E-8: Danielle's chart

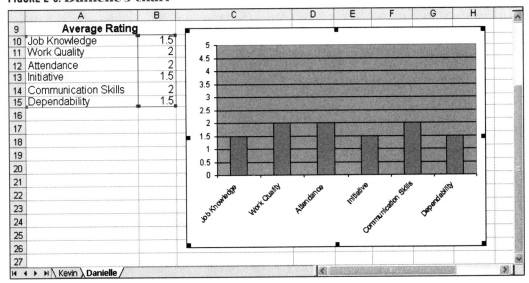

	A	B
9	**Average Rating**	
10	Job Knowledge	1.5
11	Work Quality	2
12	Attendance	2
13	Initiative	1.5
14	Communication Skills	2
15	Dependability	1.5

Kevin \ Danielle

PROJECT 1

JOB PERFORMANCE REVIEWS

activity:

Link the Form and Results

You need to copy Kevin's performance results from Excel and paste them into the Word form as linked objects. After completing Kevin's performance review form, you need to save the document as Danielle's, edit the text to reflect Danielle's information, and then change the source for the Excel performance results so the linked objects reflect Danielle's information.

steps:

1. Click the **Kevin tab**, select cells **A1:D8**, click the **Copy button** 📋 on the Standard toolbar, switch to Word, then click the **Protect Form button** 🔒 on the Forms toolbar to deselect it
You "unprotect" the form so that you can insert objects from Excel.

2. Click the **cell below Rankings**, click **Edit** on the menu bar, click **Paste Special**, click **Paste link**, click **Microsoft Office Excel Worksheet Object**, click **OK**, click the **worksheet object**, then click the **Center button** 📄 on the Formatting toolbar

3. Switch to Excel, select cells **A9:B15**, click 📋, switch to Word, click the cell below **Ranking Summary**, click **Edit** on the menu bar, click **Paste Special**, click **Paste link**, click **Microsoft Office Excel Worksheet Object**, click **OK**, then **center** the copied worksheet object

4. Switch to Excel, select the **chart**, click 📋, switch to Word, use **Paste Special** and **Paste link** to insert the chart in the **cell below Ranking Chart**, click the **chart**, click **Format** on the menu bar, click **Object**, click the **Size tab**, change the height to **2.3"**, click **OK**, then click 📄

5. Switch to Excel, change Kevin's ranking for Attendance to **5** from both the Supervisor and the Peers (cell B4 and cell D4), switch to Word, notice that the Attendance rankings have changed, save the document, then print a copy
Kevin's rankings for Attendance and the column chart are both updated in the Word document because the data is linked to the Excel workbook.

6. Save the Word document as **Performance Review_Danielle Shaw**, click 🔒, then enter text for Danielle in the Employee Information and Written Evaluation sections as shown in Figure E-9

7. Click 🔒, click **Edit** on the menu bar, click **Links**, click **Change Source**, click **Item**, select **Kevin** and type **Danielle** in the Set Item dialog box as shown in Figure E-10, click **OK**, click **Job Performance Reviews.xls** in the list of files, then click **Open**

8. Repeat the process in Step 7 to change the source for the other two links listed in the Links dialog box, noting that for the chart link, you need to replace Kevin with Danielle in two places, then click **OK**

9. Save the document, print a copy, then close the document
The completed performance review for Danielle appears as shown in Figure E-9. If the updated chart appears with other cells from the worksheet, delete the object, then copy the chart from Danielle's worksheet, paste it as a linked object, then reduce the height to 2.3". If you later open either linked document to make changes, a message box will appear advising you that the document is linked to an Excel workbook. Click Yes to maintain the link between the document and the workbook.

Trouble

If the links do not update automatically, right-click the object you want to update, then click Update Link.

Additional Practice

For additional practice with the skills presented in this project, complete Independent Challenge 1.

Vanguard Industries
Job Performance Review

Employee Information

Employee Name:	Danielle Shaw	Date:	March 25, 2006
Job Title:	Service Agent	Employee ID:	6655
Department:	Customer Service	Manager:	Your Name
Review Period:	March 1, 2005	To:	March 1, 2006

Rankings

Supervisor Rating		Peer Rating	
Job Knowledge	2	Job Knowledge	1
Work Quality	3	Work Quality	1
Attendance	1	Attendance	3
Initiative	1	Initiative	2
Communication Skills	2	Communication Skills	2
Dependability	2	Dependability	1
	11		10

Ranking Summary

Average Rating	
Job Knowledge	1.5
Work Quality	2
Attendance	2
Initiative	1.5
Communication Skills	2
Dependability	1.5

Ranking Chart

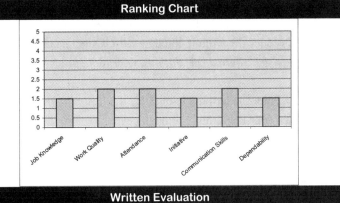

Written Evaluation

Supervisor Comments:
Danielle needs to develop a more conventional work ethic.

Goals (as agreed upon by employee and manager):
Danielle will meet weekly with the manager until June 2006.

FIGURE E-10: Set Item dialog box

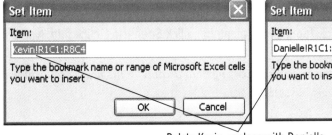

Delete Kevin, replace with Danielle

Word and Excel

Sales Report for Paradise Resorts

Paradise Resorts manages a chain of hotels on four islands: Antigua, Bermuda, Jamaica, and Puerto Rico. As the sales manager for the chain, you want to attract more guests to the hotels in the off-season months of April, May, and June. To determine your projected revenue and expenses should you attract more clients in these months you need to **Summarize Sales**, **Calculate Projected Sales**, and **Create the Sales Report**. The completed sales report appears as shown in Figure E-16 on page 113.

activity:

Summarize Sales

You need to enter labels and values in an Excel worksheet and then calculate total sales.

steps:

1. Start Excel, enter and enhance the labels and values so that the worksheet appears as shown in Figure E-11, then save the workbook as **Data for Sales Report** to the location where you are storing the files for this book

2. Click cell **B8**, enter the formula to multiply the **Average Cost per Room** by the **Total Number of Rooms Rented**, copy the formula through cell **E8**, then increase the column widths, if necessary

As you complete the required calculations, refer to Figure E-12 to verify your totals.

3. Click cell **B13**, enter the formula to multiply the **Number of Rooms Available** by the **Operating Cost per Room**, then copy the formula through cell **E13**

4. Click cell **B15**, enter the formula to add the **Total Operating Costs** to the **Advertising Costs**, then copy the formula through cell **E15**

5. Calculate the Net Revenue in cell **B17** as the **Total Expenses** subtracted from the **Total Room Rental Revenue**, then copy the formula through cell **E17**

The hotels in Antigua and Bermuda lost money in April, May, and June. Only the Puerto Rico and Jamaica hotels made a profit.

6. Select cells **B7:F8**, click the **AutoSum button** Σ on the Standard toolbar, then widen **Column F** as needed

7. Select cells **B13:F17**, click Σ, then verify that **$374,800.00** appears in cell F17

8. Select cells **B7:E7**, click **Tools** on the menu bar, click **Scenarios**, click **Add**, type **2006 Rentals**, click **OK**, click **OK**, then click **Close**

You create a scenario to preserve the existing data because in the next lesson you will change the data in order to calculate projected sales.

9. Save the workbook

The worksheet appears as shown in Figure E-12.

FIGURE E-11: **Worksheet setup**

Forte font, 26 point

14-point, bold, italic

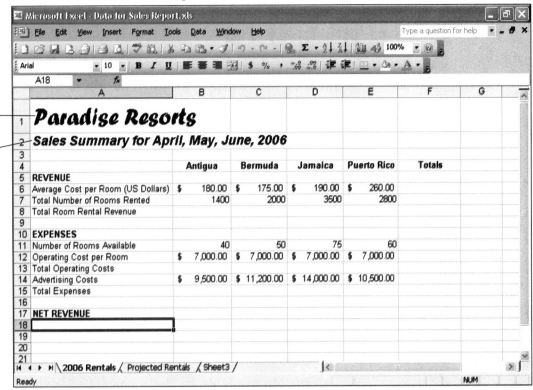

FIGURE E-12: **Worksheet complete with calculations**

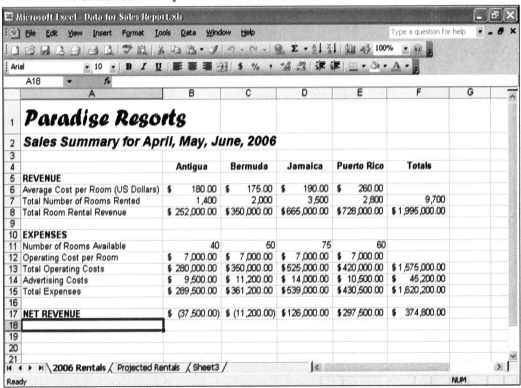

activity:

Calculate Projected Sales

You use the Goal Seek feature to determine how many rooms you should rent at the Antigua and Bermuda hotels to increase the net revenue from these hotels next year. You then create a bar chart that compares current and projected income from the rental of rooms at the Antigua and Bermuda hotels.

steps:

1. Click cell **B17** (the net revenue for the Antigua hotel), click **Tools** on the menu bar, click **Goal Seek**, click the text box next to **To value:**, type **100000**, press **[Tab]**, type **B7** as shown in Figure E-13, click **OK**, then click **OK** again

   You use Goal Seek to determine how many rooms you need to rent at the Antigua hotel to increase the net revenue to $100,000. The value needed, 2163.888889, appears in cell B7.

2. Click cell **C17**, click **Tools**, click **Goal Seek**, enter **120000** as the **To value** and **C7** as the cell to change, click **OK**, click **OK**, select cells **B7** through **F7**, click the **Comma Style button** [,] on the Formatting toolbar, then click the **Decrease Decimal button** [.00→.0] twice

   You need to rent 2,164 rooms at the Antigua hotel to make a profit of $100,000 and you need to rent 2,750 rooms at the Bermuda hotel to make a profit of $120,000.

3. Click **Tools**, click **Scenarios**, click **Add**, type **Projected Rentals**, enter **B7:C7** as the changing cells, click **OK**, click **OK**, then click **Close**

   You want the sales report to include a bar chart that compares the current and projected revenue at the four hotels. Before you can create the bar chart, you need to have access to both scenarios.

4. Double-click the **Sheet1** tab, type **2006 Rentals**, click the **Select All button** in the upper-left corner of the worksheet frame to select all the data, click the **Copy button** [icon] on the Formatting toolbar, click the **Sheet2** tab, click the **Paste button** [icon] on the Formatting toolbar, double-click the **Sheet2** tab, type **Projected Rentals**, then press **[Enter]**

5. Show the **2006 Rentals** worksheet, click **Tools** on the menu bar, click **Scenarios**, click **2006 Rentals**, click **Show**, then click **Close**

   The net revenue in cell F17 of the 2006 Rentals sheet is again $374,800.00. Next, you create a bar chart in the Projected Rentals sheet that includes data from the 2006 Rentals sheet.

6. Show the **Projected Rentals** worksheet, click cell **A20**, click the **Chart Wizard button** [icon] on the Standard toolbar, click **Bar**, click **Next**, click the **Collapse Dialog box button** [icon], click the **2006 Rentals tab**, use **[Ctrl]** to select cells **B4:E4** and cells **B8:E8**, then click the **Restore Dialog Box button** [icon]

7. Click the **Series tab**, click the **Name text box**, type **Current Room Rentals** as shown in Figure E-14, click **Add**, type **Projected Room Rentals** in the Name text box, click [icon] next to the Values text box, select cells **B8:E8** in the **Projected Rentals sheet**, then restore the dialog box

8. Click **Next**, click the **Titles tab**, type **Comparison of Current and Projected Room Rentals** as the chart title, click the **Legend tab**, click the **Bottom option button**, click **Finish**, move the chart down so that it starts at cell **A20**, then resize it so that it extends to cell **G40**

9. Right-click the **value axis (x-axis)** in the bar chart, click **Format Axis**, click the **Font tab**, change the font size to **10 point**, click the **Number tab**, select the contents of the **Decimal places text box**, type **0**, click **OK**, reduce the font size of the **category axis** and the **Legend** text to **10 point**, reduce the font size for the chart title to **16 point**, then save the workbook

   The bar chart appears in the worksheet as shown in Figure E-15.

FIGURE E-13: **Goal Seek dialog box**

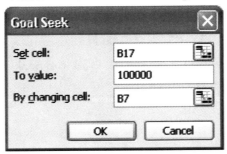

FIGURE E-14: **Chart Wizard dialog box**

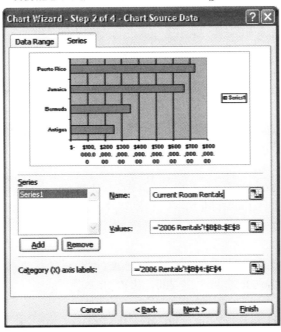

FIGURE E-15: **Bar chart resized and positioned**

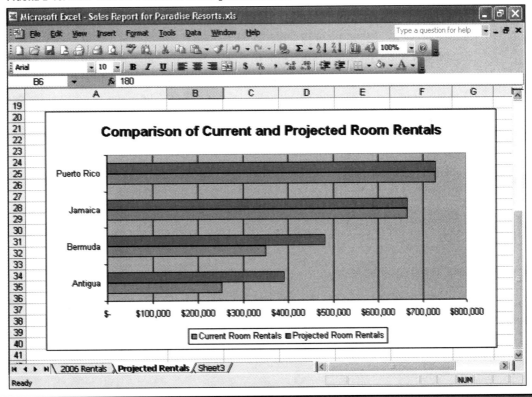

activity:

Create the Sales Report

You need to compile all the data from the Excel workbook in a report you create in Word. The completed report is shown in Figure E-16.

steps:

1. Start Word, change the bottom margin to .6", type **Sales Report for Paradise Resorts**, press **[Enter]**, enhance the title with the **Forte** font, **24-point**, **bold**, and **centered**, then save the document as **Sales Report for Paradise Resorts** to the location where you are storing the files for this book

2. Type the first paragraph of text as shown in the completed sales report in Figure E-16

3. Switch to Excel, select cells **A1:F17** in the **Projected Rentals** worksheet, click the Copy button 🗐, switch to Word, verify you are at the end of the paragraph you just typed, press **[Enter]** twice, click **Edit** on the menu bar, click **Paste Special**, click **Paste link**, click **Microsoft Office Excel Worksheet Object**, then click **OK**

4. Click the **copied worksheet object** in Word, click **Format** on the menu bar, click **Object**, click the **Size tab**, reduce the width to **6"**, click **OK**, type the paragraph of text under the copied worksheet object as shown in Figure E-16, then press **[Enter]** twice

5. Double-click the **copied worksheet object**, click cell **A2**, select **Summary** in the formula bar, type **Projections**, select **2006**, type **2007**, then press **[Enter]**

6. Scroll to the chart, click the chart, click the Copy button 🗐, switch to Word, paste the chart as a link into the Word document, then reduce the width of the chart to **6"**

7. Click the **Drawing button** 🔷 on the Standard toolbar to show the Drawing toolbar, click **AutoShapes** on the Drawing toolbar, point to **Callouts**, select the **Rounded Rectangular Callout** shape, draw the shape next to the projected rentals for Bermuda, type **Increase to 2,750 rooms**, select the text and change the font size to **10 pt**, then drag to resize the callout and position it as shown in Figure E-16
You will need to drag the yellow diamond handle on the callout shape to position the pointer correctly.

8. Draw the callout box for the Antigua bar, then fill it with the required text as shown in Figure E-16

Additional Practice

For additional practice with the skills presented in this project, complete Independent Challenge 2.

9. Type and center your name at the bottom of the page, save the document, print a copy, close the document, then switch to Excel and save and close the workbook
If you later open the document to make changes, a message box will appear advising you that the document is linked to an Excel workbook. Click Yes to maintain the link between the document and the workbook.

Sales Report for Paradise Resorts

In April, May, and June of 2006, both the Antigua and Bermuda Paradise Resorts lost money. To increase revenue at the Antigua resort, we need to rent 2,164 rooms instead of the current 1,400 rooms. To increase revenues at the Bermuda resort, we need to rent 2,750 rooms instead of the current 2,000 rooms. By so doing, we will realize a net revenue increase of $100,000 from the Antigua resort and $120,000 from the Bermuda resort.

Paradise Resorts
Sales Projections for April, May, June, 2007

	Antigua	Bermuda	Jamaica	Puerto Rico	Totals
REVENUE					
Average Cost per Room (US Dollars)	$ 180.00	$ 175.00	$ 190.00	$ 260.00	
Total Number of Rooms Rented	2,164	2,750	3,500	2,800	11,214
Total Room Rental Revenue	$ 389,500.00	$ 481,200.00	$ 665,000.00	$ 728,000.00	$ 2,263,700.00
EXPENSES					
Number of Rooms Available	40	50	75	60	
Operating Cost per Room	$ 7,000.00	$ 7,000.00	$ 7,000.00	$ 7,000.00	
Total Operating Costs	$ 280,000.00	$ 350,000.00	$ 525,000.00	$ 420,000.00	$ 1,575,000.00
Advertising Costs	$ 9,500.00	$ 11,200.00	$ 14,000.00	$ 10,500.00	$ 45,200.00
Total Expenses	$ 289,500.00	$ 361,200.00	$ 539,000.00	$ 430,500.00	$ 1,620,200.00
NET REVENUE	$ 100,000.00	$ 120,000.00	$ 126,000.00	$ 297,500.00	$ 643,500.00

The bar chart shown below compares the current room rentals in April, May, and June of 2006 with the projected room rentals in April, May, and June of 2007.

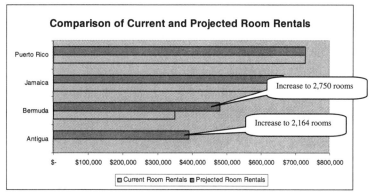

Your Name

Marketing Update for Northern Sun Tours

Northern Sun Tours hosts five 2-week tours of Scandinavia. As the office manager, you've decided to create a one-page marketing update that describes the tours offered by the company and summarizes current sales. You need to **Create the Update in Word** and then **Add Linked Data from Excel**. The completed document is shown in Figure E-20 on page 117.

activity:

Create the Update in Word

You need to enter the text for the marketing update. Then you use the Research feature to find a picture of a map of Scandinavia, which you insert into the Word document. Finally, you need to enter data in Excel that relates to the sales of Northern Sun Tours.

Hint

You will replace the "xx" references with values in a later lesson.

steps:

1. Start Word, change the Top and Bottom margins to .6", type and format the text as shown in Figure E-17, then save the document as **Northern Sun Tours Marketing Update** to the location where you are storing the files for this book

2. Click at the beginning of paragraph 1, then click the **Research button** on the Standard toolbar to open the Research task pane

3. Type **Scandinavia map** in the Search for text box, click the **All Reference Books list arrow**, click **Encarta Encyclopedia: English (North America)**, then click the link **Dynamic Map-Encarta Encyclopedia**

   Your browser opens and a map of Scandinavia appears.

4. Scroll down slightly to view the picture of the map, right-click the map, click **Save Picture As**, navigate to the location where you are saving the files for this book, type **Scandinavia** in the File name text box, click **Save**, close the browser, return to Word, then close the Research task pane

   The picture is saved as an image file in the .gif format.

5. Click **Insert** on the menu bar, point to **Picture**, click **From File**, navigate to the location where you are saving the files for this book, click **Scandinavia**, then click **Insert**

Trouble

If the Picture toolbar does not appear, right-click the picture, then click Show Picture toolbar.

6. Click the picture to select it, click the **Crop button** on the Picture toolbar, then use the Cropping tool to drag the corners and sides of the picture until the picture appears as shown in Figure E-18

   You cropped the picture to show only the portion containing the Scandinavian countries.

7. Right-click the picture, click **Format Picture**, click the **Layout tab**, click **Square**, click the **Right option button**, click **OK**, then save the document

8. Start Excel, then enter and enhance the labels and values as shown in Figure E-19

9. Select cells **B3:C8**, click the **AutoSum button** on the Standard toolbar, then save the workbook as **Marketing Update Data** to the location where you are storing the files for this book

FIGURE E-17: Text for marketing update

Arial, 16-point, bold

Northern·Sun·Tours¶
¶
Northern·Sun·Tours·conducts·five·tours·each·year·to·various·destinations·in·Scandinavia.·These·tours·are·*Scandinavian·Odyssey,·Norwegian·Fjords,·Finlandia,·Icelandic·Sagas,*·and·*Above·the·Arctic·Circle.*·All·of·Northern·Sun's·tours·are·two·weeks·in·duration.¶
¶
Since·its·incorporation·in·1982,·Northern·Sun·Tours·has·consistently·sold·virtually·all·of·the·*Scandinavian·Odyssey*·and·*Above·the·Arctic·Circle·*tours.·In·most·years,·80%·of·the·*Finlandia·*and·*Norwegian·Fjords·*tours·are·sold.·The·*Icelandic·Sagas·*tours·were·first·offered·in·2001·and·are·steadily·gaining·in·popularity.·Shown·below·is·a·breakdown·of·tour·sales·by·category.¶
¶
In·2006,·Northern·Sun·Tours·offered·a·total·of·xx·tours·and·sold·xx·tours.·The·Cylinder·chart·shown·below·displays·the·number·of·tours·sold·in·each·category·relative·to·the·number·of·tours·available.·*Scandinavian·Odyssey·*tours·rank·the·highest·in·terms·of·the·number·of·tours·sold·relative·to·the·tours·available.·*Icelandic·Sagas·*tours·rank·the·lowest.¶

FIGURE E-18: Cropped picture

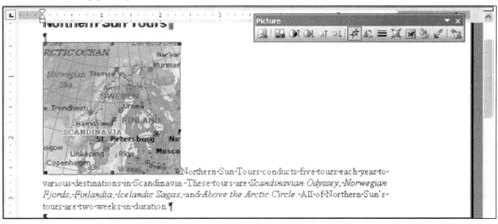

FIGURE E-19: Excel worksheet

16-point, bold, centered across cells A1:C1, filled with Gold

Bold

	A	B	C
1	**2006 Sales by Category**		
2	**Tour Name**	**Tours Available**	**Tours Sold**
3	Scandinavian Odyssey	50	48
4	Norwegian Fjords	35	28
5	Finlandia	45	36
6	Icelandic Sagas	22	14
7	Above the Arctic Circle	30	29

PROJECT **3**

MARKETING UPDATE FOR NORTHERN SUN TOURS

activity:

Add Linked Data from Excel

You need to create a chart in Excel and then insert the sales data and chart into Word as linked objects. The completed Marketing Update is shown in Figure E-20.

steps:

1. Select cells A2:C7, click the Chart Wizard button 📊 on the Standard toolbar, click Cylinder (you will need to scroll down), click Next, click Next, click the Titles tab if it is not already selected, type Tours Sold Compared to Tours Available as the chart title, click the Legend tab, click the Bottom option button, click Next, click the As object in list arrow, select Sheet2, then click Finish

2. Size and position the chart so that it extends from cell A1 through cell J21, right-click the category axis, click Format Axis, click the Font tab, click 10, follow the same process to change the font size of the value axis and Legend text to 10 point and the font size of the chart title to 14 point, click the Sheet1 tab, then save the workbook

3. Switch to Word, click after the second paragraph, press [Enter] twice, click Insert on the menu bar, click Object, click the Create from File tab, click Browse, navigate to the location where you are saving the files for this book, double-click Marketing Update Data.xls, click the Link to file check box, then click OK

   The worksheet is inserted into the Word document as a linked object.

4. Right-click the worksheet, click Show Picture toolbar, use the Crop tool to crop the worksheet object so that it appears as shown in Figure E-20, then click the Center button 🔲 on the Formatting toolbar

5. Switch to Excel, click the Sheet2 tab, click the chart, click the Copy button 📋 on the Standard toolbar, switch to Word, click at the end of the last paragraph, press [Enter] twice, click Edit on the menu bar, click Paste Special, click the Paste link option button, then click OK

6. Drag to resize the cylinder chart so that it fits on page 1 as shown in Figure E-20, then center it

7. Switch to Excel, show Sheet1, click cell B8, click 📋, switch to Word, select the first xx in line 1 of paragraph 3, click Edit on the menu bar, click Paste Special, click the Paste link option button, click Unformatted Text, click OK, then press [Spacebar]

8. Copy cell C8 from Excel and paste it as a link (Unformatted Text) over the second xx in paragraph 3, switch to Excel, then change the number of available tours for Norwegian Fjords in cell B4 to 28

Additional Practice

For additional practice with the skills presented in this project, complete Independent Challenge 3.

9. Switch to Word, notice that the links update automatically, type your name right-aligned below the chart, save the document, print a copy, close the document, exit Word, save and close the workbook in Excel, then exit Excel

   If the links do not update automatically, right click 185 in paragraph 3, click Update Link, right-click the chart, then click Update Link. If you later open the document to make changes, a message box will appear advising you that the document is linked to an Excel workbook. Click Yes to maintain the link between the document and the workbook.

Northern Sun Tours

Northern Sun Tours conducts five tours each year to various destinations in Scandinavia. These tours are *Scandinavian Odyssey*, *Norwegian Fjords*, *Finlandia*, *Icelandic Sagas*, and *Above the Arctic Circle*. All of Northern Sun's tours are two weeks in duration.

Since its incorporation in 1982, Northern Sun Tours has consistently sold virtually all of the *Scandinavian Odyssey* and *Above the Arctic Circle* tours. In most years, 80% of the *Finlandia* and *Norwegian Fjords* tours are sold. The *Icelandic Sagas* tours were first offered in 2001 and are steadily gaining in popularity. Shown below is a breakdown of tour sales by category.

2006 Sales by Category		
Tour Name	**Tours Available**	**Tours Sold**
Scandinavian Odyssey	50	48
Norwegian Fjords	28	28
Finlandia	45	36
Icelandic Sagas	22	14
Above the Arctic Circle	30	29
	175	155

In 2006, Northern Sun Tours offered a total of 175 tours and sold 155 tours. The Cylinder chart shown below displays the number of tours sold in each category relative to the number of tours available. *Scandinavian Odyssey* tours rank the highest in terms of the number of tours sold relative to the tours available. *Icelandic Sagas* tours rank the lowest.

Your Name

Independent Challenges

Create a form in Word that you can use to record data related to a performance review for a position or situation of your choice. For example, you could create a form to review a course, a workshop, or an employee. Fill in the boxes below with the required information, then set up the form in Word. You need to insert text form fields where required to contain information that will change each time you fill in the form for a different evaluation. You then need to enter data related to the evaluation in an Excel worksheet and finally copy the data and paste it as a link in Word. The completed document in Word should also include a linked chart created from the Excel data.

1. Determine the company name and the position or situation that requires a performance review form. You also need to determine at least five categories to review. For example, if you are creating a form to review a series of workshops, the categories could be Registration Procedure, Instructor, Course Materials, Learning Outcomes, and Facilities. In the box below, write the name of your company and the five categories that you will rank in the performance review:

Company name:
Categories to review:

1. _____
2. _____
3. _____
4. _____
5. _____

2. In the box below, identify information about one individual, course, or workshop that you plan to review. If you're reviewing a person, include the name, department, and position. If you're reviewing a course or workshop, include the title, subject, instructor name, date, and location.

Review subject:
_____
_____
_____
_____

3. In Word, create an attractively formatted table to contain the performance review form. Use the performance review you created for Project 1 as your guide.
4. Enter text form fields where required in the table form. Remember that you can modify selected text form fields to specify the type of information that can be entered in the field. For example, you can specify that users enter only a four-digit number or only a date in a certain format. Type your name at the bottom of the page.
5. Protect the form (click the Protect Form button on the Forms toolbar), then save the form as **My Performance Review Form** to the location where you are storing the files for this book.

6. In Excel, enter labels for the categories you wish to review and specify a ranking scale. For example, you may wish to assign each category a mark out of 10. Set up the worksheet attractively.

7. Enter rankings for one individual or course/workshop you are evaluating.

8. Create a chart that illustrates some aspect of the data. For example, you could create a column chart that shows a ranking for each category or you could create a bar chart that compares the rankings provided by two individuals. Format the chart attractively. Remember to reduce the font sizes of labels where appropriate, and to specify the maximum value of the value axis.

9. Save the workbook as **Data for My Performance Review** to the location where you are storing the files for this book.

10. In Word, enter appropriate information in the form fields related to the individual or course/workshop you wish to evaluate, then save the form as **My Performance Review 1** to the location where you are storing the files for this book.

11. In Word, unprotect the form, then copy data from the Excel chart and paste it as links in an appropriate area of the form. Copy the chart and paste it as a link.

12. Save the document, print a copy, then close the document.

13. In Excel, copy the data to a new worksheet, then replace the data with data related to another individual, course, or workshop.

14. Modify the chart so that it references data in the second worksheet. Make sure the maximum value on the value axis scale is the same on both charts to ensure a meaningful comparison between the charted results.

15. In Word, save the document as **My Performance Review 2** to the location where you are storing the files for this book, change the form information excluding the linked data and chart to reflect who or what is being reviewed, open the Links dialog box, then change the links so that they refer to the data and chart in the second Excel worksheet.

16. Save the document, print a copy, then close the document.

17. Save and close the Excel workbook.

INDEPENDENT CHALLENGE 2

In Excel, use the Goal Seek function to analyze a specific goal related to a company of your choice. In Word, create a sales report that includes data from Excel. For example, you could decide to increase your sales in two or three states or countries or increase the number of products of a certain type that you plan to sell.

1. In the box below, write the name of your company and a short description of your business goal. For example, you could name your company "Luscious Landscaping," and describe your goal as increasing your sales of bedding plants.

Company Name: _____

Description of Business Goal: _____

_____

_____

2. Set up a worksheet in Excel similar to the worksheet created for Project 2 for Paradise Resorts. Note that you need to include two or three products or locations, the income generated from sales, and your various expenses.

3. Save the workbook as **My Company Goals** to the location where you are storing the files for this book.

4. Create a current scenario of the data that you will use Goal Seek to change. For example, if you decide to increase the total number of bedding plants you sell in May, you will need to create a current scenario of the sales data related to bedding plants.

5. Use Goal Seek to change the value in one of the cells. Note that the cell you wish to change must not contain a formula. However, the cell must be referenced in a formula contained in another cell; for example, a total. You use Goal Seek to specify a set value for the cell containing the formula. For example, you can ask Goal Seek to calculate how many bedding plants you need to sell in May if you want your net income in May to equal $30,000.

6. Create a scenario from the projected data generated by Goal Seek, name the scenario **Projected**, then show the current scenerio.

7. Copy the sales summary from the Current sheet into a new sheet called **Projected**, then show the Projected scenario sales summary.

8. In the Projected worksheet, create a bar chart that compares the relevant values in the Current scenario (Sheet1) with the new values generated by Goal Seek and shown as the Projected scenario (Sheet2).

9. Format the bar chart attractively.

10. In Word, create a new document that includes the name of the company as a heading. Enter text that describes the company and summarizes the sales data.

11. Save the report as **My Sales Report** to the location where you are storing the files for this book.

12. Copy the data in the Projected worksheet and paste it as a link into the Word report, then copy the chart from the Projected worksheet and paste it as a link into the Word report. Enter a paragraph above the chart that summarizes the information in the chart.

13. In Word, draw a callout box to highlight each value in the chart that represents projected sales.

14. In Excel, change some of the data, then check that the data is updated correctly in the Word document.

15. Save and close the workbook, include your name in the sales report, print a copy, then save and close the document.

INDEPENDENT CHALLENGE 3

Create a one-page summary in Word that provides information about the sales and marketing efforts for a company of your choice. Use the marketing update you created for Northern Sun Tours as your model. The summary should include an appropriate picture that you obtain by conducting a search of the Internet from the Research task pane. Make sure you read any copyright restrictions before downloading the picture. Crop the picture if necessary and position it attractively in the document. In Excel, enter data related to your product line and create an appropriate chart in a second worksheet. In Word, insert the data into the document as a linked object, then copy the chart and paste it as a link into the Word document. Make changes to the data in Excel, then update the links in Word. If necessary, crop the worksheet object again so only the data is displayed. Save the workbook as My Update Data to the location where you are storing the files for this book and the document as My Update to the same location. Include your name on the Word document, print a copy, then save and close all open files, and exit all programs.

Create an Excel worksheet with the projected income and expenses for Time Tunnel Books, an online bookstore that specializes in historical books, maps, and periodicals. Then use the data in the worksheet to create two charts, which you link to a Projected Sales Summary in Word. Finally, add a Clip Art picture.

1. Open a blank workbook in Excel, then create the worksheet shown in Figure E-21. Note that the heading in cell A1 is formatted with the Britannic Bold font (use a similar font if you do not have this font) and a font size of 22 point. To save time, copy the values entered in column B across through column E.

FIGURE E-21: Data For Time Tunnel Books Sales Summary

	A	B	C	D	E	F	G	H	I
1		**Time Tunnel Books**							
2		Projected Income and Expenses							
3		**April**	**May**	**June**	**July**	**Totals**			
4	**Income**								
5	Sales	28,000.00	28,000.00	28,000.00	28,000.00				
6	Total Income								
7									
8	**Expenses**								
9	Salaries	$ 5,000.00	$ 5,000.00	$ 5,000.00	$ 5,000.00				
10	Rent	1,200.00	1,200.00	1,200.00	1,200.00				
11	Advertising	600.00	600.00	600.00	600.00				
12	Equipment Lease	800.00	800.00	800.00	800.00				
13	Operating Costs	700.00	700.00	700.00	700.00				
14	Cost of Sales								
15	Total Expenses								
16									
17	**Total Profit**								
18									
19									
20									
21									
22									

Sheet1 / Sheet2 / Sheet3 /

2. Save the workbook as **Time Tunnel Books Sales Data** to the location where you are storing the files for this book.
3. Enter and copy the formulas required to calculate the following amounts:
   a. Total monthly and four month income (cell F5 and cells B6:F6).
   b. Cost of Sales: sales multiplied by 60% (i.e., B5*.6).
   c. Total monthly (cells B15:F15) and four-month expenses (cells F9:F14).
   d. Total Profit (cells B17:F17): subtract the total expenses from the total income for each month.
   When you have completed all the calculations, you should see $11,600.00 in cell F17.
4. Create a pie chart that shows the breakdown of expenses by total amount. You will need to click the Chart Wizard button, select the pie chart type, and then use the [Ctrl] key to select cells A9:A14 and cells F9:F14 as the data range. Use the chart title "Breakdown of Expenses" and show the labels as percentages.
5. Move the chart below the worksheet, then increase the chart size and modify the font sizes of the chart labels so the completed pie chart appears similar to the pie chart shown in the completed sales report in Figure E-23. Your percentages will vary.

6. Switch to Word, then enter the text for the Sales Summary, as shown in Figure E-22. Note that you will replace the various "xx" entries with values that you paste as links from the Excel worksheet.

FIGURE E-22: Text for Time Tunnel Books Sales Summary

Time·Tunnel·Books·Sales·Summary¶
Jolene·Grant,·our·accountant·at·Time·Tunnel·Books,·has·projected·the·income·and·
expenses·for·the·book·store·for·the·months·of·April·through·July,·2007.¶
¶
Projected·Expenses¶
The·total·projected·expenses·are·xx.·The·pie·chart·below·displays·a·breakdown·of·
expenses·by·total·amount.¶
¶
In·order·to·decrease·our·expenses,·Yvonne·James,·our·store·manager,·will·create·a·set·of·
brochures·to·replace·our·newspaper·ads,·thereby·cutting·our·advertising·expenses·by·
40%.¶
¶
Projected·Income¶
The·total·projected·income·for·April·through·July,·2007·is·xx.·The·projected·profit·for·
Time·Tunnel·Books·from·April·through·July,·2007·is·xx.·We·plan·to·increase·sales·of·
historical·books·related·to·the·local·area·to·capture·the·tourist·market·in·June·and·July,·
our·busiest·months.¶
¶

7. Save the document as **Time Tunnel Books Sales Summary** to the location where you are storing the files for this book.

8. Copy the pie chart and any totals required from Excel, and paste them as links into Word, using Figure E-23 as a guide. Make sure you paste the totals as unformatted text.

9. Switch to Excel, increase the salaries expense for June and July to 7,500, then increase the sales income in June and July to 50,000. Note the changes to the pie chart.

10. Switch to Word, then update the links if necessary.

11. Format the document title with Arial, Bold, and 18 point, then format the Projected Expenses and Projected Income headings with Arial, Bold, and 14.

12. Insert a ClipArt picture similar to the picture shown in Figure E-23. (*Hint*: Search for History.)

13. Type your name as shown in Figure E-23, print a copy of the sales summary, save and close the Word document, then save and close the Excel workbook.

Time Tunnel Books Sales Summary

Jolene Grant, our accountant at Time Tunnel Books, has projected the income and expenses for the book store for the months of April through July, 2007.

Projected Expenses

The total projected expenses are $131,800.00. The pie chart below displays a breakdown of expenses by total amount.

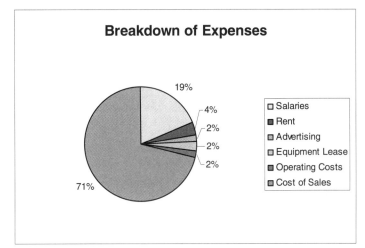

In order to decrease our expenses, Yvonne James, our store manager, will create a set of brochures to replace our newspaper ads, thereby cutting our advertising expenses by 40%.

Projected Income

The total projected income for April through July, 2007 is $156,000.00. The projected profit for Time Tunnel Books from April through July, 2007 is $24,200.00 . We plan to increase sales of historical books related to the local area to capture the tourist market in June and July, our busiest months.

Your Name

Visual Workshop

Create the worksheet shown in Figure E-24 in Excel, then save it as **High Notes Sales Data** to the location where you are storing the files for this book. Calculate the total sales of each item by multiplying the Quantity by the Price, then calculate the total sales in cell E8. Create the text for the sales report in Word as shown in Figure E-25, entering the values as links copied from the Excel workbook. Save the document as **High Notes Sales Report** to the location where you are storing the files for this book. In Excel, create a cone chart that appears similar to the completed chart shown in Figure E-25. Note that you need to remove the gray chart background. Copy the chart from Excel and paste it as a link in the Word document. In Excel, change the unit price of Haydn's Sonatas to $75, then save and close the workbook. Update the links in the sales report, print a copy, then save and close the document.

FIGURE E-24: Sales Data worksheet

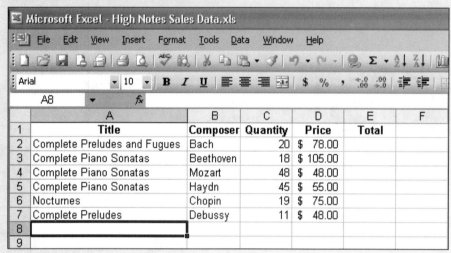

FIGURE E-25: Completed Sales Report

High Notes Music Store

1803 West Maple Avenue, North Vancouver, BC V7H 1A9

Sales of classical piano music books have been brisk in 2006. Shown below are the unit sales of our top six titles. Our best-selling composer is Haydn, with sales in 2006 of 45 units for a total of $3,375.00.

The cone chart shown below compares the sales of each of the composers.

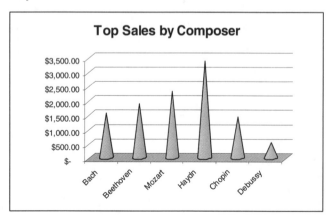

Your Name

Microsoft
► Access
Projects

Unit F

Access Projects

In this Unit You Will Create the Following:

PROJECT 1 ► **Inventory**

PROJECT 2 ► **Author Profiles**

PROJECT 3 ► **Data Access Page**

To survive and compete in the contemporary business world, companies and organizations need fast and reliable access to information about their products or services, customers, suppliers, and personnel. Suppose you own an adventure tour company and decide to offer a special incentive to all the clients who signed up for a tour in July of 2006. You could comb through all your paper files to find the clients, or you could use a relational database program, such as Access, to locate, organize, and print out a list of the clients who joined a tour in July 2006 or during any other time period you choose. A relational database program stores information in related tables that you can use to perform queries and find the information you need. To create a database, you first identify categories—called fields—that describe and organize the contents of your database, such as customers or inventory. Then you formulate queries or questions to retrieve the information you need. In this unit, you will learn how to use Microsoft Access to set up a variety of databases and then ask questions to find the information you need to perform specific tasks. You will also learn how to set up a data access page that makes data in a database accessible on the Internet.

Inventory for Global Gifts

Global Gifts sells crafts made by artisans located all over the world. As the office manager in charge of monitoring inventory levels, you need to create an inventory database containing records for 15 products and a Suppliers table containing records for four suppliers. To build the inventory database you **Set Up the Products Table**, **Set Up the Suppliers Table**, **Create Queries**, and then **Format and Print an Order Report**. The order report is shown in Figure F-13 on page 133.

activity:

Set Up the Products Table

You need to set up and then enter the data required for the Products table.

steps:

1. Start Access, click **Create a new file** in the Getting Started task pane, click **Blank database** in the New File task pane, navigate to the location where you are storing the files for this book, type **Global Gifts Inventory** in the File name text box, then click **Create**

2. Double-click **Create table by using wizard**, click **Products** in the Sample Tables list box, make sure **ProductID** is selected in the Sample Fields list box, then click the **Select Single Field button** [>]
   The ProductID field moves to the Fields in my new table list box.

Trouble

If you select the wrong field, click the Remove Single Field button to remove the field from the Fields in my new table list.

3. Verify that **ProductName** is selected, click [>], click **CategoryID**, click [>], click **Rename Field** under the Fields in my new table list box, type **Region**, click **OK**, move **ProductDescription** and rename it **Category**, then move the following fields: **SupplierID**, **UnitsInStock**, and **UnitPrice**

4. Click **Next**, type **Global Gifts Products** for the table name, accept the default to let the wizard set a primary key, click **Next**, accept the default to enter data directly into the table, then click **Finish**
   A primary key is a special kind of field that uniquely identifies each record in a table. You are currently in Datasheet view, where you enter the data required for each of the 15 products sold by Global Gifts.

5. Press [Tab] to move to the Product Name field, type **Carved Polar Bear**, press [Tab], type **North America**, then press [Tab]
   A warning message appears because you have entered the wrong kind of data into the Region field. Originally this field was called CategoryID, which Access formats as a field that contains only numbers.

6. Click **OK** to close the warning message, press [Backspace] until you erase "North America," click the **View list arrow** [icon] on the Standard toolbar, click **Design View**, click **Number** next to Region in the Data Type column, click the **Data Type list arrow**, then click **Text** as shown in Figure F-1
   You changed the data type of the field in Design view so that you can enter text data.

7. Click the **View list arrow** [icon] on the Standard toolbar, click **Datasheet View**, then click **Yes** to save the table

Hint

You can press [Shift][Tab] if you need to move back to a previous cell.

8. Press [Tab] twice to move to the Region field, type **North America**, then enter the remaining data for record 1 as shown in Figure F-2
   Just type the numbers for the Unit Price field. Access automatically formats the number in the Currency style.

9. Enter the data for records 2 to 15 as shown in Figure F-2, double-click each column divider to resize the columns as needed, click **File** on the menu bar, click **Close**, then click **Yes** in response to the Save message
   The Global Gifts Products table closed and the Global Gifts Inventory database remains open. The table is one object in a database that can contain many objects, including other tables, forms, queries, and reports.

FIGURE F-1: **Changing the data type for the Region field**

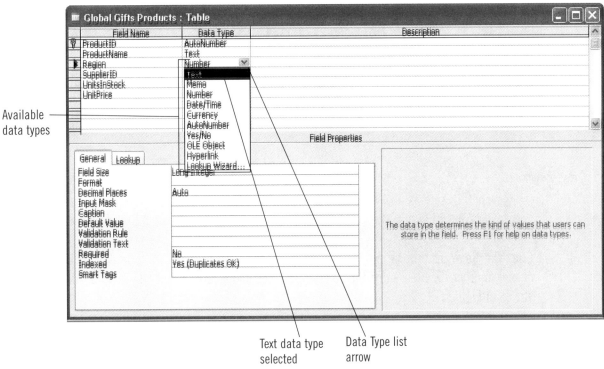

Available data types

Text data type selected

Data Type list arrow

FIGURE F-2: **Data for records 1 to 15**

Product ID	Product Name	Region	Category	Supplier ID	Units In Stock	Unit Price
1	Carved Polar Bear	North America	Art	2	15	$250.00
2	Coral Pendant	Asia	Jewelry	1	9	$220.00
3	Turquoise Earrings	North America	Jewelry	2	5	$15.00
4	Mahogany Salad Bowl	Central America	Household	4	8	$22.95
5	Smoked Salmon	North America	Food	2	15	$25.95
6	Hippo Carving	Africa	Art	3	15	$100.00
7	Jade Ring	Asia	Jewelry	1	8	$40.00
8	Soapstone Seal	North America	Art	2	4	$300.00
9	Aztec Mask	Central America	Art	4	8	$55.00
10	Maple Sugar Treats	North America	Food	2	15	$80.00
11	Ebony Carving	Africa	Art	3	12	$120.00
12	Talking Drum	Africa	Instrument	3	9	$55.00
13	Lacquer Dinner Set	Asia	Household	1	13	$85.00
14	Opal Earrings	Asia	Jewelry	1	7	$110.00
15	Hand Pipes	Central America	Instrument	4	10	$95.00
(AutoNumber)				0		

Record: 16 of 16

ProductID field entered automatically when you press Tab

Double-click between the field names to adjust column widths

Unit price field formatted automatically as Currency

PROJECT 1 **INVENTORY FOR GLOBAL GIFTS**

activity:

Set Up the Suppliers Table

You need to create the Suppliers table and then create a form to enter the data. For the Global Gifts Suppliers table, you save time by including only the name, region, and e-mail address of your four suppliers. If you were setting up a Suppliers table for a "real" business, you would also include the address, phone number(s), and Web site address of each supplier.

steps:

1. Double-click **Create table in Design view**, type **Supplier ID**, press [Tab], click the **Data type list arrow**, click **AutoNumber**, then click the **Primary Key button** 🔑 on the Standard toolbar

2. Click the **Save button** 💾 on the Standard toolbar, type **Global Gifts Suppliers**, click **OK**, click below Supplier ID, then enter the remaining three fields and select the required data types as shown in Figure F-3

3. Click **File** on the menu bar, click **Close**, click **Yes**, click **Forms** in the Objects pane of the Database window, then double-click **Create form by using wizard**

4. Click the **Tables/Queries list arrow**, click **Table: Global Gifts Suppliers**, click the **Select All Fields button** ⏩, click **Next**, click **Next** to accept the Columnar layout, click **Expedition**, click **Next**, make sure the **Open the form to view or enter information option button** is selected, then click **Finish**

5. Press [Tab], type **Far East Imports** for the Supplier Name, press [Tab], type **Asia**, press [Tab], type **sales@fareastimports.com**, then press [Tab] twice to move to the Supplier Name field in form 2

6. Enter the data for the next three forms as shown in Figure F-4, Figure F-5, and Figure F-6, then close the last form
   You can now view the data for the Global Gifts Suppliers in either individual form or in a datasheet.

7. Click **Tools** on the menu bar, click **Relationships**, click **Global Gifts Suppliers** in the Show Table dialog box, click **Add**, repeat to add the **Global Gifts Products** table to the Relationships window, close the **Show Table dialog box**, then drag the **lower-right corner** of Global Gifts Products to show all categories as needed

8. Drag **Supplier ID** from the Global Gifts Suppliers table (at the left) over Supplier ID in the Global Gifts Products table (at the right), then click **Create** in the Edit Relationships dialog box
   A relationship is created between the two tables based on Supplier ID as the common field as shown in Figure F-7.

9. Close the Relationships window, then click **Yes** to save the relationship layout

FIGURE F-3: Fields for Global Gifts Suppliers table

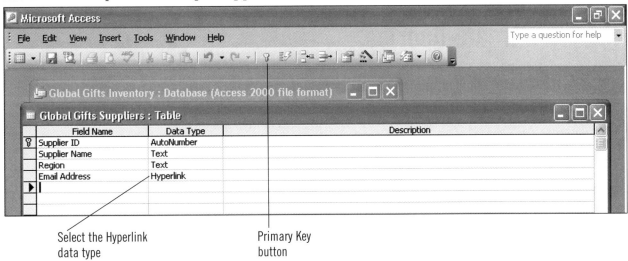

Select the Hyperlink
data type

Primary Key
button

FIGURE F-4: Data for Supplier 2

FIGURE F-5: Data for Supplier 3

FIGURE F-6: Data for Supplier 4

FIGURE F-7: Relationships window

Supplier ID
in the
Global Gifts
Suppliers
table

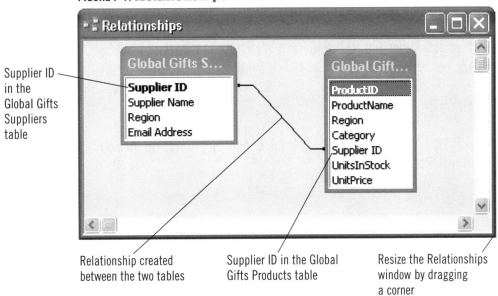

Relationship created
between the two tables

Supplier ID in the Global
Gifts Products table

Resize the Relationships
window by dragging
a corner

activity:

Create Queries

First, you need to view the records that relate to each of the four suppliers, and then you use the two tables that you've created to ask two questions, called **queries**. You create a query to find out how many products you have from Asia in the Art category, and then you create a query to determine the number of products with fewer than 10 items in the inventory.

steps:

1. Click **Tables** in the Objects pane, double-click **Global Gifts Suppliers** to open the table, then click the **Expand button** ⊞ to the left of the Far East Imports record to show the records in the Products table that share the same Supplier ID with the record in the Suppliers table as shown in Figure F-8

The one-to-many relationship created between the Suppliers table and the Products table uses the Supplier ID field as the common field. With this relationship, you can create queries that list all the products purchased from a specific supplier.

2. Click the **Close button** ⊠ in the upper-right corner of the Global Gifts Suppliers table to close it

3. Click **Queries** in the Objects pane, then double-click **Create query by using wizard**

4. Verify that **Table: Global Gifts Products** is selected in the Tables/Queries text box, click the **Select All Fields button** >> to select all the fields in the Products table, click **Next**, click **Next** to accept a Detail query, click the **Modify the query design option button**, then click **Finish**

Hint

Quotation marks appear after you exit the cell.

5. Click the **Region Criteria cell**, type **Asia**, click the **Category Criteria cell**, type **Jewelry** as shown in Figure F-9, then click the **Run button** ❗ on the Standard toolbar

Three of the products from Asia are from the Jewelry category—the Coral Pendant, the Jade Ring, and the Opal Earrings.

6. Click **File** on the menu bar, click **Close**, then click **Yes**

7. Double-click **Global Gifts Products Query**, click the **View list arrow** ◣▾, click **Design View**, delete **Asia**, delete **Jewelry**, scroll to and click the **UnitsInStock Criteria cell**, type **<10**, then click ❗

A datasheet listing all the products with fewer than 10 units in stock appears as shown in Figure F-10. These are the items that you need to order.

8. Click **File** on the menu bar, click **Save As**, type **Items to Order**, click **OK**, then close the query table

FIGURE F-8: Records in the Products table that are related to a record in the Suppliers table

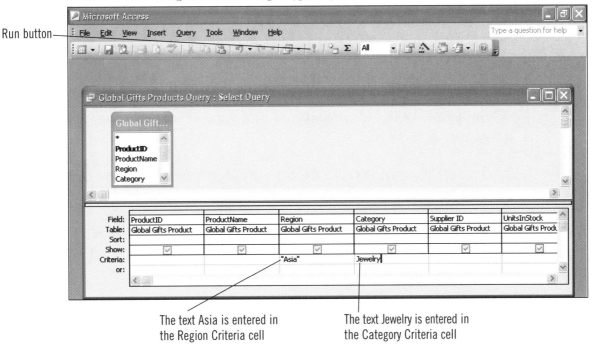

Four items in the Products table are distributed by the Far East Imports supplier

Global Gifts Suppliers : Table

	Supplier ID	Supplier Name	Region	Email Address
–	1	Far East Import	Asia	sales@fareastir

	Product ID	Product Name	Region	Category	Units In Stock	Unit Price
	2	Coral Pendant	Asia	Jewelry	9	$220.00
	7	Jade Ring	Asia	Jewelry	8	$40.00
	13	Lacquer Dinner Set	Asia	Household	13	$85.00
	14	Opal Earrings	Asia	Jewelry	7	$110.00
*	(AutoNumber)					

+	2	America Arts	North America	sales@america
+	3	Kenya Crafts	Africa	sales@kenyacr
+	4	Rainforest Coop	Central America	sales@rainfores
*	(AutoNumber)			

Record: 1 of 4

FIGURE F-9: Entering constraints for Query 1

Run button

Microsoft Access

File Edit View Insert Query Tools Window Help   Type a question for help

Global Gifts Products Query : Select Query

Global Gift...
*
ProductID
ProductName
Region
Category

Field:	ProductID	ProductName	Region	Category	Supplier ID	UnitsInStock
Table:	Global Gifts Product	Global Gifts Product	Global Gifts Product	Global Gifts Product	Global Gifts Product	Global Gifts Produ
Sort:						
Show:	☑	☑	☑	☑	☑	☑
Criteria:			"Asia"	Jewelry		
or:						

The text Asia is entered in the Region Criteria cell

The text Jewelry is entered in the Category Criteria cell

FIGURE F-10: Datasheet view of Query 2 results

Global Gifts Products Query : Select Query

	Product ID	Product Name	Region	Category	Supplier ID	Units In Stock	Unit Price
	2	Coral Pendant	Asia	Jewelry	1	9	$220.00
	3	Turquoise Earrings	North America	Jewelry	2	5	$15.00
	4	Mahogany Salad Bowl	Central America	Household	4	8	$22.95
	7	Jade Ring	Asia	Jewelry	1	8	$40.00
	8	Soapstone Seal	North America	Art	2	4	$300.00
	9	Aztec Mask	Central America	Art	4	8	$55.00
	12	Talking Drum	Africa	Instrument	3	9	$55.00
	14	Opal Earrings	Asia	Jewelry	1	7	$110.00
*	(AutoNumber)					0	

Record: 1 of 8

8 products meet the criteria of the query

All products listed have fewer than 10 in stock

activity:

Format and Print an Order Report

To quickly locate the suppliers you need to contact to order the low-inventory products, you need to modify the Items to Order query so that it includes two fields from the Suppliers table. You then need to format and print an Order report generated from the query. The completed report is shown in Figure F-13.

steps:

1. Double-click **Items to Order**, switch to Design view, click **Query** on the menu bar, click **Show Table**, click **Global Gifts Suppliers**, click **Add**, then click **Close**

2. Scroll to the right, click **Supplier Name** in the Global Gifts Suppliers table (refer to Figure F-11), drag it to the column to the right of UnitPrice, scroll right as needed to view the next blank column, then drag **Email Address** to that blank column
   Design view of the query table appears as shown in Figure F-11.

Trouble

You may need to scroll right to view all the fields in the query table.

3. Click the **SupplierName Sort cell**, click the **Sort cell list arrow**, click **Ascending**, then click the **Run button** ⚡ on the Standard toolbar
   You have your list of eight products to order and the names and e-mail addresses of the suppliers to contact sorted by supplier name.

4. Close and save the query table, click **Reports** in the Objects pane, then double-click **Create report by using wizard**

5. Click the **Tables/Queries list arrow**, click **Query: Items to Order**, then select and move the following fields to the Selected Fields list box: **ProductName**, **Region**, **Category**, **UnitPrice**, **Supplier Name**, and **Email Address**

6. Click **Next**, click **by Global Gifts Products** if necessary, click **Next**, click **Supplier Name** in the list of groupings, click the **Select Single Field button** ▷ , click **Next**, click **Next** again (you don't need to sort), click the **Align Left 2 option button**, click the **Landscape option button**, click **Next**, click **Soft Gray**, click **Next**, type **Inventory Items to Order** and your name, then click **Finish**
   The report is shown in Print Preview. Too much space appears between the Category and the Unit Price fields.

7. Click the **Zoom list arrow** on the Print Preview toolbar, then click **Fit**

8. Click the **View list arrow** 🔽, click **Design View**, click the **Unit Price label**, press and hold [Shift], click the **Unit Price field**, move the mouse over a selected label until the 🖐 pointer appears, release [Shift], then drag the 🖐 pointer to move the two selected labels about ½" to the left as shown in Figure F-12

Additional Practice

For additional practice with the skills presented in this project, complete Independent Challenge 1.

9. Click the **Print Preview button** 🔍 on the Standard toolbar, maximize the report window, switch to 75% view, compare the completed report to Figure F-13, click the **Print button** 🖨 on the Standard toolbar, close the report, click **Yes**, then close the database and Access

FIGURE F-11: New fields inserted in Design view

Global Gifts Suppliers table

Supplier Name and Email Address fields inserted

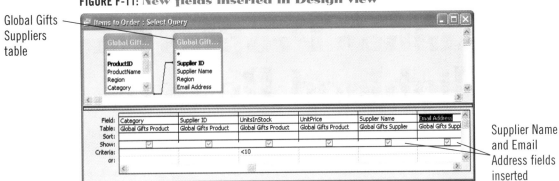

FIGURE F-12: Position of the Unit Price labels in Design view

Move icon

Unit Price label and field selected and dragged approximately ½" to the left

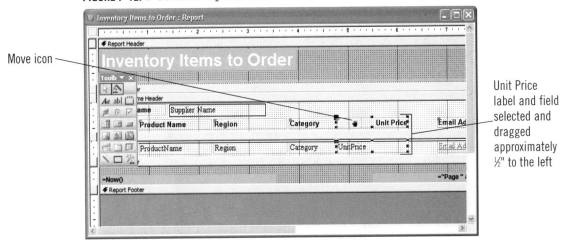

FIGURE F-13: Completed report in Print Preview

Your name appears here

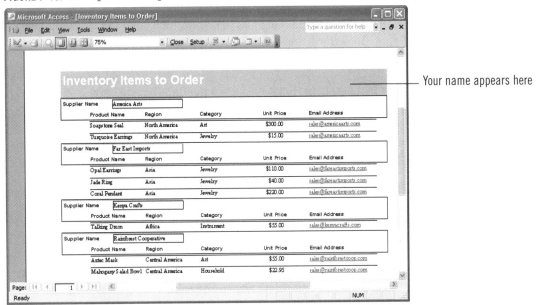

Clues to Use

Formatting Reports

If you want to modify the placement of the Unit Price labels or any other labels, switch back to Design view, make the adjustments required, and then view the results in Print Preview. To format a report in Access, you need to switch frequently between Design view and Print Preview.

Author Profiles for Highland Books

Based in Edinburgh, Scotland, Highland Books publishes books in various fiction genres by authors living and working in Scotland and Northern England. As the managing editor, you decide to set up a database that you can use to identify the authors who have sold the most books, the authors who have sold more than €13,000 worth of books (in the Euro currency) during the last year, and the most popular book genres purchased. To create the database, you **Create the Bookstore Sales and Genres Tables, Create and Modify a Query,** and then **Create and Format a Report.** The completed report is shown in Figure F-21 on page 139.

activity:

Create the Bookstore Sales and Genres Tables

Your first task is to create the two tables in the Highland Books database.

steps:

Hint

Press [Tab] three times after entering each field name or press [↓].

Trouble

Enter only numbers in the Sales column.

1. Start Access, click **Create a new file** in the Getting Started task pane, click **Blank database** in the New File task pane, navigate to the location where you are saving the files for this book, enter **Highland Books** as the filename, then click **Create**

2. Double-click **Create table in Design view**, then enter the following field names: **Book Title, Author Name, Bookstore,** and **Sales**

   Access automatically assigns Text as the data type for each field.

3. Click **Text** next to the Sales field, click the **Data Type list arrow**, click **Currency**, click **Currency** to the right of Format on the General tab, click the **list arrow**, then select **Euro** as shown in Figure F-14

4. Switch to Datasheet view, save the table as **Bookstore Sales**, click **Yes** to create a primary key, then enter the data and increase the column widths as shown in Figure F-15

5. Click **Author Name**, then click the **Sort Ascending button** ⬆ on the Standard toolbar

6. Click **Author Name** again, click the **Copy button** 📋 on the Standard toolbar, close the table, click **Yes** to save changes, then double-click **Create table by entering data**

7. Click **Field1**, click the **Paste button** 📋 on the Standard toolbar, click **Yes**, double-click **Field1**, type **Author Name**, press [Enter], widen the column so that you can see all the names, click the **Save button** 💾 on the Standard toolbar, type **Genres**, click **OK**, then click **Yes** to create a primary key

8. Right-click the row selector to the left of the second occurrence of Ferguson, Fiona, click **Delete Record** on the pop-up menu, click **Yes**, then repeat the process to delete duplicate occurrences of the remaining authors

9. Switch to Design view, type **Genre** in the Field Name column under Author Name, switch to Datasheet view, save the table, enter the genre for each author as shown in Figure F-16, close the table, then click **Yes** to save changes if necessary

FIGURE F-14: Euro currency format selected

Euro currency ——

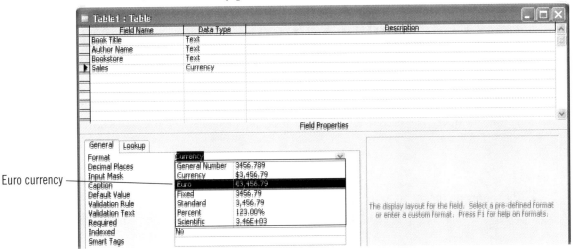

FIGURE F-15: Records for the Bookstore Sales table

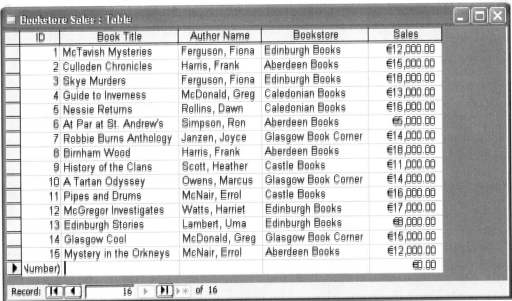

ID	Book Title	Author Name	Bookstore	Sales
1	McTavish Mysteries	Ferguson, Fiona	Edinburgh Books	€12,000.00
2	Culloden Chronicles	Harris, Frank	Aberdeen Books	€15,000.00
3	Skye Murders	Ferguson, Fiona	Edinburgh Books	€18,000.00
4	Guide to Inverness	McDonald, Greg	Caledonian Books	€13,000.00
5	Nessie Returns	Rollins, Dawn	Caledonian Books	€16,000.00
6	At Par at St. Andrew's	Simpson, Ron	Aberdeen Books	€5,000.00
7	Robbie Burns Anthology	Janzen, Joyce	Glasgow Book Corner	€14,000.00
8	Birnham Wood	Harris, Frank	Aberdeen Books	€18,000.00
9	History of the Clans	Scott, Heather	Castle Books	€11,000.00
10	A Tartan Odyssey	Owens, Marcus	Glasgow Book Corner	€14,000.00
11	Pipes and Drums	McNair, Errol	Castle Books	€18,000.00
12	McGregor Investigates	Watts, Harriet	Edinburgh Books	€17,000.00
13	Edinburgh Stories	Lambert, Uma	Edinburgh Books	€8,000.00
14	Glasgow Cool	McDonald, Greg	Glasgow Book Corner	€15,000.00
15	Mystery in the Orkneys	McNair, Errol	Aberdeen Books	€12,000.00
(Number)				€0.00

Record: 16 of 16

FIGURE F-16: Records for the Genres table

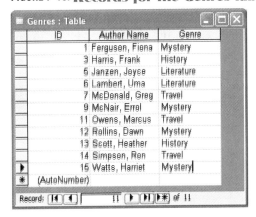

ID	Author Name	Genre
1	Ferguson, Fiona	Mystery
3	Harris, Frank	History
5	Janzen, Joyce	Literature
6	Lambert, Uma	Literature
7	McDonald, Greg	Travel
9	McNair, Errol	Mystery
11	Owens, Marcus	Travel
12	Rollins, Dawn	Mystery
13	Scott, Heather	History
14	Simpson, Ron	Travel
15	Watts, Harriet	Mystery
(AutoNumber)		

Record: 11 of 11

activity:

Create and Modify a Query

Your market researchers have found that readers want more titles in the mystery and travel genres, so you decide to create a query that shows how many titles from these genres you have in stock. You then modify this query to list only those authors who sold more than €13,000 worth of books. Before you can create the query, you need to establish a relationship between the Bookstore Sales and Genres tables.

steps:

1. Click **Tools** on the menu bar, click **Relationships**, click **Add** in the Show Table dialog box to add the Bookstore Sales table, click **Genres** in the Show Table dialog box, click **Add**, then click **Close**
   You have selected the two tables that you need to create a relationship between.

2. Click **Author Name** in the Bookstore Sales table, drag it across to **Author Name** in the Genres table, click **Create** in the Edit Relationships dialog box, close the Relationships window, then click **Yes** to save the changes

3. Click **Queries** in the Objects pane, double-click **Create query by using wizard**, verify that **Table: Bookstore Sales** is selected in the Tables/Queries text box, then click the **Select All Fields button** [>>] to move all the fields to the Selected Fields list box

4. Click the **Tables/Queries list arrow**, click **Table: Genres**, add the **Genre** field to the Selected Fields list box, click **Next**, click **Next** again, click the **Modify the query design option button**, then click **Finish**

5. Click the **Genre Sort cell** (you may need to scroll right to view it), click the **Sort cell list arrow**, click **Ascending**, then click the **Run button** [!] on the Standard toolbar
   The query results appear as shown in Figure F-17.

6. Switch to Design view, click the **Sales Criteria cell**, type **>13000**, press **[Tab]**, type **Mystery**, then complete the criteria as shown in Figure F-18

7. Click [!]
   Six books match the criteria.

8. Switch to Design view, click the **Sales Sort cell**, click the **Sales Sort list arrow**, click **Ascending**, click [!], then compare your screen with Figure F-19

9. Close the Query Results window, then click **Yes** to save the modified query

FIGURE F-17: Data sorted by Genre

	ID	Book Title	Author Name	Bookstore	Sales	Genre
▶	9	History of the Clans	Scott, Heather	Castle Books	€11,000.00	History
	8	Birnham Wood	Harris, Frank	Aberdeen Books	€18,000.00	History
	2	Culloden Chronicles	Harris, Frank	Aberdeen Books	€15,000.00	History
	13	Edinburgh Stories	Lambert, Uma	Edinburgh Books	€8,000.00	Literature
	7	Robbie Burns Anthology	Janzen, Joyce	Glasgow Book Corner	€14,000.00	Literature
	12	McGregor Investigates	Watts, Harriet	Edinburgh Books	€17,000.00	Mystery
	5	Nessie Returns	Rollins, Dawn	Caledonian Books	€16,000.00	Mystery
	15	Mystery in the Orkneys	McNair, Errol	Aberdeen Books	€12,000.00	Mystery
	11	Pipes and Drums	McNair, Errol	Castle Books	€16,000.00	Mystery
	3	Skye Murders	Ferguson, Fiona	Edinburgh Books	€18,000.00	Mystery
	1	McTavish Mysteries	Ferguson, Fiona	Edinburgh Books	€12,000.00	Mystery
	6	At Par at St. Andrew's	Simpson, Ron	Aberdeen Books	€5,000.00	Travel
	10	A Tartan Odyssey	Owens, Marcus	Glasgow Book Corner	€14,000.00	Travel
	14	Glasgow Cool	McDonald, Greg	Glasgow Book Corner	€15,000.00	Travel
	4	Guide to Inverness	McDonald, Greg	Caledonian Books	€13,000.00	Travel

Record: |◀ ◀ | 1 | ▶ ▶| ▶* | of 15

FIGURE F-18: Sales and Genre criteria

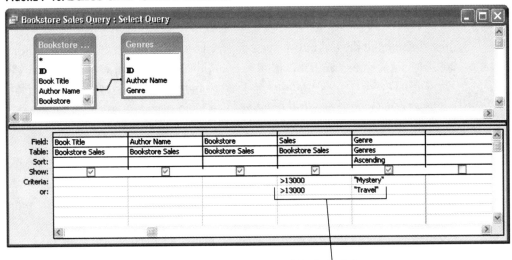

Criteria for Sales
and Genre

FIGURE F-19: Completed Bookstore Sales query

	ID	Book Title	Author Name	Bookstore	Sales	Genre
▶	10	A Tartan Odyssey	Owens, Marcus	Glasgow Book Corner	€14,000.00	Travel
	14	Glasgow Cool	McDonald, Greg	Glasgow Book Corner	€15,000.00	Travel
	5	Nessie Returns	Rollins, Dawn	Caledonian Books	€16,000.00	Mystery
	11	Pipes and Drums	McNair, Errol	Castle Books	€16,000.00	Mystery
	12	McGregor Investigates	Watts, Harriet	Edinburgh Books	€17,000.00	Mystery
	3	Skye Murders	Ferguson, Fiona	Edinburgh Books	€18,000.00	Mystery

Record: |◀ ◀ | 1 | ▶ ▶| ▶* | of 6

activity:

Create and Format a Report

You need to create a report and then format it to present to your colleagues at a meeting. Your finished report will look similar to the one shown in Figure F-21.

steps:

1. Click **Reports** in the Objects pane, double-click **Create report by using wizard**, click the **Tables/Queries** list arrow, click **Query: Bookstore Sales Query**, then click the **Select All Fields** button **>>**

2. Click the **ID field**, then click the **Remove Single Field button** **<**

3. Click **Next**, click **Author Name**, click the **Select Single Field button** **>** to insert Author Name as a header, click **Next**, click **Next**, click the **Stepped option button** if necessary, click **Next**, click **Casual**, click **Next**, type **Highland Books Best Sellers** and your name, then click **Finish**

4. Switch to Design view, click the **Text Box button** **ab|** in the Toolbox, point below the Report Footer bar and below the Sales field, then click and drag to draw a text box as shown in Figure F-20

5. Click **Unbound** in the text box you just drew, type **=Sum(Sales)**, select the text **Text16:** in the label box, type **Total sales:**, switch to Print Preview, then scroll down to see the total sales
   The total book sales (96000) appears in the unbound control you created. An unbound control contains data that is not related to a field contained in a table.

6. Return to Design view, right-click the **text box** containing =Sum([Sales]), click **Properties**, click the **text box** next to Format, click the **Format list arrow**, click **Euro** (you'll need to scroll down), then close the Properties dialog box
   The 96000 is formatted in the Euro currency format to match the other currency values in the report.

7. Click **Author Name** in the Author Name Header area, click the **Font Size list arrow** on the Formatting toolbar, click **12**, click the **Bold button** **B** on the Formatting toolbar, click **Book Title** in the Detail area, then click the **Italic button** **I** on the Formatting toolbar

8. Move and resize labels and text boxes so that the completed report appears as shown in Figure F-21 in Print Preview view
   You will need to spend quite some time modifying the positions and sizes of the various objects. For example, you'll need to increase the width of the Book Title text box so that none of the text is cut off in the printed report, and you'll need to position the unbound control containing the sum calculation so that it lines up below the entries in the sales field. As you work, switch frequently to Print Preview to monitor your progress.

9. When you are satisfied that the previewed report appears similar to Figure F-21, click the **Print** button on the Standard toolbar, close and save the report, then close the database

FIGURE F-20: Drawing an unbound control

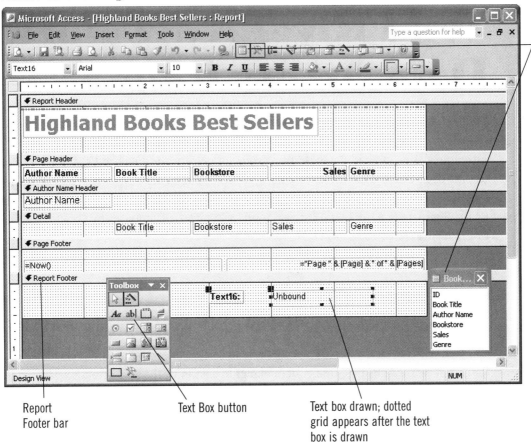

If the Field list is not showing, you can click the Show Field list button

Report Footer bar

Text Box button

Text box drawn; dotted grid appears after the text box is drawn

FIGURE F-21: Completed report for Highland Books

Your name appears here

Author Name	Book Title	Bookstore	Sales	Genre
Ferguson, Fiona				
	Skye Murders	Edinburgh Books	€18,000.00	Mystery
McDonald, Greg				
	Glasgow Cool	Glasgow Book Corner	€15,000.00	Travel
McNair, Errol				
	Pipes and Drums	Castle Books	€16,000.00	Mystery
Owens, Marcus				
	A Tartan Odyssey	Glasgow Book Corner	€14,000.00	Travel
Rollins, Dawn				
	Nessie Returns	Caledonian Books	€16,000.00	Mystery
Watts, Harriet				
	McGregor Investigates	Edinburgh Books	€17,000.00	Mystery
	Total Sales:		€96,000.00	

Page: 1

Wild River Adventures Data Access Page

Wild River Adventures offers canoe-camping adventure tours on the wilderness rivers of Quebec and Ontario for clients from all over the world. You are responsible for updating the Wild River Adventures Web site and database from your home office in Quebec City. To enable you to view records from the database over the Internet, you decide to create a data access page. A **data access page** is a special type of Web page designed in an Access database and used for viewing database data on the Internet or an intranet. First, you need to **Create the Database and Query**, and then you need to **Create the Data Access Page**.

activity:

Create the Database and Query

You need to create the database. Then you need to create a query that uses a calculation field to multiply the cost of each tour by the number of bookings to determine the total revenue generated by each tour.

steps:

Hint
You need to designate the Tour Cost field as a Currency field and the Bookings field as a Number

Hint
Press [Ctrl]['] to enter duplicate information.

1. Start Access, create a database called **Wild River Adventures** and saved to the location where you are storing the files for this book, double-click **Create table in Design view**, type **Tour ID**, press [Tab], select the **AutoNumber** data type, then click the **Primary Key button** on the Standard toolbar

2. Click **File** on the menu bar, click **Save**, type **2006 Tour Bookings**, then enter the remaining field names and select the required data types as shown in Figure F-22

3. Switch to Datasheet view, save the table, enter the data for the table as shown in Figure F-23, then close the table

4. Click **Queries** in the Objects pane, double-click **Create query in Design view**, click **Add**, then click **Close**

5. Click **Tour Name** in the list of fields, press and hold the [Shift] key, scroll down, then click **Bookings**

6. Drag the selected fields into the query grid, click **File** on the menu bar, click **Save**, type **Total Bookings**, then click **OK**

7. Click the **blank field** to the right of Bookings, type **Total Revenue: [Tour Cost]*[Bookings]**, then press [Enter]
   The formula you entered will multiply the value in the Tour Cost field by the value in the Bookings field.

8. Click the **Run button** on the Standard toolbar
   The query calculates the total revenue from each tour as shown in Figure F-24.

9. Close and save the query

FIGURE F-22: Field names for 2006 Tour Bookings table

Field Name	Data Type	Description
Tour ID	AutoNumber	
Tour Name	Text	
Location	Text	
Date	Text	
Duration	Text	
Tour Cost	Currency	
Bookings	Number	

2006 Tour Bookings : Table

Field Properties

FIGURE F-23: Records for 2006 Tour Bookings table

2006 Tour Bookings : Table

Tour ID	Tour Name	Location	Date	Duration	Tour Cost	Bookings
1	Restigouche River	Quebec	June 10	5 days	$500.00	5
2	Matapedia River	Quebec	July 15	5 days	$650.00	8
3	Sand River	Ontario	June 25	5 days	$450.00	8
4	Chochocouane River	Quebec	July 5	5 days	$550.00	12
5	Dumoine River	Quebec	July 10	7 days	$800.00	5
6	Missinaibi River	Ontario	July 18	10 days	$900.00	5
7	Petawawa River	Ontario	July 25	8 days	$700.00	12
8	Coulonge River	Quebec	July 26	14 days	$1,300.00	8
9	Bonaventure River	Quebec	August 2	12 days	$1,200.00	3
10	Moisie River	Quebec	August 15	10 days	$1,100.00	9
(AutoNumber)					$0.00	0

Record: 11 of 11

FIGURE F-24: Total Bookings query

Total Bookings : Select Query

Tour Name	Location	Date	Duration	Tour Cost	Bookings	Total Revenue
Restigouche River	Quebec	June 10	5 days	$500.00	5	$2,500.00
Matapedia River	Quebec	July 15	5 days	$650.00	8	$5,200.00
Sand River	Ontario	June 25	5 days	$450.00	8	$3,600.00
Chochocouane River	Quebec	July 5	5 days	$550.00	12	$6,600.00
Dumoine River	Quebec	July 10	7 days	$800.00	5	$4,000.00
Missinaibi River	Ontario	July 18	10 days	$900.00	5	$4,500.00
Petawawa River	Ontario	July 25	8 days	$700.00	12	$8,400.00
Coulonge River	Quebec	July 26	14 days	$1,300.00	8	$10,400.00
Bonaventure River	Quebec	August 2	12 days	$1,200.00	3	$3,600.00
Moisie River	Quebec	August 15	10 days	$1,100.00	9	$9,900.00
*				$0.00	0	

Record: 1 of 10

WILD RIVER ADVENTURES DATA ACCESS PAGE

activity:

Create the Data Access Page

You need to create a data access page that includes fields from the 2006 Tour Bookings table.

steps:

Trouble

If the Watermark theme is not available, select a different theme.

1. Click **Pages** in the Objects pane, double-click **Create data access page by using wizard**, click the **Select All Fields button** [>>], click **Next**, click **Tour Name**, click the **Select Single Field button** [>], click **Next**, then click **Next**

   The page is automatically named 2006 Tour Bookings.

2. Click the check box next to **Do you want to apply a theme to your page?**, click **Finish**, scroll down and select the **Watermark** theme as shown in Figure F-25, then click **OK**

   The data access page appears in Design view.

3. Click the **Click here and type title text box** at the top of the window, type **Wild River Adventures Bookings** and your name, click the **View list arrow** [▣▾], then click **Page View**

   The data access page appears in Page view. All the fields included in the data access page are displayed for the selected record. You use the buttons on the Navigation toolbar to modify data, add or delete records, sort records, and filter records.

4. Click the **Next button** [▸] on the Navigation toolbar until **Missinaibi River** appears, then click the **Expand button** [+] next to Tour Name

5. Click the **Duration text box**, change the duration to **5 days**, click the **Tour Cost text box**, change the cost to **$500.00**, click the **Bookings text box**, then change the bookings to **6**

6. Compare the modified data access page to Figure F-26, click the **Save button** [▣] on the Record Navigation toolbar, then click the **Print button** [▤] on the Standard toolbar to print

   The data access page prints.

7. Click the **Save button** [▣] on the Standard toolbar, navigate to the location where you are saving the files for this book, click **Save**, click **OK** to accept each warning, then close the window to return to the Database window

Additional Practice

For additional practice with the skills presented in this project, complete Independent Challenge 3.

8. Click **Queries** in the Object pane, then double-click **Total Bookings**

9. Verify that the Missinaibi River tour now lasts for 5 days, costs $500, has 6 bookings, and has generated a total revenue of $3,000, close the table, then close the database and exit Access

FIGURE F-25: Selecting the Watermark theme

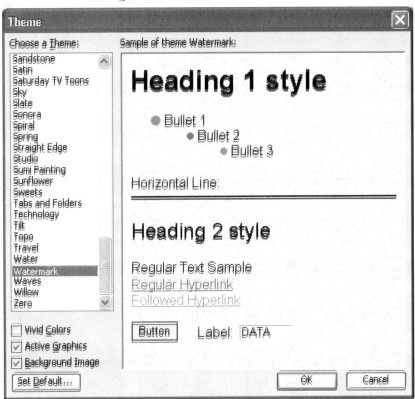

FIGURE F-26: Revised data access page

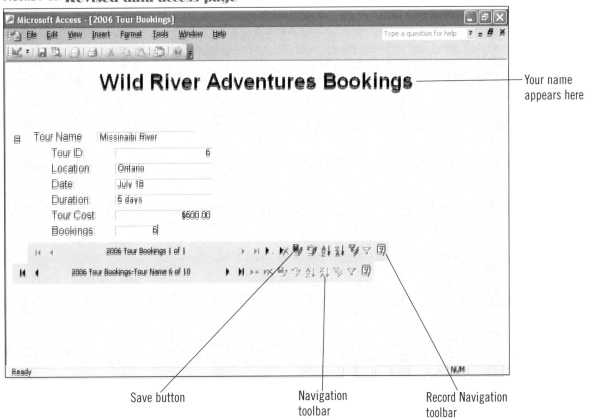

Your name appears here

Save button

Navigation toolbar

Record Navigation toolbar

Independent Challenges

Create a report based on tables that contain information about 20 to 30 products stocked by a company of your choice. Follow the steps provided to create the database, create a Products table and a Suppliers table, make two or three queries, and then create a report.

1. Choose a name for your company and determine the type of products it sells. For example, you could call your company Tee to Green and describe it as a retail operation that sells golf equipment and accessories, such as golf clubs, bags, shoes, umbrellas, and clothing. Write the name of your company and a brief description of the products it sells in the box below:

   Company name: _____

   Description: _____

   _____

   _____

2. Start Access, then create a database called **My Inventory**, and save it to the location where you are storing the files for this book.
3. Create a Products table. Use the Table Wizard to create a Products table similar to the table you created for Project 1. Include at least six fields, including the UnitsInStock field. If necessary, rename some of the fields to match the type of data you need to enter for the products in your company.
4. Create a Suppliers table, using the Form Wizard to enter the data. Include at least four fields. Make sure that at least one of the fields in the Suppliers table is the same as a field in the Products table. Use the Copy and Paste commands to minimize typing time.
5. Create a relationship between the two tables.
6. In the box below, write three queries you plan to make based on the Products and Suppliers tables. For example, you could ask which products are handled by a certain supplier, which products conform to a specific category, and which suppliers are located in a specific area. The queries you make will depend upon the type of data you included in your Products and Suppliers tables and the relationship you have created between the two tables.

   Query 1: _____

   _____

   Query 2: _____

   _____

   Query 3: _____

   _____

7. Use the Query Wizard to create the queries. Make sure you specify the criteria for each query in Design view.
8. Select the query table that you will use to create your inventory report.
9. Use the Report Wizard to create a report that will show items you need to reorder. Experiment with the many features available in Reports Design view. Remember that you will need to switch frequently between Reports Design view and the Print Preview screen to check your progress.
10. Be sure the report title includes your name, print the report, and then close the database.

INDEPENDENT CHALLENGE 2

Create an Events database that contains information about a series of related events, such as all the Vancouver-area running events in Spring 2006 or all the plays featured in a season. Plan and then create the database as follows.

1. Start Access, then create a database called **My Event**, and save it to the location where you are storing the files for this book.
2. Create a table by using a wizard, and then select Events from the Sample Tables list.
3. Plan your database on paper. Spend a fair bit of time planning your Events database so that when you begin working in Access, you will know exactly what kinds of fields and records you need in order to create the type of report you require.
   a. Write down the fields from the Events sample table that you plan to include in your table.
   b. Determine additional fields for a second table.
   c. Ensure that the two tables share one common record; use that common record to create a one-to-many relationship between the two tables. Recall that in a one-to-many relationship a field in one table can include one or many entries in the related table. For example, the Vancouver-area running events database could contain two tables: one listing the Event Name, Location, StartDate, StartTime, CostPerPerson, and a new field named CategoryID; and the other including CategoryID, RaceDistance (5K, 10K, marathon, etc.), and AvailableSpaces. Figure F-27 shows how these two tables could be related through the CategoryID field.

FIGURE F-27: Running Events tables

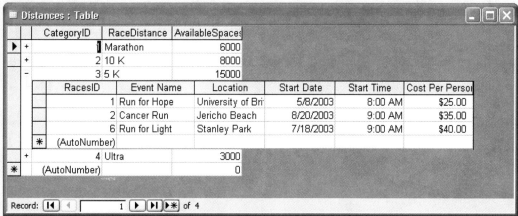

   d. Determine two or three queries that you could make based on the data in the two tables.
   e. Identify the information that you would like to show in a report. For example, you could create a report that lists all the 10K running events held in June.
4. Create the tables required for your database.
5. Establish a relationship between the tables.
6. Make two or three queries based on the data in the two tables.
7. Create and print an attractively formatted report based on one of the query tables you created. Include your name in the report title.

INDEPENDENT CHALLENGE 3

Create a database called **My Sales Information** *that contains information about all the sales made in the past month by a company of your choice, and then generate a data access page. Suppose, for example, that you owned a pet store. You could create a table called Pet Sales that appears similar to the table shown in Figure F-28.*

Once you have created a table in your database, create a data access page containing all of the fields contained in the table. Apply the theme of your choice. Add a title to the page and your name. Change some of the data in the data access page, save it as **Sales.htm** *to the location where you are storing the files for this book, then check the table in Access to verify that the changes have been made. Print a copy of the data access page and a copy of the changed table.*

FIGURE F-28: *Sales table*

	ID	Sales Date	Animal	Category	Price
	1	10/1/2006	Spaniel Puppy	Dog	$450.00
	2	10/2/2006	Persian Kitten	Cat	$230.00
	3	10/4/2006	Gerbil	Rodent	$15.00
	4	10/5/2006	Parrot	Bird	$100.00
	5	10/5/2006	Budgie	Bird	$120.00
	6	10/7/2006	Iguana	Reptile	$75.00
	7	10/10/2006	Basset Hound Puppy	Dog	$400.00
	8	10/11/2006	Siamese Kitten	Cat	$350.00
	9	10/12/2006	Terrier	Dog	$600.00
	10	10/15/2006	Ferret	Rodent	$20.00
▶	(ber)				$0.00

Record: ◄◄ ◄ 11 ► ►► ►* of 11

INDEPENDENT CHALLENGE 4

You've decided that you would like to investigate the possibility of studying in a foreign country for a summer, an academic term, or even a full year. From the hundreds of programs offered, you need to select one that suits your academic interests and is located in a country to which you want to travel. To help you choose the best program, you will search the World Wide Web for information about programs for studying abroad, and then you will create an Access database that contains data related to at least three programs.

1. Start Access, then create a database called **Study Abroad**, and save it to the location where you are storing the files for this book.
2. In Design view, enter field names and select data types as shown in Figure F-29. Note that the data type for the Description field is Memo. You select this data type so that you can enter several lines of text into the table. The data type for the Web Address field is Hyperlink. When you copy the address of a Web page into this field it will be formatted as a hyperlink that you can click and follow to open the related Web page.

FIGURE F-29: Field names and data types for Study Abroad Programs table

3. Save the table with the name **Study Abroad Programs**.
4. Connect to the Internet and then conduct a search for studying abroad programs. Use keywords such as **study abroad**, **international study**, and **overseas study**. To narrow your search further, include the field of study and location that interests you. For example, you could search for "art history programs in Italy." You could also explore study abroad Web sites such as www.studyabroad.com.
5. Identify a field of study and two or three countries that interest you. For example, you could decide to investigate archeological study programs in Italy, France, and Israel, or anthropology programs in Belize, Mexico, and Ecuador.
6. Explore some of the Web sites you've found to gather information about three programs that you think look interesting. As you explore the sites, copy and paste relevant information to the Study Abroad Programs table in the Study Abroad database. Note that you can copy and then edit a paragraph of text into the Description field because you chose the Memo data type, which allows you to enter unlimited text. You will need to follow several links to find the information required for each program. In some cases, you will not find all the information; for example, you may not be able to find cost information. You can enter N/A where applicable in the table.
7. For the Web Address field, enter the Web page address (URL) of the page that contains most of the information you've gathered about a particular program. To copy a URL, click the Address box in your browser, press [Ctrl][C], return to Access, click the appropriate cell in the Web Address field, and then press [Ctrl][V]. The Web site address appears as a hyperlink because you selected the Hyperlink data type for the field.
8. When you have gathered information about at least three programs, create a report. Include your name on the report. Select Landscape orientation, the Align Left 1 layout, and the style of your choice.
9. Format the report attractively, print a copy, and then close the Study Abroad database.

Visual Workshop

Start Access, and then create a database called **Staff Travel** using the table shown in Figure F-30. Save the database to the location where you are storing the files for this book. Create a data access page that designates the Region field as the grouping level and uses the Capsules theme. Include your name in the title. Navigate to the records for the Europe region, then modify the record for Ron Vernon as shown in Figure F-31. Print a copy of the data access page, save the changes, save the data access page as Travel Expenses.htm, and then close the database and exit Access.

FIGURE F-30: Travel Expenses table

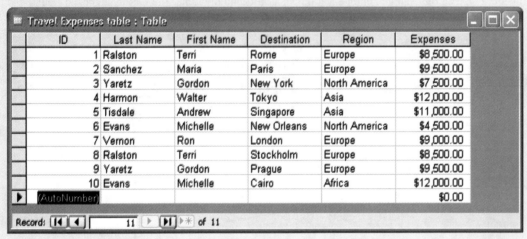

	ID	Last Name	First Name	Destination	Region	Expenses
	1	Ralston	Terri	Rome	Europe	$8,500.00
	2	Sanchez	Maria	Paris	Europe	$9,500.00
	3	Yaretz	Gordon	New York	North America	$7,500.00
	4	Harmon	Walter	Tokyo	Asia	$12,000.00
	5	Tisdale	Andrew	Singapore	Asia	$11,000.00
	6	Evans	Michelle	New Orleans	North America	$4,500.00
	7	Vernon	Ron	London	Europe	$9,000.00
	8	Ralston	Terri	Stockholm	Europe	$8,500.00
	9	Yaretz	Gordon	Prague	Europe	$9,500.00
	10	Evans	Michelle	Cairo	Africa	$12,000.00
	(AutoNumber)					$0.00

Record: 11 of 11

FIGURE F-31: Travel Expenses data access page

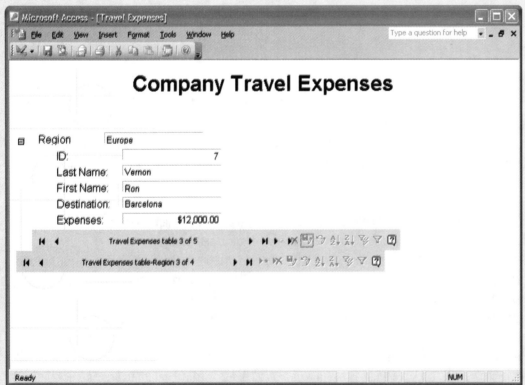

Microsoft Access - [Travel Expenses]

File Edit View Insert Format Tools Window Help

Company Travel Expenses

Region   Europe

ID: 7
Last Name: Vernon
First Name: Ron
Destination: Barcelona
Expenses: $12,000.00

Travel Expenses table 3 of 5

Travel Expenses table-Region 3 of 4

Ready   NUM

Microsoft
► Word, Excel, and Access
Projects

Unit **G**

Integration Projects II

In this Unit You Will Create the Following:

Job Search Database

Proposal for Eco Smart Cosmetics

Art Collection Catalogue

You can use Word, Access, and Excel in a variety of ways in order to perform business tasks quickly and easily. The key is to use each program in the Office suite efficiently. You often start by building an Access database that contains the names and addresses of customers and suppliers, information about inventory, and sales records. You can then combine the database information in Word to produce form letters, labels, and other documents such as reports and proposals. You can also analyze database information in Excel so that you can then create charts and spreadsheets. In this unit you will use Access, Word, and Excel to create a variety of common business documents.

PROJECT 1

Job Search Database for Wendy Trent

Wendy Trent needs to find a job in the Miami area as an office manager or management trainee. To help coordinate her job search efforts, you need to Create the Contacts Table, Create the Results Form, Create the Job Application Letter, and then Analyze the Job Search Results. The form letter is shown in Figure G-10 on page 155.

activity:

Create the Contacts Table

First, you need to create the Job Search database, and then you need to create a table to contain information about Wendy's job contacts. You design the Contacts table to include a lookup field.

steps:

1. Start Access, click **Create a new file** in the Getting Started task pane, click **Blank database** in the New File task pane, navigate to the location where you are storing the files for this book, type **Job Search** in the File name text box, then click **Create**

2. Double-click **Create table in Design view**, type **Job ID**, press **[Tab]**, click the **Data Type list arrow**, click **AutoNumber**, then click the **Primary Key button** 🔑 on the Standard toolbar

3. Click the **Save button** 🖫 on the Standard toolbar, type **Contacts**, click **OK**, click **below Job ID**, then enter the remaining fields as shown in Figure G-1

Hint

Wendy makes Miami, FL the default value because every company she has contacted is located in Miami.

4. Click the **Data Type cell** for City/State, click the **Default Value text box** in the General tab of the Field Properties area, then type **"Miami, FL"** including the quotation marks

5. Click the **Data Type cell** for Position, click the **list arrow**, click **Lookup Wizard**, click the **I will type in the values that I want option button**, then click **Next**

6. Click **below Col 1**, type **Junior Manager**, press the **[↓]**, type **Trainee**, enter the remaining positions as shown in Figure G-2, then click **Finish**

7. Click the **View list arrow** 🔽 on the Standard toolbar, click **Datasheet View**, then click **Yes**

8. Press **[Tab]** to move to the First Name field, type **Andrea**, press **[Tab]**, type **Black**, press **[Tab]**, type **100 Main Street**, press **[Tab]** two times (Miami, FL will be entered automatically), type **33172**, press **[Tab]**, type **First Fashions**, press **[Tab]**, click the **list arrow**, then select **Trainee**

9. Enter the data for the remaining records in the Contacts table as shown in Figure G-3, adjust column widths as needed, then close and save the table

FIGURE G-1: Field names for the Contacts table

Contacts : Table		
Field Name	**Data Type**	**Description**
🔑 Job ID	AutoNumber	
First Name	Text	
Last Name	Text	
Address	Text	
City/State	Text	
Zip	Text	
Company Name	Text	
▶ Position	Text	

FIGURE G-2: Lookup Wizard

Lookup Wizard

What values do you want to see in your lookup column? Enter the number of columns you want in the list, and then type the values you want in each cell.

To adjust the width of a column, drag its right edge to the width you want, or double-click the right edge of the column heading to get the best fit.

Number of columns: 1

	Col1
	Junior Manager
	Trainee
	Sales Trainee
✔	Office Manager
✱	

Cancel   « Back   Next »   Finish

FIGURE G-3: Records for the Contacts table

Contacts : Table							
Job ID	First Name	Last Name	Address	City/State	Zip	Company Name	Position
1	Andrea	Black	100 Main Street	Miami, FL	33172	First Fashions	Trainee
2	Derek	Chang	24 Front Street	Miami, FL	33133	Datalink	Sales Trainee
3	Maria	Sanchez	68 West Road	Miami, FL	33134	Techno Works	Junior Manager
4	Lewis	Eliot	202 State Street	Miami, FL	33135	Coral Utilities	Sales Trainee
5	Harriet	Weber	180 1st Street	Miami, FL	33165	Florida Insurance	Office Manager
6	Jason	Lynx	440 7th Avenue	Miami, FL	33167	Southeast Foods	Junior Manager
7	Karen	Morrison	400 Byron Place	Miami, FL	33156	Express Freight	Trainee
8	Marianne	Tilney	303 2nd Avenue	Miami, FL	33178	Key West Foods	Junior Manager
9	Ramon	Ramirez	200 Palm Drive	Miami, FL	33165	Everglades Foods	Office Manager
▶ (AutoNumber)				Miami, FL			

Record: |◀ ◀ 10 ▶ ▶| ▶✱ of 10

activity:

Create the Results Form

You need to create a form that Wendy can use to keep track of the results of her job search efforts. The form needs to include all the fields from the Contacts table as well as two new fields. One field is a check box that Wendy can click if she receives a positive response to her job application; the other field is a Date/Time field that Wendy can use to enter each interview date. You create the form in Design view so that you can customize its appearance.

steps:

1. Double-click Contacts to open the Contacts table, switch to Design view, click below Position, type Response, press [Tab], click the Data Type list arrow, then click Yes/No
   The Yes/No data type inserts a check box in the field.

2. Press [Tab] twice, type Interview Date, press [Tab], select the Date/Time data type, click the Format text box in the General tab, click the list arrow and select Medium Date, then close and save the Contacts table

3. Click Forms in the Objects pane, click New, click the list arrow and select Contacts as shown in Figure G-4, then click OK
   A blank grid appears. You use the grid and rulers to position the labels and text boxes representing the fields from the Contacts table.

4. Click Job ID in the Contacts field list, press and hold [Shift], scroll down, then click Interview Date so that all the fields are selected

5. Drag the selected fields to the design grid so the left edge of the labels lines up with 2 on the horizontal ruler bar and the top edge lines up with .5 on the vertical ruler bar as shown in Figure G-5

Trouble

When the label box is selected, you should see the grid behind the label text.

6. Click the Label button ![Aa] in the Toolbox, point just below 1 on the horizontal ruler bar, click and drag to create a box between 1 and 4 that is approximately .4" in height, type Job Search Results, click a blank area of the grid, click the label, then format the text as shown in the completed form in Figure G-6

7. Click the text box for Job ID, drag to reduce the width to approximately .5" as shown in Figure G-6, then modify the widths of the other text boxes as shown in Figure G-6

8. Switch to Form view, click the Response check box in form 1 for First Fashions, enter June 1 as the interview date, click the Next Record button ![▶] on the Navigation bar twice to move to form 3, then enter the responses and the dates for selected records as shown below:

Company Name	Response	Interview Date
Techno Works	Yes	June 2
Coral Utilities	Yes	June 3
Florida Insurance	Yes	June 6
Everglades Foods	Yes	June 8

9. Click the Save button ![💾] on the Standard toolbar, type Job Search Results, click OK, compare the form for Everglades Foods to Figure G-7, then close the form

FIGURE G-4: **Selecting the Contacts table**

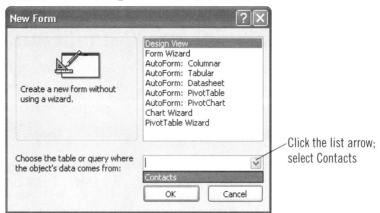

Click the list arrow;
select Contacts

FIGURE G-5: **Positioning fields on the design grid**

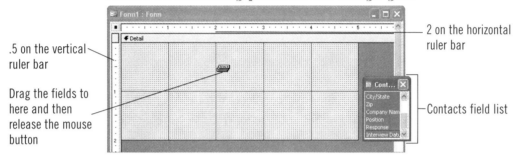

.5 on the vertical
ruler bar

Drag the fields to
here and then
release the mouse
button

2 on the horizontal
ruler bar

Contacts field list

FIGURE G-6: **Completed form in Design view**

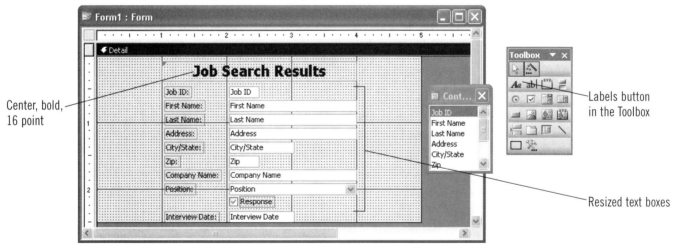

Center, bold,
16 point

Labels button
in the Toolbox

Resized text boxes

FIGURE G-7: **Completed form for Everglades Foods in Form view**

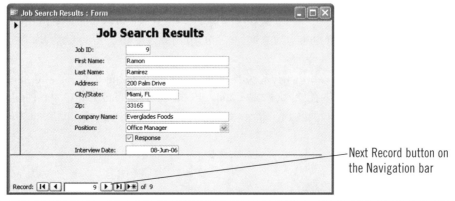

Next Record button on
the Navigation bar

activity:

Create the Job Application Letter

You need to switch to Word and create the letter that Wendy plans to send to each job prospect. You then need to merge the letter with the Job Search database to produce individually addressed letters.

steps:

Hint

Text in square brackets is placeholder text for the merge fields.

1. Start Word, navigate to the location where you are storing the files for this book, open **Application Letter.doc**, then save the document as **Job Search Form Letter**

2. Close the document and Word, return to Access, click **Tables** in the Objects pane, verify that Contacts is selected, click the **OfficeLinks list arrow** 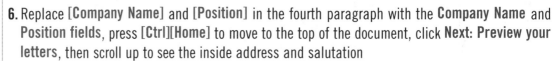 on the Standard toolbar, click **Merge It with Microsoft Office Word**, click **OK** to use an existing Microsoft Word document, navigate to the location where you are storing the files for this book, click **Job Search Form Letter.doc**, then click **Open**

   Word starts with the Mail Merge task pane open.

Trouble

If a warning appears, click OK, then close and reopen the database.

3. Verify that Use an existing list is selected in the Mail Merge task pane, click **Next: Write your letter**, replace **Current Date** in the letter with the current date, press **[Enter]** twice, click **Address block** in the task pane, then click **OK**

   When you run the mail merge, the address will be inserted in place of the field code.

4. Click after **Dear** in the letter, click **Greeting line** in the task pane, then click **OK**

5. Select **[Position]** in the first paragraph, click **More items** in the Mail Merge task pane, click **Position**, click **Insert**, click **Close**, press **[Spacebar]** if needed, select **[Company Name]**, then replace it with the **Company Name** field

6. Replace **[Company Name]** and **[Position]** in the fourth paragraph with the **Company Name** and **Position fields**, press **[Ctrl][Home]** to move to the top of the document, click **Next: Preview your letters**, then scroll up to see the inside address and salutation

   As you can see, the address and salutation appear incorrectly. Trainee Andrea Black is the name, the city and state are missing, and the salutation includes "Dear" two times.

Hint

Click the expand arrow at the bottom of the Mail Merge task pane to expand it.

7. Click **Previous: Write your letter**, select **<<AddressBlock>>** in the letter, press **[Delete]**, click **Address block** in the Mail Merge task pane, click **Match Fields**, make changes in the Match Fields dialog box as shown in Figure G-8, click **OK**, click **OK**, then press **[Enter]** if necessary

8. Select and delete **<<GreetingLine>>**, click **Greeting line** in the task pane, make changes to the Greeting line dialog box as shown in Figure G-9, then click **OK**

9. Click **Next: Preview your letters**, verify that the address and salutation text appear as shown in Figure G-10, click **Next: Complete the merge**, click **Print**, type 1 in the From box, type 2 in the To box, click **OK**, click **OK**, close the merged letters without saving them, then save and close the document

FIGURE G-8: Match Fields dialog box

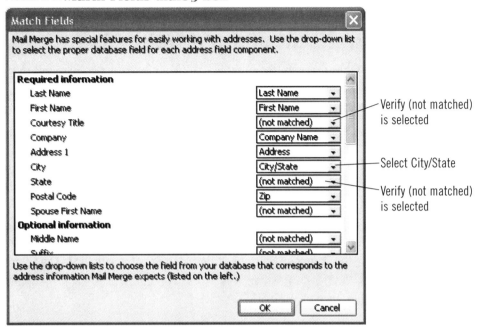

Verify (not matched) is selected

Select City/State

Verify (not matched) is selected

FIGURE G-9: Greeting Line dialog box

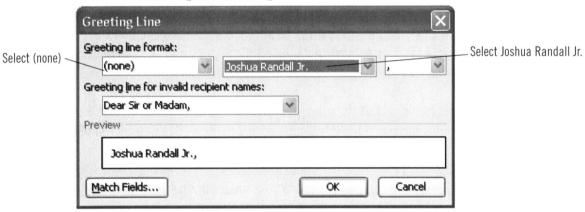

Select (none)

Select Joshua Randall Jr.

FIGURE G-10: Letter for Andrea Black

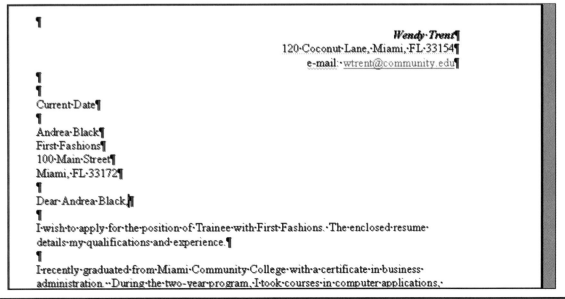

activity:

Analyze the Job Search Results

All of the companies that interviewed Wendy have offered her employment. Now she needs to decide which company to accept. To help her make a wise decision, you create a query table in Access that lists only those companies that interviewed her. Then you need to add several new fields that can be used to rank each company in terms of its location, pay, benefits, and opportunities for advancement. Wendy decides on a rating scale as follows: 3=Poor, 6=Good, 9=Excellent. Once you have completed the table, you need to analyze it in Excel and then create a chart to illustrate the overall ranking for each company.

steps:

1. Return to Access, click **Queries** in the Objects pane, double-click **Create query by using wizard**, move the **Company Name**, **Position**, and **Response** fields to the Selected Fields list box, click **Next**, click **Next**, type **Positive Results** as the query title, click the **Modify the query design option button**, then click **Finish**

2. Click the **Response Criteria cell**, type **Yes**, then click the **Run button** ! on the Standard toolbar
   All five of the companies that responded positively to Wendy's form letter appear.

3. Select the **Company Name** and **Position columns**, click the **Copy button** 🖹 on the Standard toolbar, close the query, click **Yes** to save changes, click **Tables** in the Objects pane, double-click **Create table by entering data**, select the **Field1** and **Field2** columns, click the **Paste button** 🖺 on the Standard toolbar, then click **Yes** to paste the records

4. Double-click **Field1**, type **Company Name**, double-click **Field2**, type **Position**, increase the column widths, then enter the labels and records for fields 3 to 6 as shown in Figure G-11

5. Close the table, save it as **Ratings**, click **Yes** to create a Primary Key, click **Ratings**, click the **OfficeLinks list arrow** 🗐 ▾ on the Standard toolbar, then click **Analyze It with Microsoft Office Excel**
   In a few moments, Excel launches.

6. Select cells **D2:H6**, click the **AutoSum button** Σ on the Standard toolbar, then click away from the selected cells

7. Click the **Chart Wizard button** 📊 on the Standard toolbar, click **Next**, click the **Collapse Dialog Box button** 📉, select cells **B2:B6**, type a **comma (,)**, then select cells **H2:H6**

8. Click the **Restore Dialog Box button** 🗔, click **Next**, click the **Chart title text box**, type **Employer Ratings** as the chart title, click the **Legend tab**, click the **Show legend check box** to deselect it, then click **Finish**

Additional Practice

For additional practice with the skills presented in this project, complete Independent Challenge 1.

9. Increase the size of the column chart so that all the data is clearly visible as shown in Figure G-12, print a copy of the worksheet, save and close the worksheet, close the database, then exit all programs
   Wendy can see at a glance that the job offered by Coral Utilities most closely matches her employment criteria.

FIGURE G-11: **Records for Ratings table**

	Company Name	Position	Location	Pay	Benefits	Advancement
	First Fashions	Trainee	3	3	6	3
	Techno Works	Junior Manager	3	3	3	3
	Coral Utilities	Sales Trainee	9	6	9	9
	Florida Insurance	Office Manager	6	3	3	3
▶	Everglades Foods	Office Manager	9	6	3	3

Table1 : Table

Record: 5 of 21

FIGURE G-12: **Completed chart in Excel**

Proposal for Eco Smart Cosmetics

You are the owner of Eco Smart Cosmetics, a small business that sells organically made beauty products. To increase sales, you've decided to propose a partnership with Fountain Spa, a local health resort. To create the proposal, you need to **Import an Excel Workbook, Create the Proposal in Word,** and then **Add Excel and Access Objects to Word.** The three pages of the completed proposal are shown in Figure G-19 on page 163.

activity:

Import an Excel Workbook

The owner of Fountain Spa has asked Eco Smart Cosmetics to supply a product database. Information about the aromatherapy products that most interest Fountain Spa is currently stored in an Excel workbook. You need to import the Excel data into a table in an Access database that contains information about the other products distributed by Eco Smart Cosmetics.

steps:

1. Start Access, then create a new database called **Partnership Products.mdb** and saved to the location where you are storing the files for this book

2. Double-click **Create table in Design view**, type **Product #**, press [Tab], select the **Number data type**, click the **Primary Key button** 🔑 on the Standard toolbar, save the table as **Products**, then enter the remaining fields as shown in Figure G-13

3. Switch to Datasheet view, enter the data as shown in Figure G-14, then close and save the table

4. Start Excel, open the file **Eco Smart Products.xls** from the location where you are saving the files for this book, then save the file as **Partnership Data.xls**

   The worksheet contains three columns. Before you can import this worksheet into the Access table, you need to ensure that both the Excel worksheet and the Access table contain the exact same column headings and data types.

5. Select **column C**, click the **right mouse button**, click Insert, type **Category** in cell **C1**, click cell **C2**, type **Essential Oil**, then drag the fill handle to cell **C32** to fill all the cells with the Essential Oil label

6. Save and close the workbook, return to the Partnership Products database window in Access, click **File** on the menu bar, point to **Get External Data**, then click **Import**

7. Navigate to the location where you are storing the files for this book, click the **Files of Type** list arrow, click **Microsoft Excel (*.xls)**, click **Partnership Data.xls**, then click **Import**

8. Click **Next**, click **Next**, click the **In an Existing Table option button**, click the **list arrow**, click **Products**, click **Next**, click **Finish**, then click **OK**

9. Double-click the **Products** table to open it, verify that the records from the Excel workbook appear as shown in Figure G-15, scroll down to view the records you entered, then close the table

Hint

If prompted to save, click Yes.

FIGURE G-13: **Fields for the Products table**

Field Name	Data Type	Description
Product #	Number	
Description	Text	
Category	Text	
Price	Currency	

Select the Currency data type

FIGURE G-14: **Records for the Products table**

Product #	Description	Category	Price
7888	Peppermint Bath Oil	Bath	$4.50
7889	Lavender Spray	Bath	$5.50
7890	Citrus Wash	Cleansing	$6.50
7891	Lemon Mist	Cleansing	$4.50
7892	Raspberry Wash	Cleansing	$5.50
7893	Mango-Papaya Spray	Bath	$6.50
7894	Sage Bath Oil	Bath	$5.50
7895	Green Apple Soap	Cleansing	$4.50
7896	Orange Body Scrub	Cleansing	$5.50
			$0.00

Record: 10 of 10

FIGURE G-15: **Excel data imported into the Products table**

Product #	Description	Category	Price
3550	Anise Seed	Essential Oil	$7.50
3551	Basil	Essential Oil	$7.00
3552	Cedarwood	Essential Oil	$5.50
3553	Clary Sage	Essential Oil	$6.50
3554	Clove	Essential Oil	$5.50
3555	Coriander	Essential Oil	$6.00
3556	Cypress	Essential Oil	$6.00
3557	Eucalyptus	Essential Oil	$5.50
3558	Fir Balsam	Essential Oil	$5.00
3559	Frankincense	Essential Oil	$5.50
3560	Geranium	Essential Oil	$6.00
3561	Ginger	Essential Oil	$5.50
3562	Grapefruit	Essential Oil	$5.50
3563	Hyssop	Essential Oil	$5.50
3564	Jasmine	Essential Oil	$6.00
3565	Juniper	Essential Oil	$6.50
3566	Lavender	Essential Oil	$6.00
3567	Lemon	Essential Oil	$5.50
3568	Lemon Grass	Essential Oil	$5.00
3569	Lime	Essential Oil	$5.00
3570	Myrrh	Essential Oil	$7.00

Record: 1 of 40

activity:

Create the Proposal in Word

The proposal consists of three pages that include objects copied from Excel and Access. First, you need to set up the document in Word and then insert the text. You will insert the objects in the next lesson.

steps:

1. Start Word, change the Left margin to **2.5** and the Right margin to **1**, then save the document as **Partnership Proposal.doc** to the location where you are storing the files for this book

2. Show the Drawing toolbar, click **View** on the menu bar, click **Header and Footer**, click the **Insert WordArt button** ▲ on the Drawing toolbar, click **OK**, type **Proposal**, select the **Arial** font, click the **Bold button** **B**, click the **Italic button** *I*, then click **OK**

3. Click the **WordArt object** to select it, click the **Format WordArt button** ✍ on the WordArt toolbar, then, as shown in Figure G-16, select **Gray-25%**, change the transparency to **50%**, and remove the border line

Trouble

Drag the sizing handles to adjust the width and height of the WordArt object.

4. Click **OK**, click the **WordArt Vertical Text button** ᵇᵇ on the WordArt toolbar, click the **Text Wrapping button** ▥ on the WordArt toolbar, click **Square**, switch to Whole Page view, then size and position the WordArt object as shown in Figure G-17

5. Switch back to 100% view, click the **Switch Between Header and Footer button** 🖰 on the Header and Footer toolbar, type your name at the left margin, press **[Tab]** twice, click the **Insert Page Number button** 🔢 on the Header and Footer toolbar, drag the **Right tab marker** on the horizontal ruler to the left until it is even with the right edge of the footer, then click **Close** on the Header and Footer toolbar

6. Click **Insert** on the menu bar, click **File**, navigate to the location where you are storing the files for this book, then double-click **Partnership Proposal Text.doc**

The text required for the proposal is inserted into the document.

7. Scroll to the top of the document, select **INTRODUCTION**, click the **Styles and Formatting button** 🔠 on the Formatting toolbar, then click **Heading 1**

8. Format all the headings in uppercase with the Heading 1 style, then format all the headings in title case with the Heading 2 style

Figure G-18 shows some of the formatted headings.

9. Close the Styles and Formatting task pane, then save the document

FIGURE G-16: Formatting options for the WordArt object

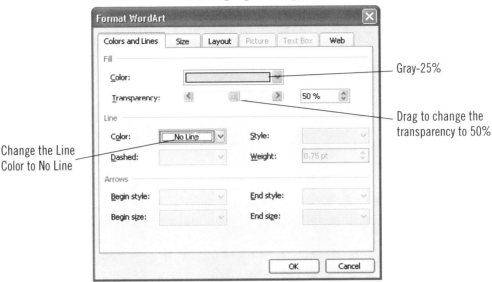

Gray-25%

Drag to change the transparency to 50%

Change the Line Color to No Line

FIGURE G-17: Completed WordArt object in Whole Page view

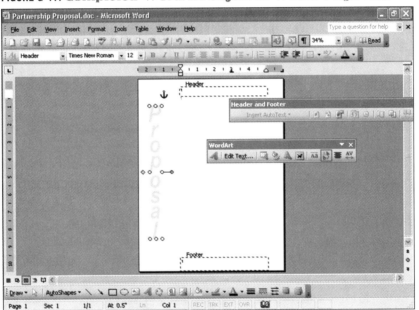

FIGURE G-18: Heading styles applied to selected text

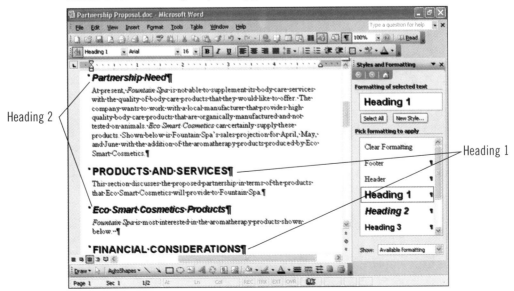

Heading 2

Heading 1

PROPOSAL FOR ECO SMART COSMETICS

activity:

Add Excel and Access Objects to Word

To produce the three pages of the completed proposal shown in Figure G-19, you need to insert spreadsheet data, create a query table in Access and publish it in Word, copy a chart from Excel, and finally, generate a table of contents.

steps:

1. Switch to Excel, open the file **Fountain Spa.xls** from the location where you are storing the files for this book, save the file as **Fountain Spa Partnership Data.xls**, select cells **A1:E14**, click the **Copy button** on the Standard toolbar, switch to Word, click at the end of the **Partnership Need paragraph**, press [Enter] twice, then click the **Paste button** on the Standard toolbar

2. Switch to Access, click **Queries** in the Objects pane, double-click **Create query by using wizard**, move all the records in the Products table to the Selected Fields list box, click **Next**, click **Next**, then click **Finish**

3. Switch to Design view, type **Essential Oil** in the Criteria cell for Category, click the **Run button**, then close and save the query

4. Click the **OfficeLinks list arrow** on the Standard toolbar, then click **Publish It with Microsoft Office Word**

   The table is pasted into a new document named Products Query.rtf.

5. Select the **table**, click , click **Window** on the menu bar, click **Partnership Proposal**, click at the end of the **Eco Smart Cosmetics Products paragraph** on page 2, press [Enter] twice, then click

6. Select the table, click **Table** on the menu bar, click **Table AutoFormat**, select the **Table Columns 1** format, click **Apply**, double-click the **column divider** between Category and Price to automatically reduce the widths of all the columns, then click the **Center button** on the Formatting toolbar

7. Switch to Excel, click the **Projected Revenue tab**, select cells **A1:E3**, click the **Chart Wizard button** on the Standard toolbar, then create the chart shown on page 3 of the completed proposal

8. Click the **chart** in Excel (make sure the ScreenTip says "Chart Area" when you click), click , switch to the Word Partnership Proposal document, click at the end of the **Projected Revenues paragraph**, press [Enter] twice, then click

Additional Practice

For additional practice with the skills presented in this project, complete Independent Challenge 2.

9. Type **ECO SMART COSMETICS AND FOUNTAIN SPA** at the top of the document as shown in Figure G-19, add a **page break** above the FINANCIAL CONSIDERATIONS heading if it does not start on a new page, print a copy of the completed proposal, save and close the document, then save and close all files and all programs

FIGURE G-19: Completed Partnership Proposal

Excel chart

Access table

Excel table

ECO SMART COSMETICS AND FOUNTAIN SPA

INTRODUCTION

Eco Smart Cosmetics has an opportunity to partner with *Fountain Spa*, a salon-style service that provides body care treatments. This proposal describes the partnership issues in terms of three factors: Partnership Requirements, Products and Services, and Financial Considerations.

PARTNERSHIP REQUIREMENTS

This section provides background information about *Fountain Spa* and discusses how the partnership could benefit both companies.

Background Information

Fountain Spa has made steady progress in a receptive marketplace. It specializes in providing a broad range of affordable and ecologically sensitive body care services. This focus on ecology has led *Fountain Spa* to seek out distributors and other related companies with similar commitments to the environment.

Partnership Need

At present, *Fountain Spa* is not able to supplement its body care services with the quality of body care products that they would like to offer. The company wants to work with a local manufacturer that provides high quality body care products that are organically manufactured and not tested on animals. *Eco Smart Cosmetics* can certainly supply these products. Shown below is Fountain Spa's sales projection for April, May, and June with the addition of the aromatherapy products produced by Eco Smart Cosmetics.

Fountain Spa
Sales Projection

	April	May	June	Total
Revenue				
Aromatherapy Products	$50,000.00	$45,000.00	$80,000.00	$175,000.00
Spa Treatments	$80,000.00	$110,000.00	$130,000.00	$180,000.00
	$130,000.00	$155,000.00	$210,000.00	$495,000.00
Expenses				
Salaries	$14,000.00	$14,000.00	$14,000.00	$42,000.00
Advertising 15.0	00.00	15,000.00	15,000.00	45,000.00
Operating Costs	18,000.00	18,000.00	18,000.00	54,000.00
Cost of Sales 60%	78,000.00	93,000.00	126,000.00	297,000.00
Total Expenses	$125,000.00	$140,000.00	$173,000.00	$438,000.00
Net Revenue	$5,000.00	$15,000.00	$37,000.00	$57,000.00

Your Name

1

PRODUCTS AND SERVICES

This section discusses the proposed partnership in terms of the products that Eco Smart Cosmetics will provide to Fountain Spa.

Eco Smart Cosmetics Products

Fountain Spa is most interested in the aromatherapy products shown below.

Product #	Description	Category	Price
3550	Anise Seed	Essential Oil	$7.50
3551	Basil	Essential Oil	$7.00
3552	Cedarwood	Essential Oil	$5.50
3553	Clary Sage	Essential Oil	$6.50
3554	Clove	Essential Oil	$5.50
3555	Coriander	Essential Oil	$6.00
3556	Cypress	Essential Oil	$6.00
3557	Eucalyptus	Essential Oil	$5.50
3558	Fir Balsam	Essential Oil	$5.50
3559	Frankincense	Essential Oil	$5.50
3560	Geranium	Essential Oil	$6.00
3561	Ginger	Essential Oil	$5.50
3562	Grapefruit	Essential Oil	$5.50
3563	Hyssop	Essential Oil	$6.00
3564	Jasmine	Essential Oil	$6.50
3565	Juniper	Essential Oil	$6.00
3566	Lavender	Essential Oil	$5.50
3567	Lemon	Essential Oil	$6.00
3568	Lemon Grass	Essential Oil	$5.00
3569	Lime	Essential Oil	$5.00
3570	Myrrh	Essential Oil	$7.00
3571	Patchouli	Essential Oil	$6.50
3572	Peppermint	Essential Oil	$6.00
3573	Pine Needle	Essential Oil	$4.50
3574	Rosemary	Essential Oil	$5.00
3575	Rosewood	Essential Oil	$4.50
3576	Sandalwood	Essential Oil	$7.00
3577	Spearmint	Essential Oil	$5.00
3578	Tea Tree	Essential Oil	$5.50
3579	Vanilla	Essential Oil	$5.50
3580	Ylang Ylang	Essential Oil	$6.50

Your Name

2

FINANCIAL CONSIDERATIONS

Fountain Spa has provided information related to the sales of products it received from its former distributor, Beauty Care, Inc. Based on this information, *Eco Smart Cosmetics* could expect a minimum 20% increase in revenues on the sale of products used by *Fountain Spa*.

Projected Revenues

The column chart illustrated below shows the revenues projected for each quarter in the first year of the proposed partnership with *Fountain Spa*.

CONCLUSION

Eco Smart Cosmetics has the opportunity to increase its market share by partnering with *Fountain Spa*. Both companies are seriously committed to the environment and to providing their customers with high quality body care products and services. The market is growing daily as more and more consumers recognize the value of products that promote relaxation and well-being.

Your Name

3

Art Collection Catalogue

As the office manager of the Pacific Crest Art Gallery, you decide to create a database that lists the art pieces currently being shown at the gallery, produce identification labels to affix to each piece, and create a chart showing the breakdown of paintings by price category. First, you need to Create the Art Database and Set Up the Merge, and then you need to Merge the Labels and Create a Chart.

activity:

Create the Art Database and Set Up the Merge

You need to create the database by copying a table from Word. Then you need to create a query and merge the data in the query with identification labels you create in Word.

steps:

1. Create a new database called **Art Collection.mdb** and saved to the location where you are storing the files for this book, then double-click **Create table by entering data**

2. Open Word, open **Art Collection.doc** from the location where you are storing the files for this book, select the **table**, click the **Copy button** on the Standard toolbar, switch to **Table1: Table** in Access, select the **first 7 columns**, click the **Paste button**, then click **Yes**
   The column labels appear as the first record in the pasted data.

3. Right-click to the left of **row 1**, click **Delete Record**, click **Yes**, replace the Field labels with the labels and adjust column widths as shown in Figure G-20, close the table, save it as **Art List**, then click **Yes** to create a primary key

4. Click **Queries** in the Objects pane, double-click **Create query by using wizard**, select all the fields *except* the ID and Price Category fields, click **Next**, click **Next**, name the query **Identification Labels**, then click **Finish**

5. Switch to **Design view**, click the **Date Sort cell**, click the **list arrow**, select **Ascending**, click the **Run button** on the Standard toolbar, close and save the query, then close the database

Hint

If a warning appears, click Yes, then click Open.

6. Open **Art Collection.mdb**, click the **OfficeLinks list arrow**, click **Merge It with Microsoft Office Word**, click the **Create a new document and then link the data to it option button**, then click **OK**

7. Click the **Labels option button** in the Mail Merge task pane, click **Next: Starting document**, click **Label options**, select **5163 - Shipping** as shown in Figure G-21, then click **OK**

8. Save the document as **Art Identification Labels** to the location where you are storing the files for this book, scroll left to view the left edge of the table, then compare the Word window to Figure G-22

FIGURE G-20: **Field labels for the Art List table**

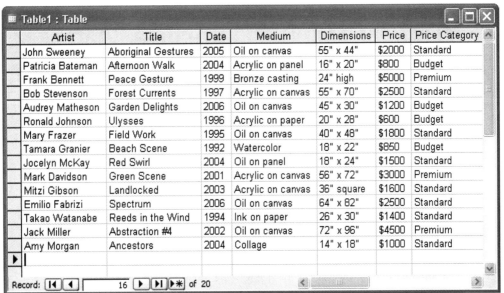

Artist	Title	Date	Medium	Dimensions	Price	Price Category
John Sweeney	Aboriginal Gestures	2005	Oil on canvas	55" x 44"	$2000	Standard
Patricia Bateman	Afternoon Walk	2004	Acrylic on panel	16" x 20"	$800	Budget
Frank Bennett	Peace Gesture	1999	Bronze casting	24" high	$5000	Premium
Bob Stevenson	Forest Currents	1997	Acrylic on canvas	55" x 70"	$2500	Standard
Audrey Matheson	Garden Delights	2006	Oil on canvas	45" x 30"	$1200	Budget
Ronald Johnson	Ulysses	1996	Acrylic on paper	20" x 28"	$600	Budget
Mary Frazer	Field Work	1995	Oil on canvas	40" x 48"	$1800	Standard
Tamara Granier	Beach Scene	1992	Watercolor	18" x 22"	$850	Budget
Jocelyn McKay	Red Swirl	2004	Oil on panel	18" x 24"	$1500	Standard
Mark Davidson	Green Scene	2001	Acrylic on canvas	56" x 72"	$3000	Premium
Mitzi Gibson	Landlocked	2003	Acrylic on canvas	36" square	$1600	Standard
Emilio Fabrizi	Spectrum	2006	Oil on canvas	64" x 82"	$2500	Standard
Takao Watanabe	Reeds in the Wind	1994	Ink on paper	26" x 30"	$1400	Standard
Jack Miller	Abstraction #4	2002	Oil on canvas	72" x 96"	$4500	Premium
Amy Morgan	Ancestors	2004	Collage	14" x 18"	$1000	Standard

Record: 16 of 20

FIGURE G-21: **Label Options dialog box**

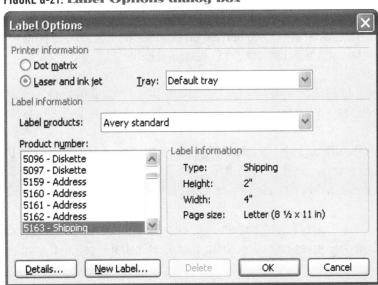

FIGURE G-22: **Label sheet in Word**

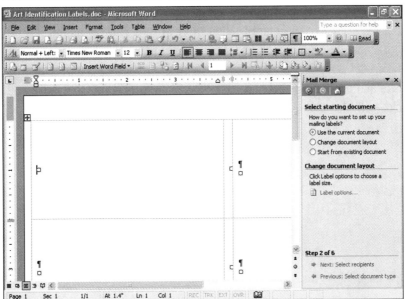

PROJECT 3

ART COLLECTION CATALOGUE

activity:

Merge the Labels and Create a Chart

You need to add fields to the identification labels, and then print the sheet of completed labels. Then you need to analyze the Art List table in Excel so that you can create a separate chart that shows the breakdown of paintings by price category.

steps:

1. Click **Next: Select recipients**, click **Next: Arrange your labels**, click **More items**, click **Insert**, then click **Close**

   The Artist field is inserted

2. Press **Enter**, insert the **Title field**, press **[Enter]** twice, insert the remaining fields as shown in Figure G-23, then format the field labels as shown in Figure G-24

3. Click the expand arrow ▼ at the bottom of the Mail Merge task pane to expand it, click **Update all labels**, click **Next: Preview your labels**, click **Next: Complete the merge**, close the Mail Merge task pane, compare the completed label sheet to Figure G-25, print a copy of the document, save and close it, then close the Art Collection.doc file

4. Switch to Access, open the **Art List table**, click **Price Category** on the table frame, click the **Sort Ascending button** ⬇ on the Standard toolbar, then close and save the table

5. Click the **OfficeLinks list arrow** ▼, click **Analyze It with Microsoft Office Excel**, widen columns as necessary, select cells **A1:H16**, click **Data** on the menu bar, click **Subtotals**, click the **At each change in list arrow**, click **Price Category**, click **OK**, then click cell **G21** to deselect the table

6. Click the **Chart Wizard button** 📊, click **Doughnut**, click **Next**, click the **Collapse Dialog box button** 📑, press and hold **[Ctrl]**, then click cell **H6**, cell **H10**, and cell **H19**

7. Click the **Restore Dialog box button** 🔲, click the **Series tab**, click 📑 next to the Category Labels text box, press and hold **[Ctrl]**, then click cells **H2**, **H7**, and **H11**

8. Click 🔲, click **Next**, enter **Breakdown by Price Category** as the chart title, click the **Data Labels tab**, click the **Value check box**, then click **Finish**

Additional Practice

For additional practice with the skills presented in this project, complete Independent Challenge 3.

9. Size and position the doughnut chart as shown in Figure G-26, save and print the workbook, then close all files and exit all programs

FIGURE G-23: Fields for the art identification labels

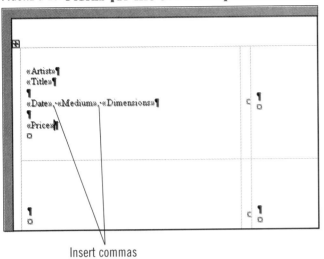

Insert commas

FIGURE G-24: Formatted fields

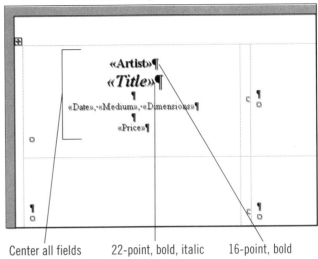

Center all fields   22-point, bold, italic   16-point, bold

FIGURE G-25: Completed label sheet

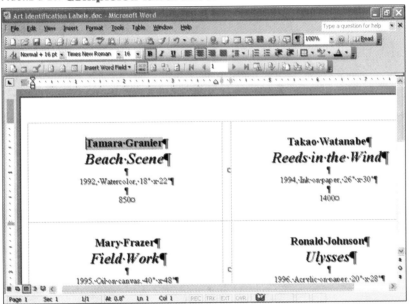

FIGURE G-26: Completed doughnut chart in Excel

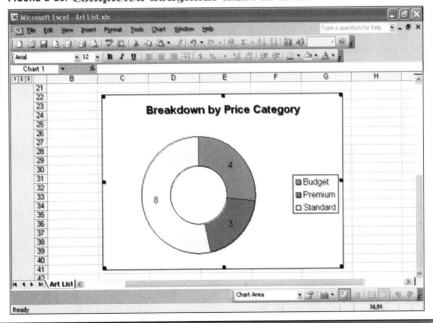

Independent Challenges

INDEPENDENT CHALLENGE 1

Create a Job Search database similar to the database you created for Project 1 to track your own job search efforts. Even if you are not currently seeking employment, create a practice database and accompanying form letter for your dream job. You can then modify these files when you are ready to seek employment. Follow the steps provided to create the database, merge it with a form letter you create in Word, and then create a chart in Excel that graphically displays your ratings of the companies that responded positively to your form letter.

1. Your first task is to determine the type of job position you are seeking and the type of company or organization you would like to work for. For example, you could seek a job as an office manager at real estate or architectural companies. In the box below, write the job positions you are seeking and the types of companies you would like to work for:

Job Positions:_____

Companies: _____

2. You need at least ten employers for your job search database. Look through the employment advertisements in your local paper to find potential employers, or, if you can't find advertisements for the specific jobs you require, look through the Yellow Pages to find the names and addresses of at least ten companies that you think you would like to work for and that may be interested in an applicant with your qualifications. Try to include as many realistic records in your job search database as possible.

3. Create a database called **My Job Search.mdb** in the location where you are saving the files for this book.

4. Create a **Contacts** table similar to the Contacts table you created for Project 1. Include at least six fields and make one field a lookup field. Make sure you include a primary key in the table.

5. Switch to Word and set up an application form letter. Use the form letter you created in Project 1 to help you determine the information to include. Make sure you fully describe your qualifications and experience. Select the records in the Contacts table as the data source for the form letter, and include the appropriate fields.

6. Merge the data source with the form letter, print two or three of the letters, then save the form letter as **My Job Application Letter.doc** in the location where you are saving the files for this book.

7. Switch back to Access and create a custom form called **Job Search** that includes the fields from the Contacts table and two additional fields: a Yes/No field called **Response**, and a text field for a date. Remember that you need to add the new fields to the Contacts table first and then you can create the form in Design view.

8. Use the form to enter positive responses for at least five of the employers.

9. Create a query that lists only the companies that responded positively to your form letter.

10. Copy the Company Name and Position records from the query to a new table called **My Ratings**, then enter your ratings for each company in terms of four criteria of your choice. For example, you could rank the employers on Location, Pay, Benefits, and Advancement.

11. Analyze the My Ratings table in Excel, then create a pie chart that shows the breakdown of companies according to your ratings. Remember that you will need to total the ratings for each company and then use the Chart Wizard to create a pie chart that includes only the company names and the total ratings.

12. Print the workbook containing the Excel chart, then close all the files and applications. Be sure the Excel workbook is saved as **My Ratings.xls** in the location where you are storing the files for this book.

13. Save all files, and close all applications.

INDEPENDENT CHALLENGE 2

Write a three-page proposal that discusses partnership opportunities between two companies of your choice. For example, you could write about the benefits of a partnership between a small computer store and a bookkeeping business. For ideas, refer to the proposal you created for Project 2. Follow the steps provided to create data in Excel, import it into an Access database, create an attractively formatted proposal in Word, and then add objects from Excel and Access.

1. Start Excel, then in Sheet1 create a product list that contains information about some of the products you plan to mention in the proposal. Save the Excel file as **My Partnership Data.xls** to the location where you are saving the files for this book.
2. Start Access, create a new database called **My Partnership.mdb**, save it to the location where you are storing the files for this book, then import the Excel worksheet.
3. Name the new table **My Products**.
4. Start Word, then save the new document as **My Partnership Proposal.doc** to the location where you are storing the files for this book.
5. Show the Header and Footer toolbar, then use WordArt to create an interesting background for your proposal similar to the background you created in Project 2. You can choose to create "Proposal" or the name of your company as shaded text behind or to the left of the proposal text.
6. Switch to the footer, enter your name at the left margin, then insert the page number at the right margin.
7. Write approximately one page of text for the proposal. Make sure that you include text that introduces a table that you'll publish from Access, a worksheet that you'll copy from Excel, and a chart that you'll copy from Excel.
8. Include several headings and subheadings that you format with the Heading 1 or Heading 2 style.
9. Switch to the My Partnership Data.xls workbook, enter appropriate financial data regarding revenue and expenses in Sheet2, then enter projected quarterly data and create a chart in Sheet3.
10. Copy the cells containing the financial data to an appropriate place in the proposal.
11. Copy the chart to an appropriate place in the proposal.
12. From Access, publish the My Products table in Word. Be sure the table is saved as **My Products.rtf** to the location where you are storing the files for this book.
13. Copy the table that appears in Word to an appropriate place in the proposal, then format it attractively by applying one of the available Table AutoFormats.
14. Add a title at the top of the first page, scroll through the document, add page breaks where appropriate, print a copy of the completed proposal, save and close the document, then save and close all files and all programs.

INDEPENDENT CHALLENGE 3

Create a database that contains information about your personal collection of CDs, records, tapes, videos, photographs, or a collection of your choice. Use the database to create labels for items in your collection. Plan and create the database as follows.

1. In Word, create a table containing headings that will differentiate the various records in your collection in terms of genre, category, or type, as appropriate. If your table lists all your videos, for example, you could include fields for Title, Genre, Date, and Price.
2. Save the Word document as **My Collection.doc** to the location where you are storing the files for this book.
3. Create a database called **My Collection.mdb** and save it to the location where you are storing the files for this book, create a table for entering data, then copy the table from the Word document into the Access table.
4. Replace the field labels with the labels in the first record, then remove the first record.
5. Save the table as **Collection List**.
6. Merge the table in Word, and then follow the steps in the Mail Merge task pane to select a label, insert fields, and then format the label. Look through the list of labels available in the Label Options dialog box to find a label appropriate for the items in your collection.
7. Complete the merge and print one sheet of labels. Save the label sheet as **My Collection Labels.doc** to the location where you are storing the files for this book.

8. Switch back to Access, sort one of the fields in the table alphabetically, then analyze the table in Excel and create a chart that shows the breakdown of items, for example, by genre. Print the Excel chart and worksheet, then save it as **My Collection Analysis.xls**.

9. Save and close all open files, and exit all programs.

INDEPENDENT CHALLENGE 4

You work for a company called Diversion, Inc. that creates imaginative computer games for teens and adults. The games sell worldwide on the Internet. You've decided to analyze the types of customers who have purchased your games in the past month in terms of occupation and country. Follow the instructions provided to create the report shown in Figure G-28. This document includes a table published from Access and a cone chart created in Excel.

1. Start Access, create a database called **Diversion Customers.mdb**, and save it to the location where are you saving the files for this book.

2. Create a table called **Customers** as shown in Figure G-27. Note that the ID field is the primary key.

FIGURE G-27: Customers table

ID	Last Name	First Name	Occupation	Country	Product
1	Janzen	David	Teacher	United Kingdom	Trail Blazer
2	Yaretz	Wanda	Lawyer	Canada	Venus Voyager
3	Pryce	Wyndam	Consultant	United Kingdom	Grand Prix Racer
4	Singh	Manjit	Manager	India	Medieval Odyssey
5	O'Brian	Sean	Teacher	Ireland	Art Quest
6	St. Pierre	Brigitte	Manager	Canada	Trail Blazer
7	Wallace	Diane	Artist	United States	Star Gazer
8	Knutson	Olga	Lawyer	United Kingdom	Venus Voyager
9	Morrison	Dawn	Lawyer	United States	Medieval Odyssey
10	Li	Doris	Teacher	United States	Deep Sea Diver
11	Stephensen	Hugh	Manager	Canada	Art Quest
12	McDonald	Ewan	Teacher	United States	Animalia
13	Reilly	Patrick	Teacher	Ireland	Roman World
14	Kanaka	Hiromi	Teacher	Canada	Art Quest
15	Fuentes	Diego	Consultant	United States	Deep Sea Diver

Record: 16 of 16

3. Sort the records by Country in ascending order.

4. Analyze the Customers table in Excel, and then save the file as **Diversion Analysis.xls**. Create a pyramid chart that shows the breakdown of customers by country. You will need to create a Subtotals list to count the number of records in each occupation before you create the pyramid chart. In the Subtotal dialog box, you'll need to select Country as the At each change in selection.

5. Format the chart so that it appears as shown in the completed report in Figure G-28.

6. Start Word, enter just the text shown in Figure G-28, and then apply similar formatting.

7. Save the document as **Diversion Report.doc** to the location where are you storing the files for this book.

8. Switch to Access, publish the table in Word, then save it as **Diversion Customers.rtf**.

9. Copy the table and then paste it below the first paragraph of text in the Word document.

10. Apply the Table List 7 AutoFormat, and then adjust column widths, as shown in Figure G-28.

11. Switch to Excel, and then copy the pyramid chart and paste it below the last paragraph in the Word document. Resize the chart so that it fits on page 1 of the document.

12. Add a Clip Art picture to the document (search for "computer game") as shown in Figure G-28. Make sure you format the layout as Square and Right.

13. Format the page attractively in Word, print a copy, then save and close all files and exit all programs.

Diversion, Inc.

Diversion, Inc., sells the majority of its computer games to teens and adults directly from its Web site. We have analyzed the types of customers who have bought our computer games during the month of December 2006 in terms of occupation and country. The following table shows the breakdown of customers for December 2006:

ID	Last Name	First Name	Occupation	Country	Product
14	Kanaka	Hiromi	Teacher	Canada	Art Quest
11	Stephensen	Hugh	Manager	Canada	Art Quest
6	St. Pierre	Brigitte	Manager	Canada	Trail Blazer
2	Yaretz	Wanda	Lawyer	Canada	Venus Voyager
4	Singh	Manjit	Manager	India	Medieval Odyssey
13	Reilly	Patrick	Teacher	Ireland	Roman World
5	O'Brian	Sean	Teacher	Ireland	Art Quest
8	Knutson	Olga	Lawyer	United Kingdom	Venus Voyager
3	Pryce	Wyndam	Consultant	United Kingdom	Grand Prix Racer
1	Janzen	David	Teacher	United Kingdom	Trail Blazer
15	Fuentes	Diego	Consultant	United States	Deep Sea Diver
12	McDonald	Ewan	Teacher	United States	Animalia
10	Li	Doris	Teacher	United States	Deep Sea Diver
9	Morrison	Dawn	Lawyer	United States	Medieval Odyssey
7	Wallace	Diane	Artist	United States	Star Gazer

As shown in the pyramid chart illustrated below, the majority of our customers live in Canada or the United States. A significant number of customers live in the United Kingdom and Ireland. To continue serving the British and Irish markets, Diversion plans to develop a marketing strategy in consultation with contacts in London and Dublin.

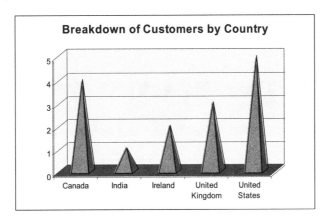

Visual Workshop

Start Word, create the table shown in Figure G-29, then save the file as **Tranquility Landscaping.doc** to the location where you are saving the files for this book. Start Access, create a database called **Tranquility Landscaping.mdb**, copy the table from the Word document to a new table in the Access database, then save the table as **Neighborhood Sales**. Add field names and a primary key as shown in Figure G-30. Analyze the table in Excel, and then create a column chart in Excel as shown in Figure G-31. Save and print the Excel worksheet, then save and close all files and exit all programs.

FIGURE G-29: Table in Word

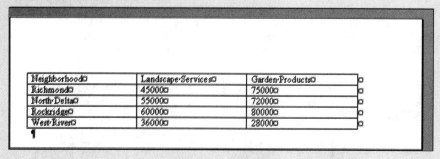

FIGURE G-30: Neighborhood Sales table

ID	Neighborhood	Landscape Services	Garden Products
1	Richmond	45000	75000
2	North Delta	55000	72000
3	Rockridge	60000	80000
4	West River	36000	28000
(AutoNumber)			

Record: ◄◄ ◄ 5 ► ►► ►* of 5

FIGURE G-31: Sales by Neighborhood

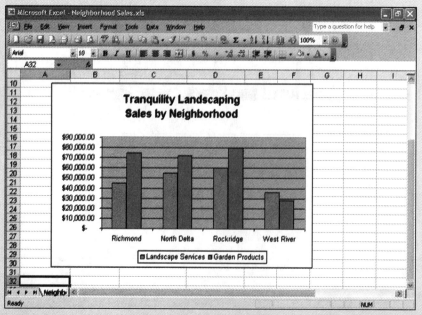

Microsoft
►PowerPoint
Projects

Unit **H**

PowerPoint Projects

In this Unit You Will Create the Following:

 ► **Training Presentation**

 ► **Poster and Web Page**

 ► **Lecture Presentation**

You use PowerPoint to create attractively formatted presentations, posters, flyers, and simple Web sites. Suppose you have been asked to present to your co-workers what you learned at a recent seminar on project management. You could, of course, just talk to your audience and perhaps hand out a sheet or two of notes. But imagine how much more compelling your lecture would be if you accompanied it with colorful slides or overheads that provided your audience with a visual backup to your words. People learn best when they can see, hear, and then write down information. You supply the words, and PowerPoint supplies the visual information. Your audience can write down some of the text you provide, but the impact of your words will be made stronger if you also include appropriate graphics illustrating what you mean. In this unit, you will learn how to create and run a PowerPoint presentation and how to use the graphics capabilities of PowerPoint to create posters, flyers, and Web pages.

Training Presentation on Oral Presentation Skills

You have been asked to teach your co-workers how to give an oral presentation. To help emphasize the points you make, you plan to accompany your lecture with an onscreen presentation that you create in PowerPoint. To complete the training presentation, you need to **Create the Presentation Outline**, **Modify the Slide Master**, **Modify Individual Slides**, and **Edit and Show the Presentation**.

activity:

Create the Presentation Outline

You need to enter the information you plan to display on the slides in the Oral Presentation Skills presentation.

steps:

Trouble

You can modify the width of the Outline pane by using the ←||→ pointer to drag the splitter bar to the left or right.

1. Start PowerPoint, then close the Getting Started task pane

2. Click the **Outline tab**, click to the right of the slide 🔲 in the Outline tab, type **Oral Presentation Skills**, then press [Enter]

3. Press [Tab] to indicate you want to type subtext on Slide 1, type your name, then save the presentation as **Oral Presentation Skills** to the location where you are storing the files for this book
   Slide 1 of the presentation appears as shown in Figure H-1. Notice how the text appears in the Outline tab and in the Slide pane.

4. Press [Enter], press [Shift][Tab] to start a new slide, type **Overview**, press [Enter], press [Tab], then type **Choose Topic**
   The text you just typed appears as the first bulleted item on the slide titled "Overview."

5. Press [Enter], type **Create Outline**, press [Enter], type **Prepare Slides**, press [Enter], type **Deliver Presentation**, then press [Enter]
   A bullet appears each time you press [Enter].

6. Press [Shift][Tab], type **Step 1: Choose Topic**, press [Enter], press [Tab], type **Persuade your audience to take a specific action or approve a specific request**, press [Enter], type **Sample Topics**, then press [Enter]

Hint

You can also click the Increase Indent button or the Decrease Indent button to change the outline level for that line.

7. Press [Tab], enter the three items under Sample Topics as shown in Figure H-2, press [Enter], then press [Shift][Tab] twice to return to the left margin

8. Enter the information for Slides 4 through 7 as shown in Figure H-2
   Remember to press [Tab] to move the insertion point to the right and [Shift][Tab] to move the insertion point to the left.

9. Click the **Spelling button** 🦋 on the Standard toolbar, make any corrections required, then save the presentation

FIGURE H-1: **Title slide**

Slides tab

Outline tab

Drag the splitter bar to change the width of the Outline tab

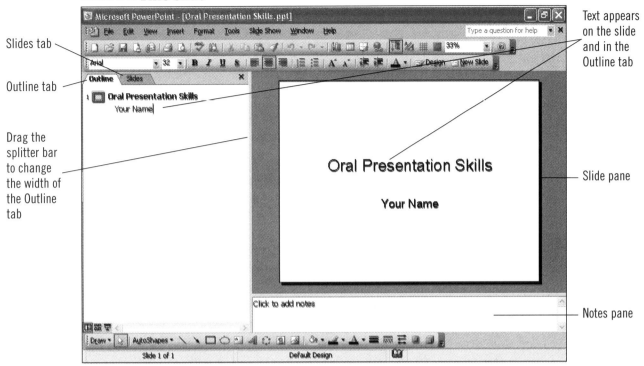

Text appears on the slide and in the Outline tab

Slide pane

Notes pane

FIGURE H-2: **Outline for Oral Presentation Skills**

Slide #

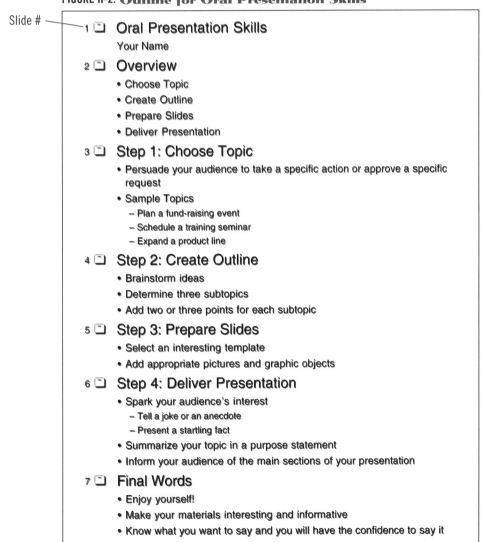

activity:

Modify the Slide Master

You need to apply the Blends design and a colored background to all the slides. Then you need to use Slide Master view to change the font style for each slide title. You also need to modify the colored boxes included with the Blends design.

Hint

When you move your pointer over a slide design, the name of the design appears as a ScreenTip.

steps:

1. Click the **Slide Design button** [⊿ Design] on the Formatting toolbar, click the **Blends** slide design (you'll need to scroll down to the bottom of the list box), then close the Slide Design task pane

2. Click **Format** on the menu bar, click **Background**, click the **Background fill list arrow**, click **More Colors**, click the **Custom tab**, enter the settings for Red, Green, and Blue (RGB) as shown in Figure H-3, click **OK**, then click **Apply to All**

3. Click **View** on the menu bar, point to **Master**, then click **Slide Master**

   The presentation switches to Slide Master view and the Slide Master View toolbar opens. Two slides appear in the Slides tab. Slide 1 is the Slide Master and Slide 2 is the Title Master. Changes you make to the objects and text in the Slide Master will affect every slide in the presentation except the Title slide. You make changes to the Title slide in the Title Master.

4. Click the **slide next to 1** in the Slides tab, click the **Click to edit Master title style placeholder text**, click the Font list arrow [Arial ▾] on the Formatting toolbar, select **Comic Sans MS**, click the **Decrease Font Size button** [A̗] once, then click the **Bold button** [B]

5. Click the **red rectangle** in the Blends design to the left of the Click to edit Master title style placeholder text, click the **Zoom list arrow** [100% ▾] on the Standard toolbar, click **150%**, click the **Fill Color list arrow** [🎨 ▾] on the Drawing toolbar, click **Fill Effects**, click the **Texture tab**, click the **Blue tissue paper** texture, then click **OK**

6. Click the **left side** of the yellow rectangle, press and hold **[Shift]**, then click the **right side** of the yellow rectangle

   Both objects that make up the yellow rectangle are selected. You use the [Shift] key to select two or more objects at once.

7. Click the **Fill Color list arrow** [🎨 ▾], click **Fill Effects**, click the **Preset option button** in the Gradient tab, click the **Preset colors list arrow**, select **Calm Water**, click the **Diagonal down option button**, select the **bottom-right Variant** as shown in Figure H-4, then click **OK**

8. Click the **Zoom list arrow** [100% ▾] on the Standard toolbar, click **Fit**, then click the **slide next to 2** in the Slides tab to display the Title master

   The changes you made to the Blends objects on the Slide Master do not affect the objects on the Title Master. You decide to delete the objects from the Title slide.

9. Click anywhere in the three colored boxes to select all three boxes and the horizontal line, press **[Delete]**, click **Close Master View** on the Slide Master View toolbar, click **Oral Presentation Skills** on Slide 1, click the **Center button** [≡] on the Formatting toolbar, save the presentation, then click a blank area of the slide

   Your screen appears as shown in Figure H-5.

FIGURE H-3: Colors dialog box

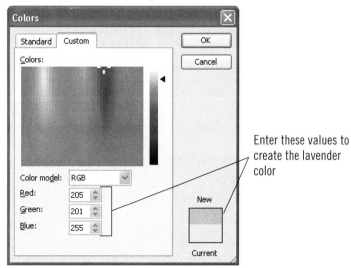

Enter these values to create the lavender color

FIGURE H-4: Fill Effects dialog box

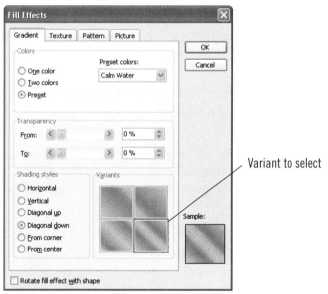

Variant to select

FIGURE H-5: Graphic object removed from the title slide

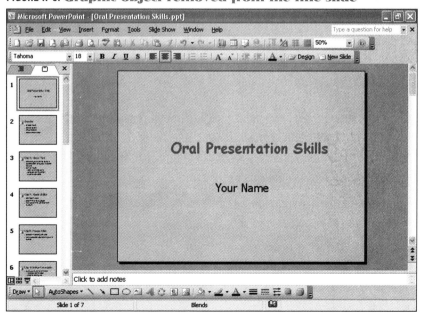

TRAINING PRESENTATION ON ORAL PRESENTATION SKILLS

activity:

Modify Individual Slides

You need to add a clip art picture on Slide 2, and then you need to insert a new slide and create a diagram on it.

Trouble

You must be connected to the Internet to use the Clip Organizer.

steps:

1. Click the **Next Slide button** ▼ on the vertical scroll bar to display Slide 2, click the **Insert Clip Art button** 🖼 on the Drawing toolbar, click the **Search for** text box, type **checkmarks**, click **Go**, right-click the **picture of the check box** (see Figure H-6) that appears, click **Insert**, then close the Clip Art task pane

2. Position the picture as shown in Figure H-6

3. Click the **Next Slide button** ▼ until Slide 6 appears (containing "Step 4: Deliver Presentation"), click the **New Slide button** 🔲 New Slide on the Formatting toolbar, select the **Title and Content** layout (the left sample in the second row of the Content Layouts section in the Slide Layout task pane), close the Slide Layout task pane, then enter **Four-Step Process** in the title text box

4. Click the **Click icon to add content text box**, click the **Insert Diagram or Organization Chart button** 🔄, select the **Radial Diagram** as shown in Figure H-7, then click **OK**

5. Click **Insert Shape** 🔲 Insert Shape on the Diagram toolbar, click the **top circle**, type **Topic**, click the **far right circle**, type **Outline**, click the **bottom circle**, type **Slides**, click the **far left circle**, type **Delivery**, click the **middle circle**, type **Great**, press [Enter], then type **Presentation**

6. Click the **AutoFormat button** 🔷 on the Diagram toolbar, select the **Square Shadows** diagram style, then click **OK**

7. Click the **top square** to select it, press and hold [Shift], click each of the remaining **four squares** so all five squares are selected, click the **Font Size list arrow** [18 ▼] on the Formatting toolbar, then click **16**

8. Click **Layout** on the Diagram toolbar, click **AutoLayout**, then deselect the radial diagram

   You turn off the AutoLayout feature so you can modify the size of just one circle (now a square) and its accompanying text box.

9. Click the **shaded border** enclosing the Great Presentation text to select the text box, drag the **lower-right sizing handle** down to increase the size of the square to fit the text, use your arrow keys to position the square as shown in Figure H-8, then save the presentation

   The completed diagram appears as shown in Figure H-8.

FIGURE H-6: **Clip art picture**

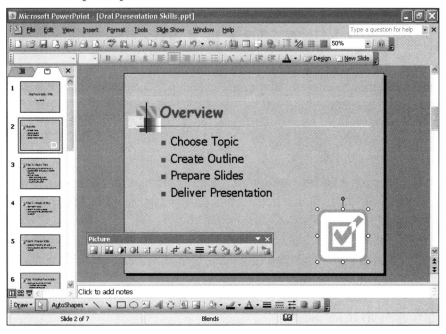

FIGURE H-7: **Diagram Gallery**

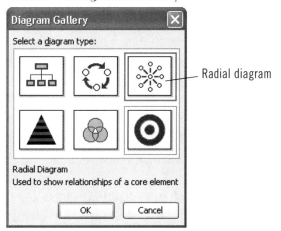

Radial diagram

FIGURE H-8: **Completed diagram**

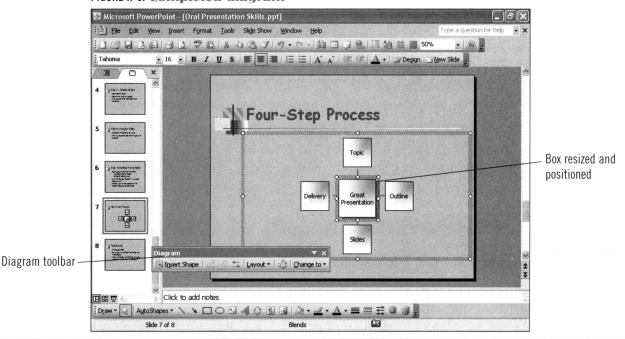

Box resized and positioned

Diagram toolbar

activity:

Edit and Show the Presentation

You need to select an animation scheme in Slide Sorter view, and then apply a custom animation scheme to the diagram. Finally, you run the presentation in Slide Show view, and then print a copy of the presentation as a sheet of handouts with all nine slides on one page.

steps:

1. Click the **Slide Sorter View button** ⊞ above the taskbar in the lower-left corner of the window, click **Slide 7**, then drag it to the left of Slide 3 as shown in Figure H-9

2. Click **Slide Show** on the menu bar, click **Animation Schemes**, scroll down the list of Animation Schemes in the Slide Design task pane, then click **Zoom** in the Moderate section
   The animation effect previews on the selected slide.

3. Click **Apply to All Slides**

4. Click the **Other Task Panes arrow** at the top of the Slide Design task pane, then click **Custom Animation**

5. Verify that **Slide 3** is still selected (it contains the diagram), then click the **Normal View button** ▣ on the taskbar at the bottom of the screen

6. Click the **diagram** to select it, click **Add Effect** in the Custom Animation task pane, point to **Entrance**, click **More Effects**, then click **Diamond** in the list of Basic effects in the Add Entrance Effect dialog box as shown in Figure H-10

7. Click **OK**, click the **list arrow** next to Diagram 2 in the Custom Animation task pane, click **Effect Options**, click the **Diagram Animation tab**, click the **Group diagram list arrow**, click **Clockwise - Inward**, then click **OK**
   The custom animation effect is previewed on the slide. As you can see, each box appears in turn, starting from the Topics box.

8. Close the Custom Animation task pane, click away from the diagram to deselect it, press **[Ctrl][Home]**, click the **Slide Show button** ☐ above the taskbar in the lower-left corner of the window, then press **[Spacebar]** or click the **left mouse button** to move through the presentation
   The animation scheme works nicely, and the custom animation effect on the diagram adds interest.

Additional Practice

For additional practice with the skills presented in this project, complete Independent Challenge 1.

9. Click **File** on the menu bar, click **Print**, click the **Print what list arrow**, click **Handouts**, click the **Slides per page list arrow**, click **9** as shown in Figure H-11, click **OK**, then save and close the presentation
   Your presentation is printed on one page.

FIGURE H-9: **Slide 7 moved in Slide Sorter view**

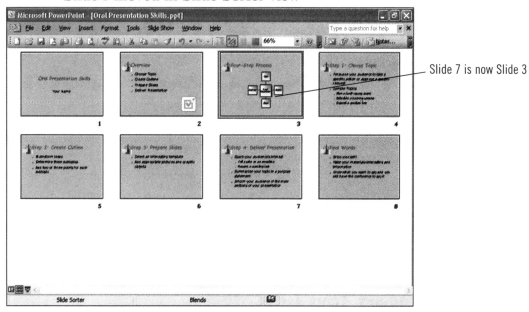

Slide 7 is now Slide 3

FIGURE H-10: **Diamond animation scheme selected**

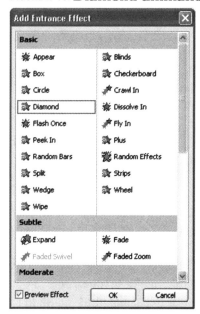

FIGURE H-11: **Print dialog box**

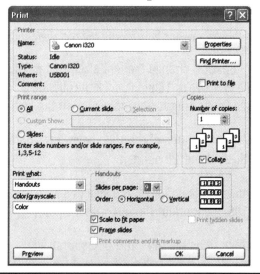

Poster and Web Page for Wings Conservation Area

You are in charge of advertising the monthly information meetings held from May through August at Wings Conservation Area in North Vancouver, British Columbia. You have decided to create a poster to advertise the dates and times of these information meetings. The poster can be displayed on bulletin boards in libraries, community centers, and other areas throughout the neighborhood and on the Wings Conservation Area's Web site. To create the poster, you need to **Insert Text Objects**, **Create a Table**, and then **Add Graphics and Save as a Web Page**. The completed poster and Web site are shown in Figures H-18 and H-19 on page 187.

activity:

Insert Text Objects

You need to start a new presentation, draw an autoshape, and then enter and format text.

steps:

1. Start PowerPoint, click the **New button** ⬜ on the Standard toolbar, click the **Blank layout** in the Content Layouts section of the Slide Layout task pane, close the Slide Layout task pane, then save the presentation as **Wings Poster** to the location where you are storing the files for this book

2. Click **AutoShapes** on the Drawing toolbar, point to **Basic Shapes**, click the **Rounded Rectangle** shape, draw a box across the screen, then type **Information Meeting**
   You do not need to worry about sizing the rectangle shape exactly at this point.

Hint

You select the border so that any changes you make will be applied to all the text in the box.

3. Click the **border** surrounding the text object, click the **Font Size list arrow** 18 ▾ on the Formatting toolbar, click **32**, then click the **Bold button** 🅱 on the Formatting toolbar

4. Right-click the **border** surrounding the text object, click **Format AutoShape**, click the **Size tab**, select the contents of the **Height text box**, type **.9"**, press [Tab], type **7.75"**, click **OK**, then drag the rounded rectangle object to position it as shown in Figure H-12

5. Click the **Text Box button** 🔲 on the Drawing toolbar, click below the rounded rectangle, type **Location**, press [Enter], then type the **address text**, as shown in Figure H-13
   You do not need to worry about positioning the rectangle shape exactly at this point.

6. Select the word **Location**, change the font size to **20 point** and apply **Bold**, select the **two address lines**, change the font size to **16 point**, click the outside border of the text box, then click the **Center button** ▤ on the Formatting toolbar to center all the text

7. Click 🔲, click in a blank area of the slide below the address, type **2006 Meeting Times**, then format the text with **Bold** and **20 point**

8. Click 🔲, click toward the bottom of the slide, type **For more information, please call Your Name at (604) 555-1188**, then format the text with **14 point**

9. Use the pointer to position the three text boxes as shown in Figure H-14, then save the presentation

FIGURE H-12: **Rounded rectangle object sized and positioned**

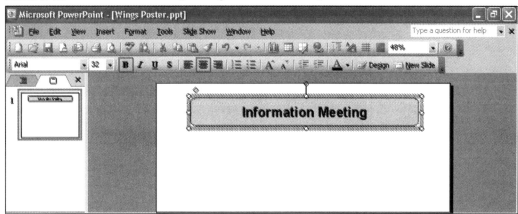

FIGURE H-13: **Address text**

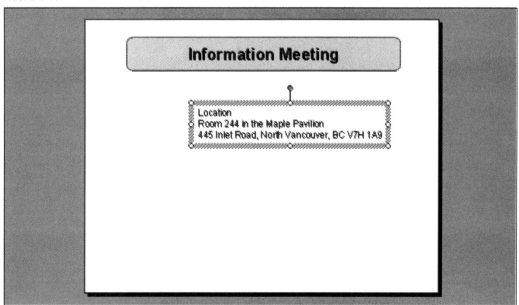

FIGURE H-14: **Completed text objects**

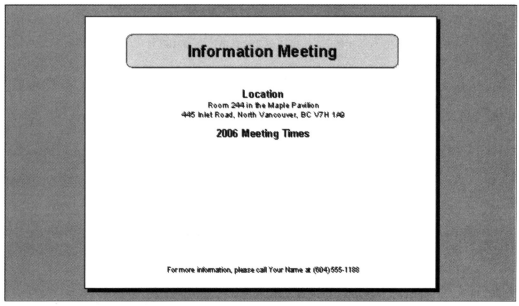

activity:

Create a Table

The poster includes a table that lists the meeting times for the months of May, June, and July. You need to use the Table feature to create the table, and then you need to modify the table using the Tables and Borders toolbar.

steps:

1. Click the **Insert Table button** 🔲 on the Standard toolbar, then drag to create a table consisting of two columns and three rows

2. Click the **border** surrounding the table, click the **Font Size list arrow** 18 ▾ on the Formatting toolbar, then click **16**

3. Move the pointer over the **top-middle sizing handle** of the table, then click and drag down to reduce the height of the table as shown in Figure H-15

4. Type the text for the table as shown in Figure H-16

5. Click the **border** surrounding the table, click the **Fill Color list arrow** ◇ ▾ on the Drawing toolbar, click **More Fill Colors**, click the **Standard tab**, click a **light yellow color**, then click **OK**

6. Select **all the text in the table**, click the **Font Size list arrow** 18 ▾, click **18** if needed, select **all the text in column 1**, click the **Bold button** **B** on the Formatting toolbar, then click the **Align Right button** ≣ on the Formatting toolbar

7. Move the pointer over the **column divider** between columns 1 and 2 to show the ←‖→ pointer, double-click ←‖→ to reduce the width of column 1, move the pointer over the right border of column 2, then double-click ←‖→ to reduce the width of column 2

8. Select the table, click the **Center Vertically button** ▤ on the Tables and Borders toolbar, then position the table so that it appears as shown in Figure H-17

9. Click the **rounded rectangle**, click the **Fill Color button** ◇ to fill the shape with light yellow, click away from the shape to deselect it, then save the presentation

FIGURE H-15: Table resized

Drag the top-middle sizing handle down

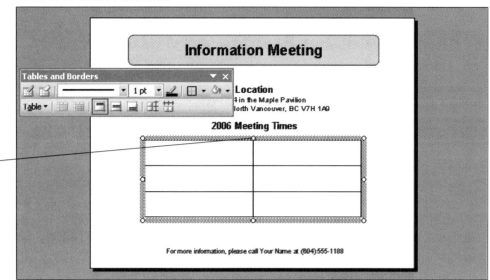

FIGURE H-16: Table text

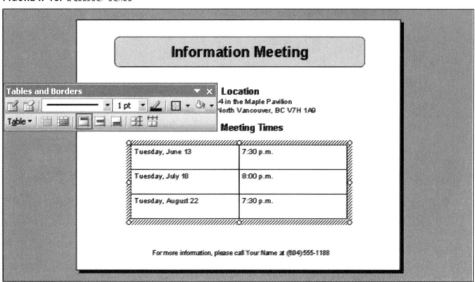

Figure H-17: Table sized and positioned

Bold, 18 point, and right-aligned

18 point

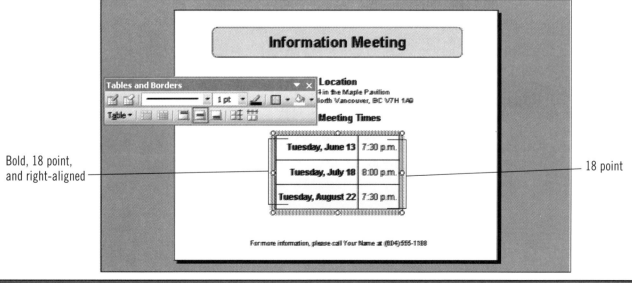

PowerPoint

PROJECT 2

POSTER AND WEB PAGE FOR WINGS CONSERVATION AREA

activity:

Add Graphics and Save as a Web Page

You need to insert two photographs and create a WordArt object using the text "Wings Conservation Area" as shown in Figure H-18. Then you need to save the poster as a Web page and view it in your Web browser.

steps:

1. Click the Insert WordArt button ◢ on the Drawing toolbar, click OK to accept the default WordArt style, type Wings Conservation Area, select the Forte font (or a similar font) and Bold, then click OK

2. Click the Fill Color list arrow ◇▾ on the Drawing toolbar, click More Fill Colors, select a dark green color, click OK, click the Line Color list arrow ✎▾, click No Line, size and position the WordArt object so that it appears as shown in Figure H-18, then click outside the WordArt

3. Click the Insert Picture button 🖼 on the Drawing toolbar, navigate to the location where you are storing the files for this book, then double-click Magnolia.jpg

4. Right-click the picture, click Format Picture, click the Size tab, change the height to 1.75", click OK, move the picture over the left side of the Information Meeting text object at the top of the poster, click Draw on the Drawing toolbar, point to Order, then click Send to Back

5. Insert the Marsh.jpg picture (from the location where you are storing the files for this book), reduce the height to 1.75", position and send the picture behind the table as shown in Figure H-18, then save the presentation

6. Click File on the menu bar, click Save as Web Page, click Change Title, type Wings Conservation Area Information Meeting, click OK, then click Save

   PowerPoint saves the file as an .mht file that you can open and view in a Web browser.

7. Click File on the menu bar, click Print, click OK, then close the presentation and launch your Web browser

8. Click File on the menu bar, click Open, click Browse, navigate to the location where you are storing the files for this book, double-click Wings Poster.mht, then click OK

   The poster appears in the Internet browser as shown in Figure H-19.

Additional Practice

For additional practice with the skills presented in this project, complete Independent Challenge 2.

9. Close the browser

FIGURE H-18: Completed poster

FIGURE H-19: Poster displayed in a Web browser

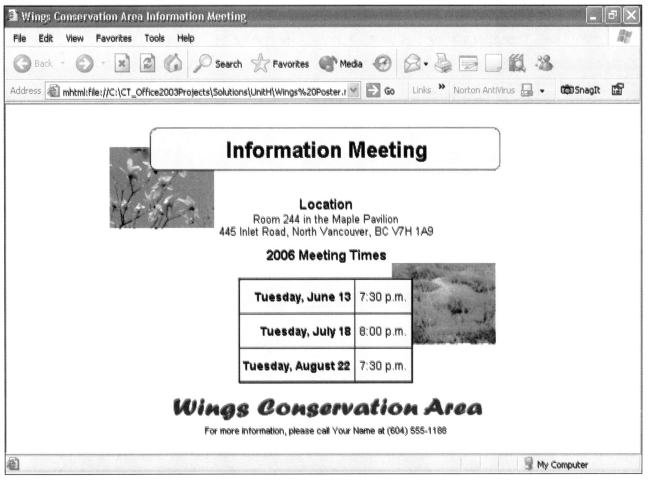

Lecture Presentation on Project Management

You need to give a presentation to your classmates on the basic concepts of project management. You decide to use PowerPoint to create overhead transparencies. You need to Set Up the Presentation and Modify Graphics. The completed presentation is shown in Slide Sorter view in Figure H-24 on page 191.

activity:

Set Up the Presentation

You need to enter and then edit text for the presentation in Outline view. Then you need to insert an organizational chart on Slide 6.

steps:

1. Start PowerPoint, use the default title slide layout, close the Getting Started task pane, click File on the menu bar, click Page Setup, click the Slides sized for list arrow, click Letter Paper (8.5 x 11 in.), click the Portrait option button in the Orientation Slides section, then click OK

2. Click the Outline tab, enter the text for the eight slides in the presentation, as shown in Figure H-20, check the spelling, then save the presentation as Project Management Lecture to the location where you are storing the files for this book

3. Click the Slide Design button [Design] on the Formatting toolbar, select the Edge design, click Color Schemes at the top of the Slide Design task pane, scroll down, click the last color scheme option (white background, teal objects), then close the Slide Design task pane

4. Move to Slide 6, click the Insert Diagram or Organization Chart button [icon] on the Drawing toolbar, then click OK to insert the organization chart type

5. Switch to 75% view, click the top box if it is not already selected, type Project Manager, click the far left box, type Department Managers, click the middle box, type Vendors, click the right box, then type Customers

6. Click the Project Manager box, click Insert Shape on the Organization Chart toolbar, click the new shape, then type Board of Directors

7. Switch to Fit view, click the Project Manager box, click Layout on the Organization Chart toolbar, click Right Hanging, click the Autoformat button [icon] on the Organization Chart toolbar, click 3-D Color, then click OK

8. Click away from the chart, compare the slide to Figure H-21, then save the presentation

FIGURE H-20: Outline for the Project Management lecture

1 ▢ **Introduction to Project Management**
Your Name
2 ▢ Overview
 ■ Characteristics of a Project
 ■ Project Manager Tasks
 ■ Project Stages
3 ▢ What is a Project?
 ■ A project is a temporary endeavor involving a
  ❑ Connected sequence of activities
  ❑ Range of resources
 ■ Designed to achieve a specific and unique outcome
 ■ Operates within time, cost, and quality constraints
4 ▢ Key Points
 ■ Temporary
 ■ Connected sequence of activities
 ■ Range of resources
 ■ Specific and unique outcome
 ■ Introduces change
5 ▣ Stakeholders
 ■ A project must meet or exceed the expectations of stakeholders
  ❑ All those with a vested interest in the project
6 ▢ Project Stakeholders
7 ▢ Project Manager Tasks
 ■ What do you deliver?
 ■ What cost?
 ■ What performance standards?
 ■ To whose satisfaction?
 ■ By when?
8 ▣ Project Stages

FIGURE H-21: Completed organization chart

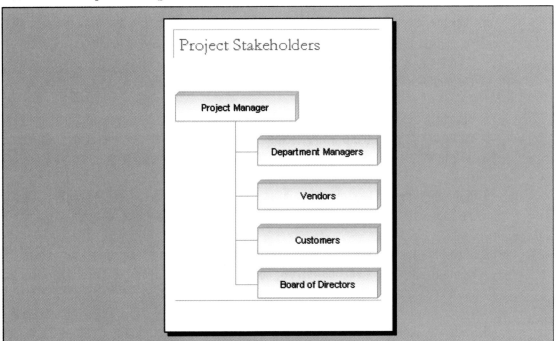

activity:

Modify Graphics

You need to insert a clip art picture and then modify it by removing an object in the picture that you do not want. You then need to create five aligned text boxes and draw arrows to connect them. The completed presentation in Slide Sorter view is shown in Figure H-24.

steps:

1. Move to Slide 5, click the Insert Clip Art button ☒ on the Drawing toolbar, type project in the Search for text box, find and insert the picture shown in Figure H-22 (except the picture you insert will include a yellow background), then close the Clip Art task pane

2. Move the picture so it fills the lower-right area of the slide, right-click the picture, point to Grouping, click Ungroup, then click Yes to convert it to a drawing object

3. Increase the zoom to 100%, click away from the picture, right-click the yellow background, point to Grouping, click Ungroup, click away from the selected objects, click the yellow background again, then press [Delete]
   Most of the picture is deleted—which isn't quite what you had in mind.

4. Click the Undo button ↶ on the Standard toolbar, right-click the yellow background, point to Grouping, click Ungroup, click away from the picture again, click the yellow background again, then press [Delete]
   Now just the yellow background object is removed from the picture.

5. Click the Select Objects button ⇖ on the Drawing toolbar, click and drag to select all the remaining objects that make up the picture, click Draw on the Drawing toolbar, click Group, then switch to Fit view
   The modified clip art object appears as shown in Figure H-22.

6. Move to Slide 8, apply the Title Only slide layout, draw a text box, type Initiating, click the Fill Color list arrow ▼ on the Drawing toolbar, click the Teal color box, select the text, change the font color to white, change the font size to 28 point, center the text, then apply bold

7. Right-click the text box, click Format Text Box, click the Size tab, set the width at 4", click OK, click the Copy button ⧉ on the Standard toolbar, then click the Paste button four times

Hint

Click the Arrow button on the Drawing toolbar to draw the arrow.

8. Space the text boxes and change the text in each of the four copied text boxes as shown in Figure H-23, draw a vertical arrow, copy it three times, then position the arrows as shown
   You will need to spend some time positioning the various objects.

Additional Practice

For additional practice with the skills presented in this project, complete Independent Challenge 3.

9. Switch to Slide Sorter view, compare the completed presentation to Figure H-24, click File on the menu bar, click Print, click the Print what list arrow, click Handouts, click OK, then save and close the presentation

FIGURE H-22: Modified clip art object

FIGURE H-23: Text boxes and arrows on Slide 8

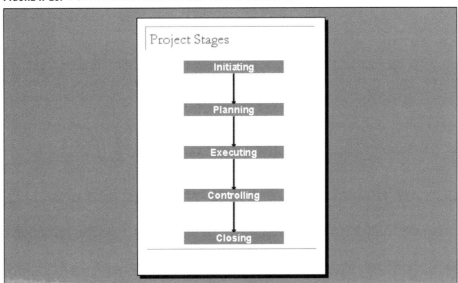

FIGURE H-24: Completed presentation in Slide Sorter view

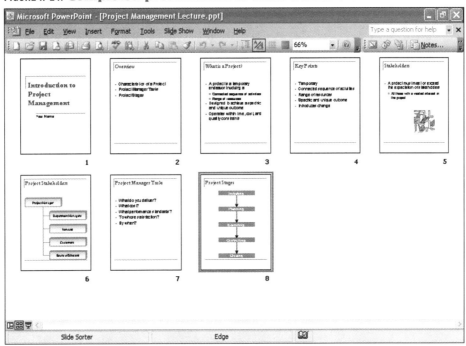

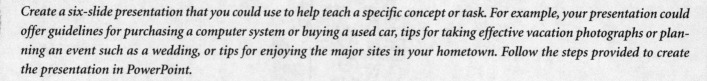

Independent Challenges

INDEPENDENT CHALLENGE 1

Create a six-slide presentation that you could use to help teach a specific concept or task. For example, your presentation could offer guidelines for purchasing a computer system or buying a used car, tips for taking effective vacation photographs or planning an event such as a wedding, or tips for enjoying the major sites in your hometown. Follow the steps provided to create the presentation in PowerPoint.

1. Your first task is to determine the topic of your presentation. Think about an activity or task that you know well and that you can present in short, easy-to-understand steps. To help get started, write the words "How to", followed by a verb and then the activity. For example, your presentation topic could be "How to Create a Balcony Garden," or "How to Plan a Backpacking Trip." In the box below, write the topic of your presentation:

Presentation Topic: _____

2. You need to determine three main sections for your presentation. Each of these sections should cover a specific activity related to your topic. For example, the three sections for a presentation titled "How to Find a Job" could be: 1. Personal Profile, 2. Employment Sources, and 3. Interview Techniques. You should present each of these sections on separate slides along with three or four bulleted points that describe it. Write the sections of your presentation in the box below:

Section 1: _____

Section 2: _____

Section 3: _____

3. Start PowerPoint and create an outline of your presentation. Save the presentation as **My Training Presentation** to the location where you are storing files for this book. Here's a suggested format:

Slide #	Slide Title	Text
1	Presentation Topic	Your Name
2	Overview	List the three sections in your presentation
3	Section 1 Title	List three or four bulleted points related to Section 1
4	Section 2 Title	List three or four bulleted points related to Section 2
5	Section 3 Title	List three or four bulleted points related to Section 3
6	Conclusion	Create a "motivational" slide to summarize your presentation

4. Apply the slide design of your choice.
5. Switch to Slide Master view and modify the appearance of the text in the placeholders. You may wish, for example, to change the font size and style of the text in the Master Title Style placeholder.
6. Add clip art pictures to selected slides. Remember that you can use the drawing tools to modify a clip art image after you have ungrouped it.
7. Insert an appropriate diagram on one slide. Insert a new slide if necessary. Modify the diagram attractively. Remember to deselect AutoLayout if you want to resize specific parts of the diagram.
8. When you are satisfied with the appearance of your slides, switch to Slide Sorter view, add an animation scheme, add a custom animation effect to the diagram, and then switch to Slide Show view and run the presentation.
9. Save the presentation, print a copy of it as handouts with four to a page, and then close the presentation.

INDEPENDENT CHALLENGE 2

Create a poster (that you'll also save as a Web page) that announces some kind of event, such as a concert series, sports tournament, or club meeting.

1. Determine the type of event you will announce. Think of your own interests. In what type of event are you most likely to participate? If you are involved in sports, you could create a poster to advertise an upcoming game or tournament. If you belong to a club, you could create a poster and Web page to advertise a special event such as a fund-raising bake sale or craft fair.
2. Think of an interesting title for your event. For example, a poster that announces a celebrity golf tournament could be called "Stars on Par," or a Web page that advertises running events for cash prizes could be called "Dash for Cash."
3. Determine the details that readers of your poster and Web page will need to know in order to participate in the event you plan to advertise. You need to specify where the event will be held, when it will be held (date and time), what activities will occur at the event, and the person readers should contact for more information.
4. On a blank piece of paper, create a rough draft of your poster. Determine where you will place the various blocks of text and one or two clip art images. If appropriate, present some information in a table.
5. Create the poster on a blank PowerPoint slide. Add at least one clip art image or photograph and a WordArt object.
6. Save the presentation as **My Poster** to the location where you are storing the files for this book, then print a copy.
7. Save the slide as a Web page called **My Web Page** to the same location. Add a page title.
8. View the Web page in your browser, then print a copy.

INDEPENDENT CHALLENGE 3

1. Create a short presentation that presents information about an academic topic of your choice. Then format and print the presentation in Portrait orientation, which is appropriate for delivery on an overhead projector. Think of courses you are currently taking or have taken in the past, and then prepare slides that could accompany a short lecture on one of the class topics that interests you. For example, you could create a presentation that outlines the three principal causes of the First World War, or presents major issues in Shakespeare's Macbeth, or provides an overview of photosynthesis. In the box below, write the topic of your presentation:

Presentation Topic: _____

2. Determine the three subtopics you will discuss in your presentation. List these subtopics on the second slide of the presentation, and title that slide **Overview**. For example, three topics for a presentation on major issues in Shakespeare's Macbeth could be "The Tragic Hero," "Dramatic Irony," and "Imagery." Write the three topics of your presentation in the box below:

Topic 1: _____

Topic 2: _____

Topic 3: _____

3. Start PowerPoint and create an outline of your presentation. Save the presentation as **My Lecture** to the location where you are storing the files for this book. Use the same format suggested for Independent Challenge 1 to organize your topics and subtopics.
4. Change the page orientation for the presentation to Portrait, and then apply the slide design and color scheme of your choice.
5. Switch to Slide Master view and modify the appearance of the text in the placeholders and of the various elements that make up the slide design. For example, you can choose to delete some objects, change the fill colors of other objects, or add a new clip art picture.
6. Enhance the presentation slides attractively with clip art, where appropriate.
7. Save the presentation, print a copy of the presentation, and then close the presentation.

INDEPENDENT CHALLENGE 4

You have helped to organize a three-day convention for home-based entrepreneurs in your state or province. This convention will include seminars, booths for the entrepreneurs to promote their products or services, a keynote speech by your state governor or provincial premier, and plenty of opportunities for entrepreneurs to network. A few months prior to the convention, you will hold a meeting for local entrepreneurs to inform them about the conference and encourage them to participate. Follow the instructions provided to create and then modify the presentation that you plan to give at this meeting.

1. Start PowerPoint and a new presentation, and then enter the slide titles and text for the presentation as shown below:

Slide #	Slide Title	Level 1 Text	Level 2 Text
1	Home-Based Entrepreneurs Convention	[Your name and the name of your town and state/province]	
2	Convention Details	Location Date Time	[Enter an appropriate location in your home town, e.g., Westside Convention Center, San Diego"] May 3 to May 5, 2006 8 a.m. to 6 p.m. Banquet on May 4 at 8 p.m.
3	Convention Activities	Seminars Booth Rentals Networking Keynote Speech	
4	Seminars	Selected Seminars:	Business on the Internet Marketing Your Service Business Basic Accounting for Small Businesses Organizing Your Home Office
5	Booth Rentals	50 square feet: $2000 100 square feet: $3400	
6	Networking	Contact hundreds of local and national distributors Form new business alliances Trade success stories	
7	Keynote Speech	[Name of your governor, premier, or other leader] will present a keynote speech on:	Government Support for Home-Based Entrepreneurs
8	Home Is Where the Business Is!	[Create a "motivational" slide to encourage attendance at the convention]	

2. Save the presentation as **Entrepreneurs Presentation** to the location where you are storing the files for this book.

3. Apply the Profile slide design.

4. Add clip art pictures to some slides. Remember that you can use the drawing tools to modify a clip art image after you have ungrouped it. Refer to the sample version of the presentation shown in Figure H-25. *Hint*: Use search keywords such as "seminar," "booth," "home," and "business." The images you choose don't have to be the same as the images shown in Figure H-25.

5. When you are satisfied with the appearance of your slides, print them as handouts (6 to a page).

6. Add an animation scheme to all slides and a custom animation scheme to the picture on Slide 3, then preview the presentation in Slide Show view.

7. Print, save, close the presentation, and then exit PowerPoint.

FIGURE H-25: *Completed presentation in Slide Sorter view*

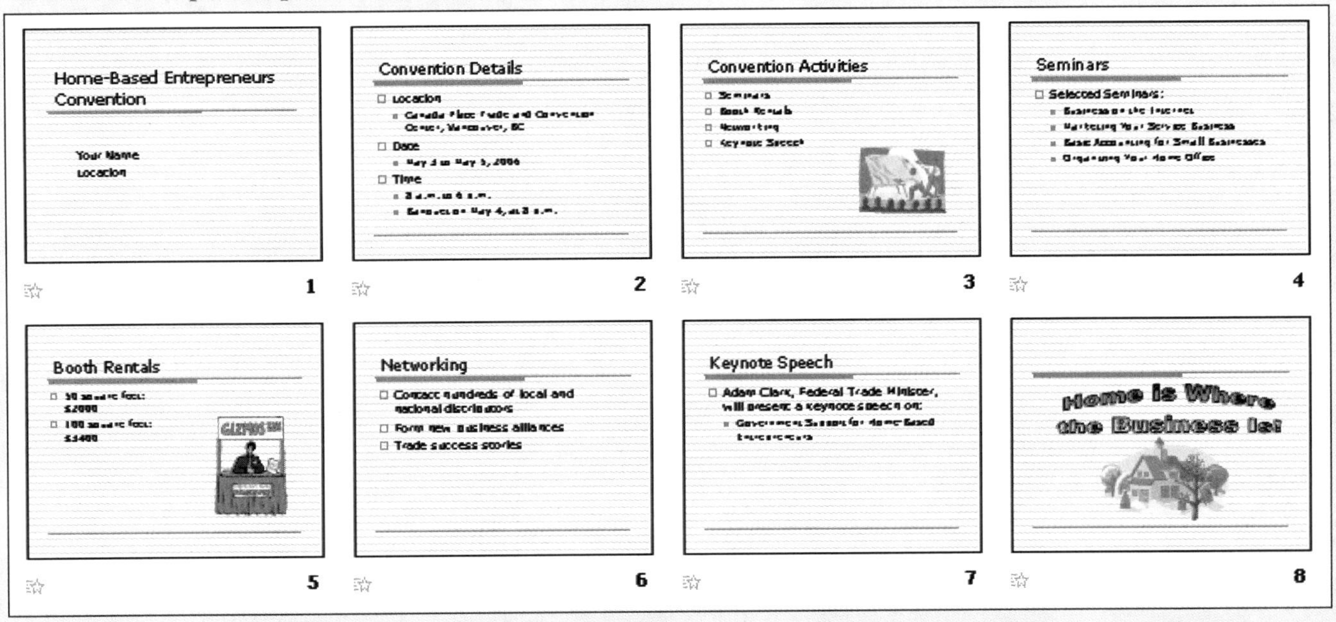

Visual Workshop

As part of a presentation on Saving the Wilderness that you are giving at a meeting of a local environmental group, you need to create the two slides shown in Figures H-26 and H-27. Enter the title and subtitle text on Slide 1, select and modify the slide design to use the light teal color scheme, and use Slide Master view to increase the title text size and apply bold. For Slide 2, change the layout to Blank, then add text and clip art as shown in Figure H-27. Note that the clip art images you select may be different. Save the presentation as **Montana Wilderness** to the location where you are storing the files for this book, print the two slides, and then close the presentation.

FIGURE H-26: Title slide

FIGURE H-27: Slide 2

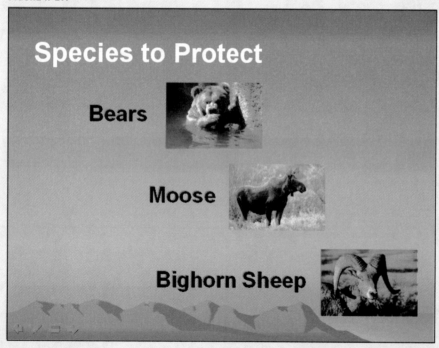

Microsoft
► PowerPoint, Word, Excel, and Access
Projects

Unit **I**

Integration Projects III

In this Unit You Will Create the Following:

 **Status Report**

 **Investor Orientation**

 **Class Party Presentation**

You can integrate Office applications to present information in a variety of ways. For example, you can compile source materials in Access and Excel and then create a report in Word or a presentation in PowerPoint that includes objects from the source materials. You can create an outline in Word and then send it to PowerPoint to create a presentation. Conversely, you can create a presentation in PowerPoint and send it to Word to create a report. You can also create links between objects from the various applications, and then you can update the links as new data becomes available. In this unit, you will integrate PowerPoint, Access, Excel, and Word to produce a report in Word and two presentations in PowerPoint.

Status Report for Evergreen Wellness Clinic

You've been asked to present a status report on the programs run by the Evergreen Wellness Clinic to the clinic's board of directors. To produce the report you need to **Format the Report in Word**, **Compile Source Materials**, **Add Excel and PowerPoint Objects**, and **Add a Report from Access**. The completed report is shown in Figure I-10 on page 205.

activity:

Format the Report in Word

You need to open and format a document containing the text for the report and placeholders that indicate the location of objects you plan to import from Excel, Access, and PowerPoint in later lessons.

steps:

1. Start Word, open the file Status Report.doc from the location where you are storing the files for this book, save the file as Evergreen Wellness Clinic June Report to the location where you are storing the files for this book, then scroll through the report to familiarize yourself with its contents and to view placeholders

2. Press [Ctrl][Home], click Insert on the menu bar, click Break, then click OK to insert a page break

3. Press [Ctrl][Home], click Insert on the menu bar, click Object, scroll the list of object types, click Microsoft PowerPoint Slide as shown in Figure I-1, then click OK

4. Click the Click to add title text, type Evergreen Wellness Clinic, click the Click to add subtitle text, type June Status Report, press [Enter], then type your name

5. Click the Slide Design button ✏ Design on the Formatting toolbar, scroll to and click the Maple template, click Color Schemes, then select the dark green color scheme shown in Figure I-2

Trouble

The remaining document headings are Running Clinics, Lifestyle Seminars, Nutrition Workshops, and Summary.

6. Click below the slide, scroll to the first page of the report text, select Introduction, click the Styles and Formatting button 🅰 on the Formatting toolbar, click Heading 1 in the Styles and Formatting task pane, apply the Heading 1 style to the remaining document headings, then close the Styles and Formatting task pane

7. Scroll to the top of page 2, click below Table of Contents, press [Enter], click Insert on the menu bar, point to Reference, then click Index and Tables

8. Click the Table of Contents tab, click the Formats list arrow, select Formal as shown in Figure I-3, click OK, then save the document

FIGURE I-1: Selecting a PowerPoint Slide object

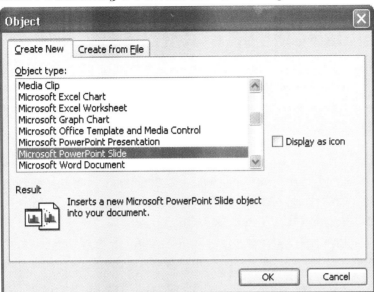

FIGURE I-2: Completed PowerPoint slide for the report title page

Dark green color scheme selected

FIGURE I-3: Formal Table of Contents format selected

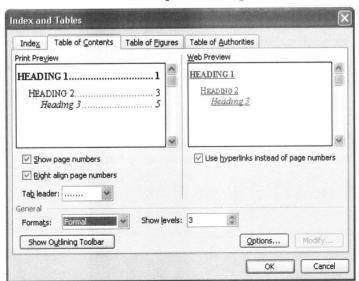

PowerPoint, Word, Excel, and Access

STATUS REPORT FOR EVERGREEN WELLNESS CLINIC

activity:

Compile Source Materials

You need to open a database that contains some of the data required for the report, and then you need to modify the format of selected fields. You also need to publish an Access table in the Word report and create two queries.

If a warning dialog box appears, click Yes, then click Open.

steps:

1. Start Access, open **Evergreen Wellness Clinic.mdb** from the location where you are storing the files for this book, double-click **June Running Clinic**, click in the blank **Start Run Time cell** for Record 1, type **14.55**, then press **[Tab]**

   The number you entered is automatically rounded up to 15. You want to show decimals so you need to modify the format of the Number data type.

2. Click the View list arrow 🖉▾ on the Standard toolbar, click **Design View**, click the **Number data type** next to Start Run Time, click **Long Integer** next to Field Size, click the **list arrow**, click **Single**, click **Auto** next to Decimal Places, click the **list arrow**, click **2**, then repeat this procedure to change the format of the Number data type for the End Run Time field

3. Click the View list arrow 🖿▾, click **Datasheet View**, click **Yes** to save the table, enter data for the Start Run Time and End Run Time fields and widen columns as shown in Figure I-4, then close and save the table

4. Click the OfficeLinks list arrow 🖳▾, then click **Publish It with Microsoft Office Word**

   The table appears in a new Word document called June Running Clinic.rtf.

[Running Times] is on page 3.

5. Select the table, click the **Copy button** 🖻 on the Standard toolbar, switch to the report in Word, select the placeholder text **[Running Times]**, then click the **Paste button** 🖺 on the Standard toolbar

6. With the table selected, click **Table** on the menu bar, click **Table AutoFormat**, select **Table 3D effects 3**, click **Apply**, click the **Center button** ≡, adjust column widths as required, click below the table, compare it to Figure I-5, then save the document

To save time, you enter only the beginning of the criteria followed by the wildcard character to tell Access to list all records in the Program Area field that contain Life as the first four letters.

7. Switch to Access, click **Queries** in the Objects pane, double-click **Create query by using wizard**, click the **Tables/Queries list arrow**, click **Table: Programs**, click the **Select All Fields button** >> , click **Next**, click **Next**, type **Lifestyle Seminars**, click the **Modify the query design option button**, click **Finish**, click the **Program Area Criteria cell**, type **Life***, click the **Run button** ▮, then close and save the query

   Three Lifestyle seminars are listed.

8. In Access, double-click **Create query by using wizard**, select the **Programs table**, select all the fields in the table *except* the Program ID field, click **Next**, click **Next**, name the query **June Programs**, click **Finish**, then view the query in Design view

9. Click the **blank field** to the right of the Fee field, then type **Total: [Attendance]*[Fee]**, click the **Criteria cell** for Date, type **June***, click the **Run button** ▮ on the Standard toolbar, compare the query to Figure I-6, then close and save the query

   The query returns a list of all the programs run in June, along with the total revenue generated from each program.

FIGURE I-4: Data for the Start Run Time and End Run Time fields

June Running Clinic : Table

	ID	Last Name	First Name	Start Run Time	End Run Time
	1	Wilson	Melody	14.55	11.55
	2	Knutson	Olga	15.35	12.35
	3	Kirkpatrick	Wendy	15.45	11.45
	4	Svensen	Lars	14.25	12.35
	5	Ralston	Patty	16.35	14.35
	6	Mason	Brenda	16.55	12.45
	7	O'Brien	Sean	17.45	15.25
	8	Evans	Adele	12.55	12.25
	9	Markoff	Catherine	15.35	12.45
	10	Mason	Donna	14.35	11.25
▶	(ber)			0	0

Record: I◀ ◀ 11 ▶ ▶I ▶* of 11

FIGURE I-5: Formatted table in Word

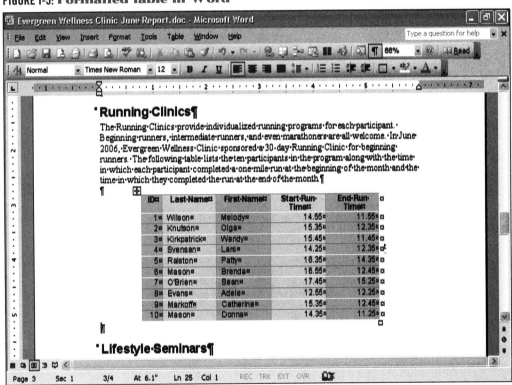

FIGURE I-6: June Programs query

June Programs : Select Query

	Date	Program Area	Attendance	Fee	Total
▶	June 1	Running Clinic	12	$45.00	$540.00
	June 4	Lifestyle Seminar	20	$75.00	$1,500.00
	June 10	Running Clinic	25	$45.00	$1,125.00
	June 20	Nutrition Workshop	40	$50.00	$2,000.00
	June 25	Nutrition Workshop	38	$50.00	$1,900.00
*			0	$0.00	

Record: I◀ ◀ 1 ▶ ▶I ▶* of 5

activity:

Add Excel and PowerPoint Objects

You need to analyze the Lifestyle Seminars query in Excel, calculate totals and then copy selected cells to the [Attendance Figures] placeholder in the Word report. You then need to copy two PowerPoint slides from an existing presentation to the [PowerPoint Slides] placeholder in the Word report.

steps:

1. Verify that **Queries** is selected in the Objects pane, click **Lifestyle Seminars**, click the **OfficeLinks list arrow** ▣, then click **Analyze It with Microsoft Office Excel**

2. When the Lifestyle Seminars table opens in Excel, click cell **F2**, type **=D2*E2**, press **[Enter]**, copy the formula through cell **F4**, then click the **Currency Style button** ⑤ on the Formatting toolbar

3. Enter **Totals** in cell **F1**, select cells **B1:F4**, click the **Copy button** ▣ on the Standard toolbar, switch to the report in Word, select the placeholder text **[Attendance Figures]**, then click the **Paste button** ▣ on the Standard toolbar

4. Select the table, double-click the **column divider** between columns 1 and 2 to resize the columns automatically, click the **Center button** ▣ on the Formatting toolbar, click below the table, then compare it to Figure I-7

5. In the Word report, click to the left of **Nutrition Workshops**, insert a new page break, select the placeholder text **[PowerPoint Slides]**, press **[Delete]**, click the **Insert Table button** ▦ on the Standard toolbar, drag to create a table that is two columns and one row, then save the document

6. Start PowerPoint, open **Nutrition Workshop.ppt** from the location where you are storing the files for this book, then click the **Slide Sorter button** ▦ to switch to Slide Sorter view

7. Verify that the title slide is selected, click ▣, switch to the Word report, click ▣, switch to PowerPoint, click **slide 3**, click ▣, switch to the Word report, press **[Tab]** to move to the second cell in the table, then click ▣

Trouble

If Object does not appear on the Format menu, click Picture.

8. Click the **slide** in cell 1, click **Format** on the menu bar, click **Object**, click the **Size tab**, set the **Width** at **3"**, click **OK**, set the width of the slide in cell 2 to **3"**

9. Select the table, click the **Outside Border list arrow** ▣ on the Formatting toolbar, click the **No Border button** ▣, click the **Summary paragraph** to deselect the table, then save the document
The two slides appear in the report as shown in Figure I-8.

FIGURE I-7: Excel data copied to Word

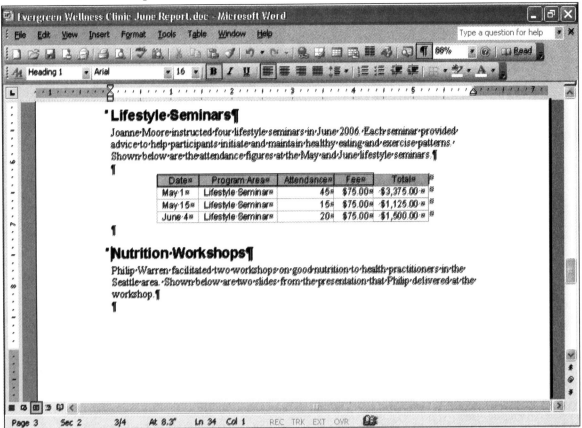

FIGURE I-8: Completed PowerPoint slides in Word

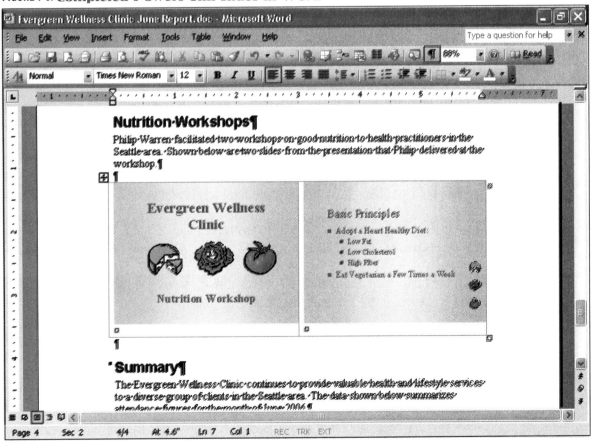

STATUS REPORT FOR EVERGREEN WELLNESS CLINIC

activity:

Add a Report from Access

You need to create a report from the June Programs query, publish the report in Word, and format it attractively. Finally, you need to update the table of contents in Word and print a copy of the report.

steps:

1. Switch to Access, click Reports in the Objects pane, double-click Create report by using wizard, select the June Programs query and all the fields in the query, click Next, click Program Area, click the Select Single Field button ⟩, click Next, click Summary Options, click the Sum check box for Total, click OK, click Next, select the Align Left 1 option button in the Layout list, click Next, click the Formal format, then click Finish

2. Switch to Design view, click the object immediately below the Program Area Footer (starts with "Summary for"), press [Delete], press and hold [Shift], click the =Sum[Total] text box in the Program Area Footer, click the =Sum [Total] text box in the Report Footer area, click the right mouse button, click Properties, click the Format list arrow, select the Currency format, close the Properties window, then close and save the report

3. Click June Programs, click the OfficeLinks button on the Standard toolbar, then click Publish It with Microsoft Office Word

   When the report is published in Word all the formatting applied to the report in Access is removed. You can convert the data into a table so that you can quickly apply formatting.

4. Delete all of the first line (contains June Programs) in the document, scroll to the bottom of the document, delete the last line of text (contains the date), press [Ctrl][A], click Table on the menu bar, point to Convert, click Text to Table, then click OK to accept the number of columns entered (5)

   By default, Word enters a number of columns equal to the maximum number of tab characters in any one line of text. The first column in the table is blank.

5. Scroll up, move the pointer over the top of column 1 to show ↓, click ↓ to select all of column 1, click the Cut button on the Standard toolbar, select the table, click Format on the menu bar, click Paragraph, set the Before and After spacing to 0, then click OK

6. Select Sum and $1,500.00 in cells 1 and 2 of row 4, drag one cell to the right, then repeat this procedure to reposition the Sum and Grand Total labels and values as shown in Figure I-9

7. Show the Tables and Borders toolbar, then modify the table so that it appears similar to Figure I-9

   As you work, refer to the directions in Figure I-9. Correct the spelling of Attendance if misspelled.

8. Select the table, copy it, switch to the report in Word, select the text [Summary Report] at the end of the report, paste the table, then center the table

9. Scroll to the table of contents, right-click the table of contents, click Update Field, click the Update entire table option button, then click OK

10. Click the Print Preview button on the Standard toolbar, click the Multiple Pages button on the toolbar, select 2 x 2 Pages, compare the four pages of the report to Figure I-10, click Close, save the document, print a copy, close it, then close and save all other files and programs

Hint

Adjust column widths before merging cells.

Additional Practice

For additional practice with the skills presented in this project, complete Independent Challenge 1.

FIGURE I-9: Formatted Access report in Word

Change the font size of all the text to 12 point; then as shown in the figure, merge cells, add 12.5% shading, and adjust text alignment and formatting

Program·Area¤	Lifestyle·Seminar¤		
Date¤	**Attendance¤**	**Fee¤**	**Total¤**
June·4¤	20¤	$75.00¤	$1,500.00¤
		Sum¤	$1,500.00¤
Program·Area¤	Nutrition·Workshop¤		
Date¤	**Attendance¤**	**Fee¤**	**Total¤**
June·25¤	38¤	$50.00¤	$1,900.00¤
June·20¤	40¤	$50.00¤	$2,000.00¤
		Sum¤	$3,900.00¤
Program·Area¤	Running·Clinic¤		
Date¤	**Attendance¤**	**Fee¤**	**Total¤**
June·10¤	25¤	$45.00¤	$1,125.00¤
June·1¤	12¤	$45.00¤	$540.00¤
		Sum¤	$1,665.00¤
		Grand·Total¤	$7,065.00¤

FIGURE I-10: Completed report in Print Preview

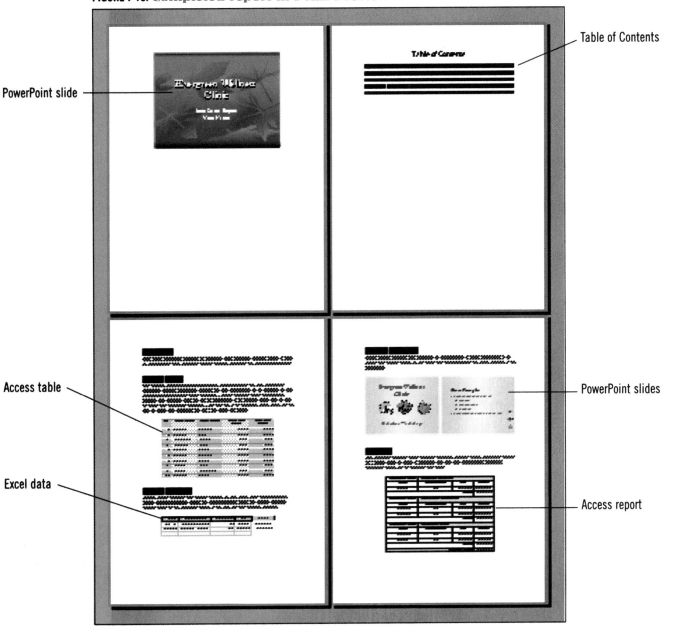

PowerPoint slide

Access table

Excel data

Table of Contents

PowerPoint slides

Access report

Investor Orientation for Orca Estates

You work for the Sales Manager of Orca Estates, a new resort development on the West Coast. You need to prepare a presentation to welcome investors and provide them with important information about the resort. For this project, you need to Create a Database, Create a Chart, Create the Presentation, and Update the Presentation. The completed presentation appears in Figure I-20 on page 213.

activity:

Create a Database

You need to enter the data in an Access table and then copy the Access table to Excel and paste it as a link.

steps:

1. Start Access, then create an Access database called Orca Estates and save it to the location where you are storing the files for this book

2. Create a table in Design view using the fields and data types shown in Figure I-11, then save the table as Home Designs

3. Enter the records for the table in Datasheet view as shown in Figure I-12, then close the table

4. Click Queries in the Objects pane, then double-click Create query by using wizard

5. Add all the fields from the Home Designs table, name the query Design Breakdown, then show the query in Design view

6. Sort the Style and Cost fields in Ascending order

7. Click the Run button ![run] on the Standard toolbar, close and save the query, then click the Copy button ![copy] on the Standard toolbar

8. Start Excel to open a blank workbook, click Edit on the menu bar, click Paste Special, click the Paste link option button, then click OK

9. Save the workbook as Orca Estates Data to the location where you are storing files for this book

FIGURE I-11: **Fields for the Home Designs table**

Field Name	Data Type	Description
🔑 Design ID	AutoNumber	
Style	Text	
Bedrooms	Number	
Location	Text	
Cost	Currency	
Quantity	Number	
Sales	Number	

FIGURE I-12: **Data for the Home Designs table**

Design ID	Style	Bedrooms	Location	Cost	Quantity	Sales
1	Contemporary	4	Waterfront	$350,000.00	10	5
2	Traditional	4	Waterfront	$380,000.00	15	4
3	Classic	2	Cliffside	$280,000.00	8	3
4	Contemporary	2	Forest	$220,000.00	12	2
5	Traditional	3	Cliffside	$250,000.00	3	0
6	Contemporary	3	Forest	$260,000.00	5	4
7	Traditional	2	Forest	$210,000.00	6	3
8	Traditional	3	Waterfront	$320,000.00	10	2
9	Classic	3	Forest	$270,000.00	7	1
10	Classic	4	Waterfront	$380,000.00	5	1
(AutoNumber)		0		$0.00	0	0

Record: ⏮ ◀ 11 ▶ ⏭ ▶* of 11

activity:

Create a Chart

You need to create a column chart to display information about the resort development. In a later lesson you will copy the column chart and paste it as a link on a slide in the PowerPoint presentation.

steps:

1. In Excel, click cell **H1**, type **Total Worth**, press **[Enter]**, type **=E2*F2**, press **[Enter]**, then copy the formula in cell H2 through cell **H11**

2. Click cell **I1**, type **Total Sales**, press **[Enter]**, type **=E2*G2**, press **[Enter]**, then copy the formula in cell I2 through cell **I11**

3. Click cell **F12**, click the **AutoSum button** Σ on the Standard toolbar, then copy the formula through cell **I12**

4. Format cells **E2:E11** and cells **H2:I12** with the Currency style

5. Click cell **B14**, enter the labels and calculations as shown in Figure I-13, then widen columns as needed
   When you copy data from an Access database and paste it as a link into an Excel workbook, you cannot use tools such as the Subtotals function to calculate totals.

6. Select cells **B14:D15**, click the **Chart Wizard button** 📊 on the Standard toolbar, click **Next** to accept the Column chart type, then click **Next** again

7. Click the **Axes tab**, click the **Value (Y) axis check box** to deselect it, click the **Legend tab**, click the **Show Legend check box** to deselect it, click the **Data Labels tab**, click the **Value check box** to select it, then click **Finish**

8. Right-click one of the **data labels**, click **Format Data Labels**, click the **Number tab**, reduce the decimal places to **0**, click the **Font tab**, apply **Bold**, then click **OK**

9. Size and position the chart as shown in Figure I-14, then save the workbook

FIGURE I-13: **Calculations of total worth**

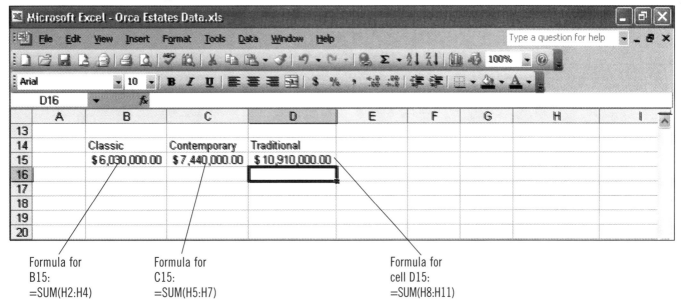

Formula for
B15:
=SUM(H2:H4)

Formula for
C15:
=SUM(H5:H7)

Formula for
cell D15:
=SUM(H8:H11)

FIGURE I-14: **Completed column chart**

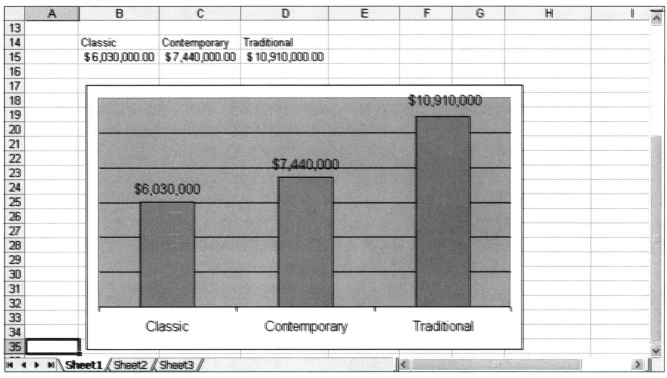

activity:

Create the Presentation

The text for the PowerPoint presentation is already stored in a Word document. You need to import the Word text into a new presentation and then modify the presentation design so that a picture appears on every slide in the presentation except the title slide.

steps:

1. Start PowerPoint, close the Getting Started task pane, click **Insert** on the menu bar, click **Slides from Outline**, navigate to the location where you are storing the files for this book, select **Orca Estates.doc**, click **Insert**, click **No** if a conversion warning appears, then save the presentation as **Orca Estates Investor Orientation** to the location where you are storing the files for this book

2. Click **Slide 1**, press [**Delete**], click **Format** on the menu bar, click **Slide Layout**, click **Title Slide**, click to the right of Investor Orientation, press [**Enter**], then type your name

3. Click the **Slide Design button** [⧉ Design] on the Formatting toolbar, select the **Ocean template**, then close the Slide Design task pane

4. Click **View** on the menu bar, point to **Master**, click **Slide Master**, click the **slide next to 1** in the Slides tab, click **Insert** on the menu bar, point to **Picture**, click **From File**, navigate to the location where you are storing the files for this book, then double-click **Arbutus.jpg**

5. Right-click the **picture**, click **Format Picture**, click the **Size tab**, change the Width to **2.5"**, click **OK**, drag the picture to the lower-right corner of the slide master as shown in Figure I-15, then click **Close Master View**

6. Move to Slide 4 in the presentation, switch to Excel, click the **column chart** if necessary, click the **Copy button** [⧉] on the Standard toolbar, switch to PowerPoint, click **Edit** on the menu bar, click **Paste Special**, click the **Paste link option button**, then click **OK**

7. Click **Format** on the menu bar, click **Background**, click the **Omit background graphics from master check box**, click **Preview**, then click **Apply**

8. Move the bullet text up and resize the text box as shown in Figure I-16, then size and position the chart attractively on the slide

9. Make sure the chart is still selected, click **Format** on the menu bar, click **Object**, click the **Picture tab**, click **Recolor**, click the **Fills option button**, click the **list arrow** next to the blue color, click **More Colors**, select a **bright yellow color**, click **OK**, compare the Recolor Picture dialog box to Figure I-17, click **OK** two times, then save the presentation

FIGURE I-15: Positioning the picture in the slide master

FIGURE I-16: Column chart sized and positioned

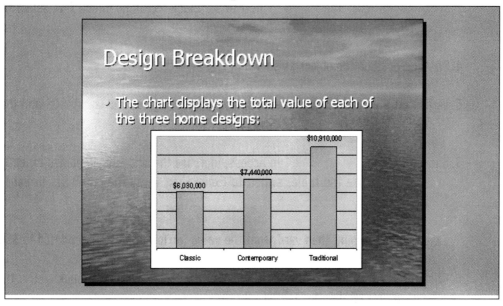

FIGURE I-17: Recolor Picture dialog box

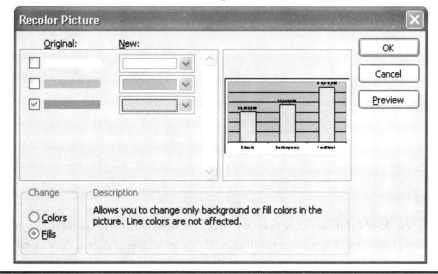

INVESTOR ORIENTATION FOR ORCA ESTATES

activity:

Update the Presentation

You need to summarize data in the Excel worksheet, copy it, and paste it as a link on Slide 5. Then, you need to change data in the Access database and update the links in Excel and PowerPoint. Finally, you need to print a copy of the completed presentation.

Trouble

Make sure you enter formulas where indicated, *not* values.

steps:

1. Switch to Excel, click cell I14, enter the labels and formulas as shown in Figure I-18, then widen the columns as needed

2. Select cells I14:J17, click the Copy button  on the Standard toolbar, switch to PowerPoint, go to Slide 5, click Edit on the menu bar, click Paste Special, click the Paste link option button, then click OK

3. Right-click the copied object, click Format Object, click the Picture tab if not already selected, click Recolor, click the list arrow next to the black rectangle under New, select the bright yellow color, click OK, then click OK

4. Size and position the object as shown in Figure I-19

5. Verify that the Total Worth of all the homes in Orca Estates is $24,380,000 and the total sales are $7,510,000

Trouble

It may take a minute before the values are updated. However, if the values do not update automatically, click Edit on the menu bar, click Links, click a link, click Update Values.

6. Show the Home Designs table in Access, increase the price of the homes in records 1, 2, and 10 to $450,000, close the table, switch to Excel, then verify that the total in cells I12 and J17 is $8,360,000

7. Switch to PowerPoint, then verify that the value for Total Sales has updated to $8,360,000

8. Click the Slide Sorter View button , click the Zoom list arrow, click 100%, then compare the completed presentation to Figure I-20

9. Print a sheet of handouts (6 slides to the page), then save and close all files and applications

Additional Practice

For additional practice with the skills presented in this project, complete Independent Challenge 2.

Clues to Use

Re-establishing Links

To re-establish links, you should start with the program that does not contain links and then open the remaining files in the order in which they are linked. For this presentation the order of files is Access, Excel, and PowerPoint.

FIGURE I-18: Total Quantity and Sales values

	D	E	F	G	H	I	J	K	L
6	Forest	$ 260,000.00	5	4	$ 1,300,000.00	$ 1,040,000.00			
7	Waterfront	$ 350,000.00	10	5	$ 3,500,000.00	$ 1,750,000.00			
8	Forest	$ 210,000.00	6	3	$ 1,260,000.00	$ 630,000.00			
9	Cliffside	$ 250,000.00	3	0	$ 750,000.00	$ =			
10	Waterfront	$ 320,000.00	10	2	$ 3,200,000.00	$ 640,000.00			
11	Waterfront	$ 380,000.00	15	4	$ 5,700,000.00	$ 1,520,000.00			
12			81	25	$ 24,380,000.00	$ 7,510,000.00			
13									
14	Traditional				Number of Homes		81		
15	$ 10,910,000.00				Total Worth		$ 24,380,000.00		
16					Number of Sales		25		
17			$10,910,000		Total Sales		$ 7,510,000.00		
18									
19									
20									
21									

=F12
=H12
=G12
=I12

FIGURE I-19: Excel object sized and positioned

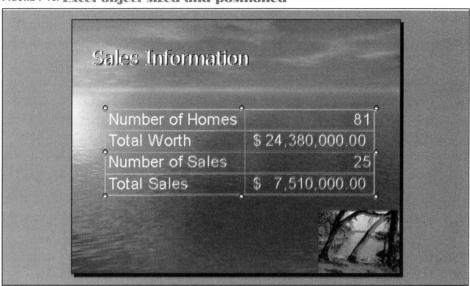

FIGURE I-20: Completed presentation in Slide Sorter view

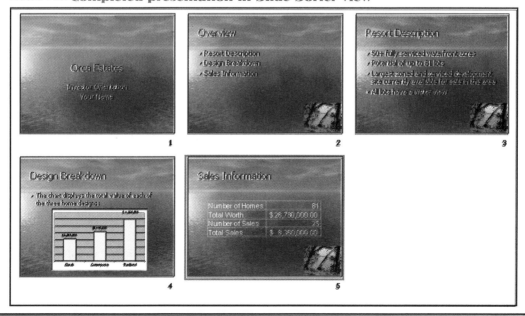

PowerPoint, Word, Excel, and Access

Class Party Presentation

You are organizing a class party to celebrate graduation from the business diploma program at Dillon Community College outside Chicago. You need to create a presentation to inform classmates about the party and a database to keep track of the students who plan to attend. For this project, you need to Create a Form and Create the Presentation. The completed presentation appears in Figure I-27 on page 217.

activity:

Create a Form

You need to create a table in Access, and then create a form to enter information about students who plan to attend the party. The form includes the title slide from the presentation.

steps:

1. Start Access, create an Access database called Class Party and saved to the location where you are storing the files for this book, create a table in Design view and enter the fields and data types as shown in Figure I-21, then close the table and save it as Attendees

2. Click Forms in the Objects pane, double-click Create form by using wizard, add all fields from the Attendees table, click Next, click Justified, click Next, select Sumi Painting, click Next, click the Modify the form's design option button, then click Finish

3. Start PowerPoint, type Class Party as the slide title, enter Business Diploma Program, Dillon Community College, and your name on three separate lines in the Subtitle area, then save the presentation as Class Party Presentation to the location where you are storing the files for this book

4. Click Insert on the menu bar, point to Picture, click From File, navigate to the location where you are storing the files for this book, then double-click Traces.jpg

5. Click the Color button 🖼 on the Picture toolbar, click Washout, right-click the picture, click Save as Picture, navigate to the location where you are storing the files for this book, type Traces_Class Party as the filename, then click Save

6. Delete the picture, click Format on the menu bar, click Background, click the Background fill list arrow, click Fill Effects, click the Picture tab, click Select Picture, navigate to the location where you stored Traces_Class Party.jpg, double-click the file, click OK, then click Apply to All

7. Switch to Slide Sorter view, click the Copy button 🖹 on the Standard toolbar, switch to Form 1 in Access, click a blank area of the form, click Edit on the menu bar, then click Paste

8. Right-click the picture, click Properties, click the list arrow to the right of Clip next to Size mode, click Stretch, close the Properties dialog box, size and position the picture and reposition the Contribution label and text box as shown in Figure I-22, then close and save the form

9. Double-click Attendees to open the form in Form view, use the form to enter data for the five attendees listed in Figure I-23, then close the form
The form for Harriet Watson (the last attendee) is shown in Figure I-24.

FIGURE I-21: Fields for the Attendees table

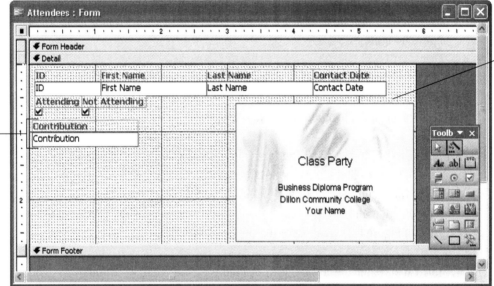

FIGURE I-22: Completed form in Design view

Reposition the Contribution label and text box

The grid area expands when you size and position the slide object

FIGURE I-23: List of attendees

ID	First Name	Last Name	Contact Date	Attending	Not Attending	Contribution
1	Mary	Jones	May 10	☑	☐	Appetizers
2	Darren	Price	May 15	☐	☑	
3	Donald	Zabrinski	May 15	☑	☐	Chips and Salsa
4	Polly	Quarles	May 20	☑	☐	Soft Drinks
5	Harriet	Watson	May 20	☑	☐	Fruit Plate

Record: ◄◄ ◄ 1 ► ►► ►✱ of 5

FIGURE I-24: Completed form for Harriet Watson

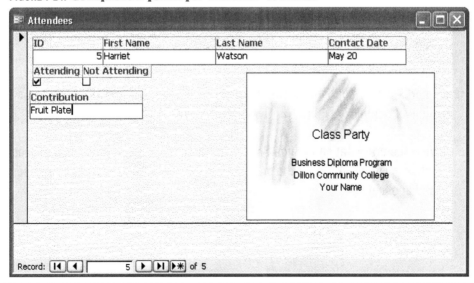

activity:

Create the Presentation

You need to complete the presentation, enter some of the data in Excel and Word, then copy the data to the presentation.

steps:

1. Switch to PowerPoint, click the **Normal View button** 🖿, click the **Outline tab**, click after your name in the Outline tab, press **[Enter]**, press **[Shift][Tab]** to start a new slide, then enter the outline as shown in Figure I-25

2. Start Word, type **Date:**, press **[Tab]**, type **June 5**, press **[Enter]**, type **Time:**, press **[Tab]**, type **7 p.m. to ??**, press **[Enter]**, type **Place:**, press **[Tab]**, type **Lakeview Terraces**, then save the document as **Class Party** to the location where you are storing the files for this book

3. Press **[Ctrl][A]** to select all the text, click the **Copy button** 🖺 on the Standard toolbar, switch to PowerPoint, view **Slide 3: Party Details**, apply the **Title Only** slide layout, click below the title, click **Edit** on the menu bar, click **Paste Special**, click **Unformatted Text**, click **OK**, increase the font size to **40**, position and size the text frame attractively on the slide as shown in the completed presentation in Figure I-27, then save the presentation

4. Start Excel, enter the data shown in Figure I-26 in cells **A1** through **D2**, widen the columns and apply the Currency style as shown, then save the workbook as **Class Party** to the location where you are storing the files for this book

5. Select cells **A1:D2**, click 🖺, switch to PowerPoint, view **Slide 4: Cost Breakdown**, apply the **Title Only** slide layout, click the **Insert Chart button** 🖾 on the Standard toolbar, click **Chart** on the menu bar, click **Chart Type**, click **Pie**, click **OK**, select columns **A** through **D** in the datasheet, click **Edit** on the menu bar, click **Paste**, delete rows 2 and 3 in the datasheet, then close the datasheet

6. Right-click the **Legend**, click **Format Legend**, click the **Placement tab**, click **Bottom**, then click **OK**

7. Click the **Chart Objects** list arrow on the Standard toolbar, click **Plot Area**, press **[Delete]** to remove the border around the pie, click **Chart** on the menu bar, click **Chart Options**, click the **Data Labels tab**, click the **Value check box**, click **OK**, click away from the pie chart to deselect it, then resize and position the pie chart so that it fills the area under the slide title as shown in Figure I-27

8. Show **Slide 5**, apply the **Blank** slide layout, then add a WordArt object and a clip art image to Slide 5, similar to Figure I-27

9. View the presentation in Slide Sorter view, switch to 100% view, compare the completed presentation to Figure I-27, print the presentation as handouts six to a page, then save and close all files and applications

Hint

Select the rainbow-colored WordArt object and the Deflate shape, and search for "balloon" to find the clip art.

Additional Practice

For additional practice with the skills presented in this project, complete Independent Challenge 3.

FIGURE I-25: **Outline for the Class Party presentation**

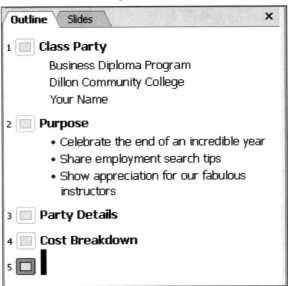

FIGURE I-26: **Data for Party Costs entered in Excel**

	A	B	C	D	E
1	Dinner Service	Decorations	Entertainment	Gifts	
2	$ 2,300.00	$ 450.00	$ 600.00	$ 800.00	
3					
4					
5					

FIGURE I-27: **Completed presentation in Slide Sorter view**

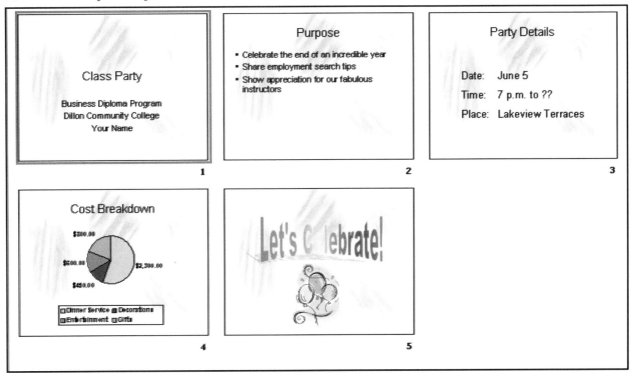

Independent Challenges

INDEPENDENT CHALLENGE 1

Create a multiple-page report in Word that includes objects from Excel, PowerPoint, and Access. Base the report on a business-oriented subject. For example, you could write a status report that describes activities over the past six months related to a company or organization of your choice, or you could write a report that proposes a change to a specific policy such as the employee dress code or the establishment of an employee recognition program. Follow the steps provided to create the report in Word and then to include objects from the other applications.

1. Determine the name of your company or organization and the type of activities it has engaged in over the past six months. For example, you could call your organization Vision Art Gallery and describe activities such as exhibitions, lectures, and auctions. Write the name and a brief description of the activities in the box below:

> **Company Name:** _____
> **Description of Activities:** _____
> _____
> _____

2. Start Word, then type text for the report. Include placeholders for objects that you will insert from other applications. Your report should include space for a worksheet or chart from Excel, a slide or two from PowerPoint, and a report from Access. You will also want to include a Table of Contents.
3. Include your name and the page number in a footer.
4. Format headings with heading styles and generate a table of contents above the first page of the report text.
   a. Save the report as **My Integrated Report.doc** to the location where you are storing the files for this book, switch to Excel, then create a worksheet containing data appropriate to a section of your report. You may also wish to use the worksheet data to create a chart.
   b. Save the Excel workbook as **My Integrated Report Data.xls** to the location where you are storing the files for this book.
   c. Copy the Excel worksheet and/or chart to the appropriate location(s) in your Word report.
   d. Create a PowerPoint slide somewhere in the report. You can choose to include the slide as your title page or in another location. Enter appropriate text and apply a slide design.
   e. Start Access, create a database called **My Integrated Report.mdb** and save it to the location where you are storing the files for this book, create a table called **My Report Data** that contains data relevant to your report, then create a query called **Query 1** and a report called **My Report** that highlights some aspect of the data. Refer to the database you created in Project 1 for ideas.
   f. Publish the report in Word (the file is saved as My Report.rtf), convert the text to a table, enhance the table attractively, then copy it to an appropriate location in the report.
   g. Update the table of contents, print a copy of the report from Word, save and close the report, then save and close all open documents and applications.

INDEPENDENT CHALLENGE 2

Create an onscreen presentation of six to eight slides that highlights sales information and recommends marketing strategies for a company or organization of your choice. For example, you could create a presentation for the continuing education department of a local college that presents the revenues from the last 10 courses offered and recommends a marketing plan for the courses that generated the most revenue. For ideas, check the business section of your local newspaper, surf the World Wide Web, or browse through the clip art categories. Follow the steps provided to create a table in Access, charts in Excel, and the presentation in PowerPoint. Data in the Access table should be linked to the Excel worksheet and the Excel objects in PowerPoint.

1. Determine the name of your company or organization and the type of products or services that it sells. For example, you could call your company Organic Planet and describe it as an online grocer that delivers organic fruits and vegetables and health food products to households in the Dallas area. Write the name and a brief description of your company in the box below:

Company Name: _____

Description: _____

2. Start Access, create a database called **My Sales Presentation.mdb** and save it to the location where you are storing the files for this book, and create a table consisting of at least four fields and 10 records. Call the table **Sales**. Include fields in the table that you will be able to use in charts. For example, a table for the Organic Planet presentation could include the following fields: Product, Category (e.g., Fruit, Vegetable, Dairy), Number of Sales, and Sale Price.

3. Copy the table and paste it as a link into Excel. Create two charts that illustrate sales information about your company. For example, you could create a pie chart that shows the breakdown of product sales by category and a column or bar chart that demonstrates the revenue from each of the 10 products listed in the Access table. Save the workbook as **My Sales Presentation Data.xls** to the location where you are storing the files for this book.

4. Switch to Word, create an outline for the presentation, then save the document as **My Sales Presentation.doc** to the location where you are storing the files for this book. Following are some ideas to help you get started:

SLIDE #	SLIDE TITLE	TEXT
1	Company Name	Sales Presentation Your Name
2	Goal	Write a one- or two-sentence description of your company's goals.
3	Product Categories	Write a one- or two-sentence description of a chart that illustrates the breakdown of sales by category.
4	Product Sales or Location	Write a one- or two-sentence description of a chart that shows the breakdown of sales by location or overall sales, depending on the type of chart you have created.
5	Marketing Plan	Write two or three points describing your marketing plan.
6	Conclusion	Create an interesting motivational slide to conclude your presentation.

5. Add additional slides to your outline, if you wish.

6. Save the outline in Word, then send it to PowerPoint. Save the presentation in PowerPoint as **My Sales Presentation.ppt** to the location where you are storing the files for this book.

7. Apply the slide design of your choice to the presentation and change the color scheme.

8. Switch to Slide Master view, and add a clip art image to the slide master or modify any images included with the slide design.

9. In Normal view, paste the charts from Excel as links to the appropriate slides and format them as necessary to make them readable and attractive.

10. Print the presentation slides as handouts (suggest 6 slides to the page).

11. Change some of the values in the Access table, then update the charts in PowerPoint.

12. Print only the slides that are updated as a result of the new values you entered in the Access table.

13. Save and close all files and applications.

INDEPENDENT CHALLENGE 3

Create a presentation that proposes a special event, entertainment, or party to a group of your choice. For example, you can create your own class party presentation similar to the presentation you created for Project 3. Alternatively, you can create a presentation that proposes a class reunion, a company picnic, or a weekend seminar.

1. Create an outline in PowerPoint that includes slide titles with the following information:
   a. Type of party or event
   b. Purpose of the party or event
   c. Location, time, and cost
   d. Chart showing the cost breakdown
   e. Motivational closing slide

2. Use as many slides as you wish. For ideas, refer to the presentation you created for Project 3. Save the presentation as **My Party Presentation.ppt** to the location where you are storing the files for this book.

3. Format the presentation attractively. If you wish, include a picture as the background on each slide in the presentation. Note that you may need to adjust the coloring of the picture so that text appears clearly.

4. In Access, create a database called **My Party Presentation.mdb** and save it to the location where you are storing the files for this book. Create a table to keep track of attendees, then create an attractive form for entering the data. Include a copy of the title slide of the presentation on the form.

5. Enter the event details in Word, save the document as **My Party Details.doc** to the location where you are storing the files for this book, copy and paste them as unformatted text into PowerPoint, then format the text to make it clear and easy to read.

6. Create a worksheet in Excel that shows the cost breakdown for the party, copy the data into a datasheet that you create in PowerPoint, then create a pie chart. Format the chart attractively. Save the worksheet as **My Party Costs.xls** to the location where you are storing the files for this book.

7. Print a copy of the presentation as handouts. Save and close the presentation, close the database, then close all open applications.

INDEPENDENT CHALLENGE 4

You need to create a presentation to welcome new employees to Food Mart, a large grocery chain in Toronto. Follow the instructions provided to create and then modify the presentation.

1. Open a blank PowerPoint presentation in Outline view, enter the slide titles and text for the presentation as shown below, then save the presentation as **Food Mart Orientation.ppt** to the location where you are storing the files for this book.

SLIDE #	SLIDE TITLE	LEVEL 1 TEXT
1	Food Mart	Employee Orientation Your Name
2	Overview	• Company History • Company Policies • Employee Benefits • Other Resources
3	Company History	• Established in 1976 by Marianne Harris
4	Sample Products	• Here are sample products in each of the eight categories carried by Food Mart:
5	Benefits	• Medical Plan • Dental Plan • Group Life Insurance • Group Disability Insurance
6	Human Resources	• Human Resources Department ° Local 3455 ° Open from 8:00 a.m. to 6:30 p.m.

2. Apply the Parchment preset background in the Gradient tab of the Fill Effects dialog box to all the slides. Select one of the horizontal variants.
3. Switch to Slide Master view, change the font in the Master Title Style placeholder to Comic Sans MS, apply Bold, then reduce the font size to 40 point.
4. Open the Insert Clip Art task pane, search for **shopping cart**, insert an appropriate clip art picture, then size and position the picture in the upper-right corner of the slide master. Refer to Figure I-29 as you work.
5. Close Slide Master view, view Slide 3, open a blank worksheet in Excel, then enter the data shown below:

1976	1986	1996	2006
1	10	35	75

6. Select the data in the Excel worksheet, click the Chart Wizard button, select the Cylinder chart, click Next, click the Series tab, click in the Category (X) axis labels text box, collapse the dialog box if necessary, then select the cells containing the years (e.g., cells A1 through D1).

7. Expand the dialog box, click Series 1, click Remove, click Next, type **Number of Stores** as the Value (Z) axis title, remove the legend, then click Finish.

8. Right-click Number of Stores, click Format Axis Title, click the Alignment tab, then change the rotation to 90 degrees.

9. Right-click the gray grid area, click Clear, right-click the chart area, click Format Chart Area, then click None in the Area section to remove the white background from the chart area.

10. Save the workbook as **Food Mart Orientation.xls** to the location where you are storing the files for this book.

11. Copy the chart and paste it as a link on Slide 3. Change the slide layout to Title and Text over Content, then size and position the chart attractively on the slide.

12. Start Access, create a database called **Food Mart Orientation.mdb** and saved to the location where you are storing the files for this book, then create the table shown in Figure I-28.

13. Publish the table in Microsoft Word (the file is saved as Product Lines.rtf), apply the Table List 1 AutoFormat, then copy the table and paste it on Slide 4.

14. Apply the Title and Text over Content layout, change the font size of the text in the table to 16 point, then size and position the table as shown in Figure I-29.

15. Switch to Excel, change the number of stores in 1996 to 50 and the number of stores in 2006 to 92, then verify that the cylinder chart is updated in PowerPoint. If necessary, click Edit on the menu bar, click Links, then update the link manually.

16. Apply the animation scheme of your choice to all the slides in the presentation.

17. View the presentation in Slide Sorter view, then compare it to the completed presentation shown in Figure I-29.

18. Preview the slide show, then print the slides in your presentation as a handout of six slides to one page.

19. Save and close the presentation, then close all open applications.

FIGURE I-28: **Product Lines**

Product Name	Category	Location	Prefix
Shampoo	Cosmetics	Aisle 2	33
Strawberries	Produce	Section 3	35
Cheese	Dairy	Aisle 9	37
Chicken Strips	Meat, Fish, Poultry	Section 1	36
Cookies	Dry Goods	Aisles 3 to 8	32
Bread	Bakery	Section 2	28
Pens	Stationery	Aisle 1	38
Ice Cream	Frozen Foods	Aisle 10	36
			0

Record: 9 of 9

FIGURE I-29: Completed presentation in Slide Sorter view

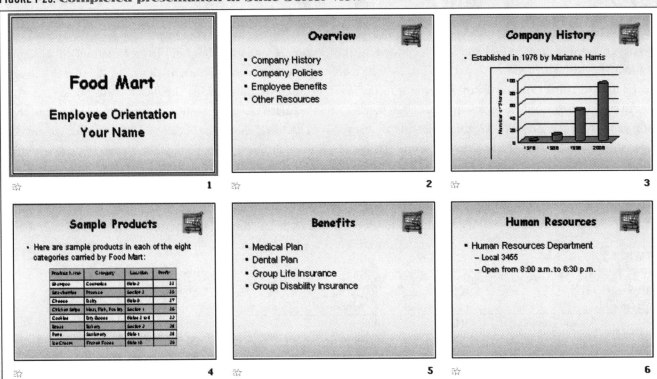

Visual Workshop

You've been asked to create a presentation on cultural tours of Europe. One of the slides in the presentation will be a pie chart that shows the breakdown of participants by tour category. Create the Tours table, as shown in Figure I-30, in an Access database called **Cultural Tours** and save it to the location where you are storing the files for this book. Create a query that sorts the records in ascending order by Theme. Copy the query table and paste it as a link into Excel. Find the total revenue for each tour (Participants*Price). Then create a pie chart that shows the percent of total revenue generated by each tour theme. (Note: At this point, your values will differ from Figure I-31.) Copy the pie chart and paste it as a link in a new PowerPoint slide. Add a title to the slide and format the slide and pie chart as shown in Figure I-31. Switch to Access, then change the number of participants in the Medieval Tuscany tour to 80. Verify that the pie chart updates in PowerPoint. Save the Excel workbook as **Cultural Tours.xls** to the location where you are storing the files for this book, and save the PowerPoint presentation as **Cultural Tours.ppt** to the same location. Close all open applications.

FIGURE I-30: Tours table

Tour ID	Tour	Theme	Country	Participants	Price
1	Ancient Rome	History	Italy	40	€3,500.00
2	Magical Provence	Culinary	France	30	€4,500.00
3	Rhineland Dreaming	Culinary	Germany	35	€4,200.00
4	Medieval Tuscany	History	Italy	20	€3,800.00
5	Van Gogh Odyssey	Art	France	25	€3,200.00
6	Mozart Madness	Music	Austria	35	€4,500.00
7	Renaissance Florence	Art	Italy	20	€2,800.00
8	Dutch Masters	Art	Netherlands	15	€3,200.00
9	The Impressionists	Art	France	20	€3,300.00
10	Megalith Builders	History	France	35	€3,800.00
(AutoN					€0.00

Record: 11 of 11

FIGURE I-31: Completed slide

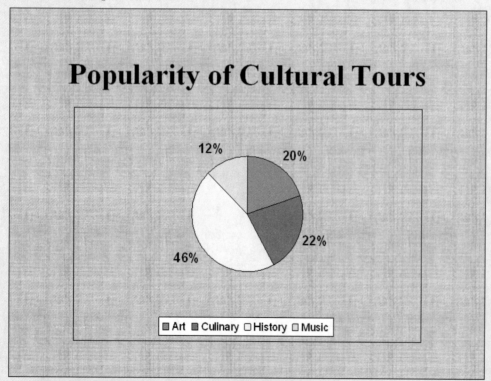

Popularity of Cultural Tours

12%   20%

22%

46%

■ Art ■ Culinary □ History □ Music

Index

3-D styles, WordArt, 16

▸ A

Access
See also databases
creating author profiles with, *134–139*
creating inventory database, *126–127*
importing Excel workbook into, *158–159*
objects, adding to Word, *162–163*
overview, *125*
wildcard character, *200*
Access Projects, *125–148*
activity schedules, creating, *20*
adding
See also inserting
graphics, *6*
linked data from Excel to Word, *116*
WordArt logo, *16–17*
Atlanta Arts newsletter
completed (fig.), *13*
creating, *9–12*
analyses
personal investment, creating, *90–93*
creating course grades, *84–89*
analyzing
customer purchases (Independent Challenge), *170*
job search results, *156–157*
Andrea Leriche resume (fig.), *43*
Animation Schemes (PowerPoint), *180*
announcement poster, creating (Independent Challenge), *193*
arrows, drawing, *190*
art
clip. *See* clip art
collection catalogue, creating, *164–165*
author profiles, creating using Access, *134–139*
AutoFormat button, Diagram toolbar, *32, 178*
AutoLayout button, Diagram toolbar, *178*
AutoNumber data type, *140, 150*
AutoShapes, using, *30, 112*
averaging values, *104, 108*

▸ B

bar charts, resized and positioned (fig.), *111*
best case scenarios, creating, *80–83*
borders
adding, *12*

adding to Word tables, *2*
applying styles, *26–27*
applying to table cells, *60*
enclosing text with, *30*
using in presentations, *182–183*
Borders and Shading dialog box (fig.), *27*
Borders, and Tables toolbar (fig.), *5*
breaks
column, *40*
page, *30, 88*
brochures
creating six-panel, *36–41, 48*
creating two-page, six-panel (Independent Challenge), *46*
Tulsa School of Drama (fig.), *49*
budgets
creating personal (Independent Challenge), *70–71*
setting up, *66–67*
business cards, creating, *14–19*
business partnership proposal, creating, *160–161*
buttons. *See specific button*

▸ C

calculating
See also formulas
advances, *64–65*
best and worst case scenarios, *80–83*
currency exchange rates, *73*
expenses, *62*
options for, *68*
present and future value, *90–91, 95–96*
results, viewing, *76*
sales total, *108–109*
sums, *60*
totals and grades, *84–85*
callouts, inserting in reports, *112*
cards, business, *14–19*
catalogs, creating, *164–165*
Chart Wizard, *86, 92*
Chart Wizard dialog box (fig.), *111*
charts
bar, *110*
creating, *82*
column, creating, *208*
cylinder, creating, *116–117*
displaying investment analysis in, *92–93*